The Death of Industrial Civilization

SUNY Series in Environmental Public Policy

Lester W. Milbrath, Editor

The Death of Industrial Civilization

The Limits to Economic Growth
and the Repoliticization of
Advanced Industrial Society

Joel Jay Kassiola

State University of New York Press

Published by
State University of New York Press, Albany

© 1990 State University of New York

For information, address State University of New York
Press, State University Plaza, Albany, N.Y., 12246

Library of Congress Cataloging-in-Publication Data

Kassiola, Joel Jay, 1945–
    The Death of Industrial Civilization : the limits to economic
growth and the repoliticization of advanced industrial society /
Joel Jay Kassiola.
        p.   cm. — (SUNY series in environmental public policy)
        ISBN 0-7914-0351-3. — ISBN 0-7914-0352-1 (pbk.)
        1. Economic development—Environmental aspects. 2. Economic
development—Social aspects. 3. Values. 4. Materialism.
5. Competition. 6. Cooperation. I. Title. II. Series.
HD75.6.K38   1990
306.3—dc20   89-37052
                                                         CIP

10 9 8 7 6 5 4 3 2 1

To Amy,
my best friend and partner
through the journey of life.

In this world there are only two tragedies. One is not getting what one wants, and the other is getting it. The last is much the worst, the last is a real tragedy!

—Oscar Wilde
Lady Windermere's Fan

Contents

Part I
Advanced Industrial Society in Crisis
Experiencing the Consequences of
Economic Growth Addiction

1

The Contemporary Industrial Crisis and the Limits-to-Growth Controversy

Western civilization is a man running with increasing speed through an air-sealed tunnel in search of additional oxygen. You can quite reasonably tell him he will survive longer if he slows down but he is not likely to do it.

—Philip Slater[1]

To punish mortals the gods grant their wishes. But whether seen as nemesis or not, the vision evoked by this interpretation of events is a frightening one: that of Western civilisation, the civilisation of the Enlightenment, the civilisation of Science, a civilisation born of high hopes and auspicious heralding...being piped gaily to the brink of the abyss. And all that yet might stay the fatal plunge lying in the mud, discarded and in decay.

—E. J. Mishan[2]

More than any time in history mankind faces a crossroads. One path leads to despair and utter hopelessness, the other to total extinction. Let us pray that we have the wisdom to choose correctly.

—Woody Allen[3]

Several years ago I began an article on the political consequences of the limits to economic growth as follows:

That current thought in the West had become pessimistic is not to be doubted and does not require discussion. Whether one consults the scholarly literature of the social and natural sciences, surveys of public opinion or the popular media, it becomes clear that the optimism which characterized industrial civilization not too long ago has been transformed into a deep-seated apprehension about our society's very survival. How one dates this dramatic shift in outlook: with the publication and worldwide reaction to the first Club of Rome Report; or in 1973 with the OPEC embargo, quadrupling of the price of oil, increasing inflation and unemployment, and devaluating the dollar; or some previous year and event, does not matter.[4]

Naturally, I was quite surprised when this assumption of mine concerning the recent pessimism in Western thought was challenged by an anonymous reviewer who demanded an accompanying discussion setting forth supporting evidence for what I took to be obvious. Rather than taking as a given the general recognition of a crisis within advanced industrial society and proceeding to attempt an explanation of this crisis, as I did in my previous briefer work, I would like to begin this discussion instead by confronting the reviewer's objection directly: What is the nature of and evidence for this supposed dramatic change in perspective toward pessimism within contemporary, advanced industrial society? (I shall use the term "advanced industrial society" with such examples as the United States, Japan, and West Germany, and for terminological variety "contemporary industrial society" and "postindustrial" will be used synonymously with it.) What factors are responsible for this turn toward discontent within the richest societies in the world?

Answering these questions will accomplish several goals. First, I will reply to any skeptical readers who, like the reviewer, doubt whether the alleged crisis and accompanying changes in outlook in advanced industrial thought and society have actually occurred. Second, since these statements are about industrial thought and civilization on the broadest level, encompassing the institutions and the underlying social values of our culture, they must be abstract and complex (owing to the complex nature of this type of society). Therefore, several different conceptions and interpretations of postindustrial institutions and values are possible.

Third, the explicit examination of the nature of the crisis within industrialism will define my understanding of the nature of the challenges to our institutions and values as we find ourselves in the last decade of the twentieth century. Also, the nature of this postindustrial type of social order and its impact upon the planet as a whole pose serious threats to its survival. These dangers provide not only the urgent issues I shall address in this volume, but are crucial to all humankind, including the approximately three billion people yet to be integrated fully into the industrial way of life.

Fourth, if we are to address the essential questions of the consequences of the industrial crisis and what, if anything, can be done about them, an examination of the nature of industrial society seems to be required. In social theory, as in medicine, an accurate case history and diagnosis must precede prescription as to the proper mode of treatment.

Therefore, this chapter will be devoted to a brief presentation of the current crisis in advanced industrial society: its nature, consequences and implications. My purpose is to lay the groundwork for the substance of this book, reflecting upon: advanced industrial society's crisis and its eventual demise; what type of social order should take its place; and, how the process of replacing the postindustrial social order may occur.

Indications of the Industrial Crisis in Brief and Introduction
to the Limits-to-Growth Controversy

The manifestations of the crisis within advanced industrial society are everywhere. A content analysis of scholarly volumes published in the last twenty years reveals a significant number of titles published in various disciplines, from different conceptual approaches, whose theme is this crisis.[5] I shall not rehash the burgeoning industrial crisis literature or what critics have termed the "doomsday" or "doom and gloom" or "neo-Malthusian" literature,[6] nor engage in a scientific dispute (which is beyond my competence) over the precise ecological state of our world and its future. Instead, I think the best strategy of exposition is to refer to a comprehensive list drawn up by Kirkpatrick Sale of the crises we face in advanced industrial society. (These crises when considered together will be called the "crisis" of our society.)

An imperilled ecology, irremediable pollution of atmosphere and oceans, overpopulation, world hunger and starvation, the depletion of resources, environmental diseases, the vanishing wilderness, uncontrolled technologies, chemical toxins in water, air, and foods, and endangered species on land and sea.

A deepening suspicion of authority, distrust of established institutions, breakdown of family ties, decline of community, erosion of religious commitment, contempt for law, disregard for tradition, ethical and moral confusion, cultural ignorance, artistic chaos, and aesthetic uncertainty.

Deteriorating cities, megalopolitan sprawls, stifling ghettoes, overcrowding, traffic congestion, untreated wastes, smog and soot, budget insolvency, inadequate schools, mounting illiteracy, declining university standards, dehumanizing welfare systems, police brutality, overcrowded hospitals, clogged court calendars, inhuman prisons, racial injustice, sex discrimination, poverty, crime and vandalism, and fear.

The growth of loneliness, powerlessness, insecurity, anxiety, anomie, boredom, bewilderment, alienation, rudeness, suicide, mental illness, alcoholism, drug usage, divorce, violence, and sexual dysfunction.

Political alienation and discontent, bureaucratic rigidification, administrative inefficiency, legislative ineptitude, judicial inequity, bribery and corruption, the use of repressive machinery, abuses of power, ineradicable national debt, collapse of the two-party system, defense overspending, nuclear proliferation, the arms race and arms sales, and the threat of nuclear annihilation.

Economic uncertainty, unemployment, inflation, devaluation and displacement of the dollar, capital shortages, the energy crisis, absenteeism, employee sabotage and theft, corporate mismanagement, industrial espionage, business payoffs and bribes, white-collar criminality, shoddy goods, waste and inefficiency, planned obsolescence, fraudulent and incessant advertising, mounting personal debt, and maldistribution of wealth.

International instability, worldwide inflation, national and civil warfare, arms buildups, nuclear reactors, plutonium stockpiles, disputes over laws of the sea, inadequate international law, the failure of the United Nations, multinational exploitation, Third World poverty and unrepayable debt, and the end of the American imperial arrangement.[7]

This lengthy list of advanced industrial crises (published in 1982) omits the current health crisis revolving around Acquired Immune Deficiency Syndrome (AIDS), and the specific detailing of the ecological aspects of the industrial crisis, some of which were just recently detected: stratospheric ozone depletion, acid rain, deforestation, and the carbon dioxide "greenhouse effect" or global warming.

Of course, such a mere listing of the multiple crises and problems within industrial culture is open to misinterpretation and objection without the necessary clarifying elaboration and supporting evidence. However, if only *half* of these claimed crises were, in fact, present in such important areas of industrial life there would be cause for concern that advanced industrial society is at a critical juncture in its history (affecting nonindustrial society as well because of its global impact). Pessimism about our ability to cope with these numerous and grave problems lead appropriately to doubts about this social order's very survival.

Indeed, such pessimism abounds today not only among the scholarly contributors to the industrial crisis literature but among the average contemporary industrial citizens as well, revealed by extensive public opinion poll results. Even that great optimist and critic of the limits-to-growth position, Herman Kahn, takes note of a Louis Harris survey entitled, "Majority Pessimistic on Reaching Ideal," and concludes that "two-thirds of the American people have been strongly influenced by the neo-Malthusian view and share many of its tenets."[8] (Although many of the references in this chapter and throughout the entire volume will be to American society, I think it should be clear that I am referring to the entire advanced industrialized world. The United States is taken as merely illustrative—even if an extreme case—of other industrialized societies. The United States is conspicuous in both its advanced state of industrial development and severity of crises and therefore has been selected for emphasis. This point is needed in order to respond to the charge of parochialism levelled against American researchers relying mainly upon American sources.[9] While the specific institutional manifestations of advanced industrial society will vary from nation-state to nation-state, my main interest in this political theoretical discussion is the deep underlying values of industrial civilization as a whole which are internationally uniform on this level of analyses.)

We even have had the rare spectacle of an American president reporting to the American public and the world via national television that America faced a:

> crisis of confidence...a crisis that strikes at the very heart and soul and spirit of our national will; [and, furthermore, that] the symptoms of this crisis of the American spirit are all around us. For the first time in the history of our country a majority of our people believe that the next five years will be worse than that [sic] past five years.[10]

If this view of Jimmy Carter's in 1979 might be considered as some misreading of the social conditions by an isolated, unperceptive American president who was eventually defeated, it should be noted that at the time "an astonishing 77 percent in the TIMES–CBS poll and 79 percent in the AP–NBC poll agreed that, yes, 'there is a moral and spiritual crisis, that is, a crisis of confidence, in the country today.'"[11]

Carter's somber remarks, even if true at the time, are vulnerable to the charge of becoming outdated by the changes in policy and successes of his opponent in 1980, Ronald Reagan, and the so-called "Reagan Revolution." I shall have more to say later about the possible criticism that indeed it was Carter's "doom and gloom" misinterpretation of the social situation in America that produced his landslide defeat at the hands of Ronald Reagan, just a little more than one year after he delivered his nationwide speech on July 15, 1979—a defeat all the more stunning considering that Carter was an incumbent. Critics of Carter's social diagnosis could contend that what was possibly true at the time was no longer so because of the change in administrations and policies begun with the first Reagan administration in 1981. This criticism raises the broader issue of whether Ronald Reagan's two enormous electoral victories in 1980 and 1984 (followed by the resounding electoral success of his vice-president, George Bush in 1988), and his administrations' exuberant endorsement of proeconomic growth policies further indicate the obsolete or erroneous nature of Carter's claim of a social crisis as well as the misconceived nature of the industrial crisis, limits-to-growth position as a whole.

At this early point in our discussion I shall state merely that one view of the Reagan-dominated 1980s and his administrations' attempt to recapture the lost optimism and glory of the America of the past is that it is the beginning of the end for such a proeconomic growth perspective and all that it entails; a "last hurrah" that reflected the American people's rejection of Carter's message of crisis because they preferred Ronald Reagan's denial of danger and embraced his "city on a hill" and "morning in America" as symbols of a more confident and once again predominant America. By electing Reagan in 1980, one could say that the American voters chose to avoid the more sobering and painful implications of Carter's assessment of the "crisis of the American spirit." However, the victorious 1988 Presidential campaign of Reagan's vice president, George Bush, nonetheless, did not reflect the exuberance and optimism of his predecessor. Bush appeared more impressed and humbled by the actual consequences, and not the mere rhetoric, of the two Reagan administrations' policies.

That the Reagan era of the 1980s may be considered merely a hiatus based on collective wishful thinking and fundamental policy errors is confirmed with the benefit of the hindsight available at the end of Mr. Reagan's term in office. As an economist wrote in an article entitled, "We're Running Out of Gimmicks to Sustain Our Prosperity: Decline Began in 1973, But We Have Concealed It": "In 1984 [presidential election] we still believed that the 1980s could be like the 1950s and '60s economically. Now we are not so sure."[12]

The pessimism of investment banker and social commentator Felix Rohatyn, contained in an article entitled, "On the Brink," and written four months *before* the October 1987 worldwide stock market crash is relevant here and reflects the discontent and foreboding characteristic of the end of the Reagan era in marked contrast with its beginning:

The United States today is headed for a financial and economic crisis. What appeared to be only a possibility five or six years ago became a probability more recently, and has now become a virtual certainty. The only real questions are when and how.[13]

The world's inhabitants must contemplate a post-Reagan America laboring under the legacies of the Reagan Administrations' social values and goals—most prominent of which was unlimited economic growth—and their policies to implement them that have brought us to "the brink of the abyss" (to use Mishan's apocalyptic language cited in the epigraph to this chapter)—and not only financially! Do not Jimmy Carter's words: "a crisis that strikes at the heart and soul and spirit of our national will" ring true now when we look at our inner cities, hospitals, schools, prisons, environment, and economy? Even the most optimistic analysts are predicting a very difficult post-Reagan period in our attempt to get out from under the huge domestic and international debt, and other disabling Reaganite policies with their adverse consequences.

The essence of the reply to those cheerful throngs of Reagan supporters of 1981 could begin by quoting Levy again:

> For the past decade and longer, Americans have been living an illusion of increasing prosperity—but in fact, we have been living on borrowed money and borrowed optimism. As a result, we are digging ourselves into a deep hole.[14]

Clearly, the optimism and high spirits associated with the beginning of the first Reagan Administration are over. Perhaps the national diagnosis of the crisis of the 1970s (reflected in Jimmy Carter's 1979 speech) can be understood and accepted by the American public in the 1990s now that our Reaganite "escapism" has ended? Certainly, few people today are prepared to argue that, economics aside, the moral and spiritual environment has been substantially improved upon or that we can optimistically look forward to the decade of the 1990s and the ensuing twenty-first century. President Bush's rhetoric and proposals both seem to reflect a much more sober view of the state of the American union as befits the chief executive responsible for alleviating the problems left by the Reagan policies, actions, and inactions, perhaps best symbolized by the Savings and Loan financial debacle likely to cost the American public upwards of $200 billion.

Not only is the supporting evidence for the industrial crisis and its accompanying despondency within the industrial public forthcoming from natural and social scientists, but students of industrial popular culture such as Kurt Vonnegut, Jr. have also observed its presence as well. Vonnegut, writing a review of the works of the science fiction writer Stanislaw Lem, calls him "one of the most popular science-fiction writers in the world [and] a master of utterly terminal pessimism appalled by all that an insane humanity may yet survive to do."[15] Vonnegut himself expresses this "utterly terminal pessimism" of contemporary industrial thought when he quotes a letter from his son, a medical student, about how:

> it is a bad time for anybody's writing just now, that the spirit in the air is this: "We're destroying the planet. There's not a damn thing that can be done about it. It's going to be very slow, drawn-out and ugly, or so fast it doesn't make any difference."[16]

Of course, the Chernobyl nuclear accident of April 1986 needs to be mentioned in this regard adding to the current pessimism. To realize that what critics of our reliance upon nuclear-generated energy have feared about the dangers of such energy could actually happen with the predicted global effects is both frightening and disheartening. Furthermore, it demonstrates one of the main themes of the environment and limits-to-growth movements: the interdependency of all life on earth. One expert writes:

> The Chernobyl accident was by any measure the most serious nuclear accident the world has ever suffered...The Chernobyl nuclear cloud showed graphically—and tragically—that we all share the global environment.[17]

In addition to the statements and the passages cited in the epigraph to this chapter, the following passages are, I think, a representative sample of the apocalyptic nature of the industrial crisis literature. From the pen of a student of international politics:

> There is a spectre haunting the world of politics, economics, and public affairs. It knows no boundaries, it ignores the old rules of international intercourse, pays no respect to the wealthy traditions of the past, and barely acknowledges the ruling tenets of international order and the norms and values that helped shape it. It cares not to emulate the past because it cannot control the future. It is the awsome ghost of a waning century, the ghost of scarcity.[18]

In their Letter of Transmittal accompanying *The Global 2000 Report To The President*—the most extensive study of current and future environmental conditions conducted by the American government—an Assistant Secretary of State for Oceans and International Environmental and Scientific Affairs, and the Chairman of The Council on Environmental Quality wrote the following to President Carter:

> Our conclusions, summarized in the pages that follow, are disturbing. They indicate the potential for global problems of alarming proportions by the year 2000. Environmental, resource, and population stresses are intensifying and will increasingly determine the quality of human life on our planet. These stresses are already severe enough to deny many millions of people basic needs for food, shelter, health, and jobs, or any hope for betterment. At the same time, the earth's carrying capacity—the ability of biological systems to provide resources for human needs—is eroding. The trends reflected in the *Global 2000* study suggest strongly a progressive degradation and impoverishment of the earth's natural resource base.[19]

It was this same paragraph that the pro-growth and crisis-denying critics of the *Global 2000 Report*, Julian Simon and Herman Kahn, chose to attack and radically rewrite in order to show their vehement opposition to this report, its methods and conclusions.[20]

Perhaps the last word of despair should go to the economist Robert Heilbroner, who writes:

> The outlook for man, I believe, is painful, difficult, perhaps desperate, and the hope that can be held out for his future prospect seems to be very slim indeed. Thus, to anticipate the conclusions of our inquiry, the answer to whether we can conceive of the future other than as a continuation of the darkness, cruelty, and disorder of the past seems to me to be no; and to the question whether worse impends, yes.[21]

Clearly, we seem to be in what even the critic of the industrial crisis literature, Herman Kahn, was forced to admit is "L'époque de Malaise" (The Era of Malaise); a period of malaise that Kahn describes present within the American, Canadian, European—West and East—and Soviet societies.[22] (The universality of the value of unlimited economic growth independent of whether capitalist or socialist social orders and its harmful consequences will be discussed later.) Perhaps it was this pervasive malaise that Ronald Reagan and his image-makers sought to take us away from. It worked for a while, but now that the illusions are destroyed the lost time and additional damage must be made up, repaired (where possible), and recognized for the dangerous fantasies that they were.

The claim of the crisis of advanced industrial society and the melancholy reaction it engendered appears to be once again, in the post-Reagan era, both intellectually fashionable and part of the contemporary popular culture (see public and media reactions to severe ecological phenomena during 1988). Nonetheless, these developments might inspire the following question: could they be taken as indications of the superficiality, exaggeration, or even complete wrongheadedness on the part of these purveyors of societal doom and gloom associated with the limits-to-growth position particularly given the faddism that characterizes industrial culture? Might not all this talk of impending disaster constitute a "doomsday syndrome" or "myth" as opponents charge,[23] or merely another popular fashion that will fade with time and change in social mood—with another Ronald Reagan type—and therefore have little lasting social significance? Are the industrial crisis view and limits-to-growth critique like horror movies portraying natural disasters that are periodically popular? And, finally, the question may be posed by someone like the skeptical reviewer of my earlier work:

are not those who claim a crisis within industrial civilization suffering from various errors in their thinking?

Let us note here, in an attempt to examine the possible replies to these questions, one important component of the limits-to-growth controversy: the essential characteristic of the progrowth argument and defenders of the status quo of their denial of the existence of a crisis within industrial culture and who, furthermore, support the existing policy of making continuous and unlimited economic growth one of the most important industrial social values and objectives.[24] Since these critics of the limits-to-growth position cannot reasonably deny many of the environmental and social problems claimed by the industrial crisis, limits-to-growth advocates (although some do in the scientific controversy regarding the biophysical or environmental limits to growth best exemplified by the Simon and Kahn volume), they are forced to make their counterattack upon this limits-to-growth critique of industrial civilization in an *ad hominem* manner. Examples of this *ad hominem* response by defenders of the progrowth status quo may be seen in several critical discussions of the claimed industrial crisis and limits to growth.

Ad hominem arguments are a main element in prominent rebuttals to the environmentally based critique of industrial society and should be useful as a means of examining the nature of the limits-to-growth debate. Perhaps the most extensive use of such fallacious tactics occurs in Wilfred Beckerman's *Two Cheers for the Affluent Society*. His view may be summarized as follows:

> How the growth of the economy is to be used, therefore, is too serious a problem to be taken over by extremists of any kind, or to become a form of psychotherapy for those more affluent members of society who want to work off their guilt complexes in a manner which, they can be sure, will never actually have any effect on their relative affluence.[25]

This single sentence combines three main countercharges by the defenders of the industrial value system and used against their opponents in the limits-to-growth debate: (1) extremism; (2) some psychological problem (usually guilt at their relative wealth); and, of most theoretical importance, (3) deceptive self-interested practices to protect their alleged comparative material advantages.

Beckerman proceeds to argue for the collective guilt of various advocates of the antigrowth position, such as:

> [scientists] The scientific community probably has a sort of collective guilt complex concerning certain scientific developments over the last

two or three decades, notably the atom bomb and also the increasing knowledge of even more destructive ways of wiping out mankind as a result of "progress" in biological and botanical sciences....

[middle classes]...the middle classes today feel more guilty about their relative affluence than has been the case in the past...Further-more, it is likely that the middle class opposition to growth reflects partly their sense that economic growth also brings a loss of various privileges.[26]

Another progrowth advocate, Herman Kahn, speaks of what he terms the "Anti-Growth Triad" composed of: "affluent radicals and reformers; Thorstein Veblen's "leisure class"; and a subgroup of upper-middle class intellectuals we refer to as neoliberal members of the New Class."[27] He further claims that this Anti-Growth Triad has adopted fourteen "new" emphases (or values)[28] and most, if not all, of his critical remarks about these purported antigrowth values will fit into the standard, tripartite pro-growth set of responses to the antigrowth challenge: extremism, psychopathology, and disguised self-service for the elite. Under the rubric of "extremism" (although these classifications of mine are not exhaustive) are Kahn's attributed values to the limits-to-growth position of: "selective risk avoidance, comfort, safety, health, happiness and hedonism;" under "psy-chopathology": "loss of nerve, will, optimism, confidence and morale;" and under "classist self-service": "localism, protection of the environment and ecology."[29]

Although specific value changes emphasized by the limits-to-growth critics of industrial society selected for counterattack by the defenders of growth may vary, we find that these three components usually characterize the defense offered by those who deny that industrial civilization is faltering as a result of its commitment to limitless economic growth. (I shall address shortly the important countercharge of elitism against the limits-to-growth detractors of industrialism by the proponents of unlimited economic growth and the industrial social order founded upon it.)

The Limits-to-Growth Formulation of the Industrial Crisis and Its Nonapocalyptic Possibilities

The controversy over the existence of limits to economic growth and the resulting challenge to the feasibility of unlimited economic growth as an industrial social value raise the following question: Are those who claim the existence of the industrial crisis and base their attack upon unlimited eco-nomic growth as a fundamental industrial social value indeed extreme and mistaken (because of psychopathologies and/or self-interest), as their opponents would have us believe? In order to answer this key question to the limits-to-growth debate we must examine in more detail the nature of the alleged crisis according to these critics of industrial growth.

First, we should observe the importance of how the nature of the crisis of industrial society was formulated. Immanuel Wallerstein, who accepts the existence of "the crisis of the demise of the capitalist world economy," nevertheless goes on to warn that, "most discussions of the crisis are too cataclysmic in tone [and] analyses of the crisis are too full of illusion and hence inevitably breed disillusion"[30] Some of the industrial critics' "doom and gloom" analyses—*even if correct*—can result in paralyzing despair and produce "utterly terminal pessimism" which will only hasten the day of disaster because of the failure to take corrective action. Relevant to this point about social paralysis and terminal pessimism, I would like to note that the law of diminishing returns may be applied to the apocalyptic descriptions typically provided by the limits-to-growth literature. In referring to apocalyptic accounts of nuclear war by antinuclear advocates, a commentator writes:

But there are limitations to this approach. The law of diminishing returns applies even to repeated presentations of the apocalypse. Ground Zero Day can be celebrated, as it were, once or perhaps twice, but it soon begins to lose its effectiveness. The numbing effect of detail, as well as the simple inability of any movement to sustain indefinitely a sense of crisis and imminent calamity, has led to the current decline in popularity of the pragmatic antinuclear case.[31]

Without going into the merits of Krauthammer's claims regarding the antinuclear war movement, surely his point here can be applied to repeated versions of humanity's (and the whole earth's) demise forecast by the limits-to-growth advocates, especially those who follow the biophysical approach from The first Club of Rome report on *The Limits to Growth*. Supporters of this view should take heed!

A critic of industrial values and an advocate of a new world order, Richard Falk, notes that such terminal pessimism might lead to a social paralysis and an inability to take the necessary social action resulting in the freezing of the *status quo*, particularly with regard to the profoundly political issue of the redistribution of wealth.[32]

It is important to note here that the limits-to-growth critique of industrial civilization does not logically require a freezing of the status quo to the benefit of the current rich only. Indeed, a quite often overlooked aspect of the influential first report to the Club of Rome specifically rejects this conservative bias as I shall show.

We must be careful not to have the limits-to-growth critiques of industrial values exist in isolation with their fearful and depressing message only. They must be combined with discussions of alternative social orders and proposals for the design and transformation processes by which these alternative societies might be realized; in short, an account of how social transformation of advanced industrial society may occur. I shall attempt to begin to do this in part 4 and thereby provide insight to and appreciation of the following crucial encouraging fact: *the end of the industrial civilization does not necessarily mean the end of human civilization in toto.*

The concern by supporters that the limits-to-growth attack might be viewed so cataclysmically as to induce inaction either because of shock or despair is illustrated by a story told by William Sloane Coffin about a Harvard scientist flying over the lake country in northern Alabama using technical instruments in an experiment measuring fish population. When the scientist discovered two fishermen out on the lake that he had just determined had no fish, he thought he would inform them of his recent finding as a friendly gesture.

They were outraged, instantly, and told the scientist in rich Southern expletives where he could take his plane and his instruments and what he could do with them, whereupon they baited their lines once again and kept on fishing. The scientist flew off, much puzzled. "I expected their disappointment," he said later, "but not their anger."[33]

Similarly, as students of industrial society knowledgeable of the requirements for social action and change, we need to be cognizant of the possible reactions of both the public and policymakers in advanced industrial societies, no matter how accurate we consider the claims about the crisis of industrial culture to be; as Krauthammer noted, the law of diminishing returns applied to repeated apocalyptic accounts might set in.

Happily, this will not mean ignoring aspects of the crisis for fear of such overkill. There is a socially significant, encouraging element to the most gloomy analysis of the threats to postindustrial society in the recognition that the death of industrial civilization need not mean the end of the world. Formulations of the industrial crisis should be as accurate as possible and should reflect the social implications and consequences of this crisis. If these goals are accomplished, along with the realization that such a treatment of the crisis need not mean a catastrophe for humanity as a whole but may actually bring about positive results through its stimulus for social action to transform advanced industrial civilization, it is unlikely that social theorists asserting the severity of the crisis will end up as Coffin's thoughtful scientist: ignored or angrily dismissed by his or her intended audience, yet puzzled by their reaction.

New Elements in the Limits-to-Growth Critique of Industrialism

The survival of industrial society, the merits of unlimited economic growth as a central component within the industrial worldview, and the acceptability of the underlying values of industrial society as a whole are not new issues. Two classical economists, Smith and Malthus, concerned themselves with the feasibility of limitless economic growth: both agreed, for different reasons, that it was not feasible.[34] Also, such nineteenth- and twentieth-century economists as J. C. L. Simonde de Sismondi, John Ruskin, John A. Hobson, and Richard H. Tawney all challenged the desirability of economic growth and the industrial civilization that was based on this belief.[35] And, of course, there were the cultural critics of industrialism such as Charles Dickens, Matthew Arnold and Ruskin.[36] Given this rich history of criticism of industrial values in general, and the central place among these values of economic growth in particular, what is new and significant about the recent version of the attack on industrial civilization singling out the limits to economic growth begun sometime in the late 1960s and early 1970s?

First, as one would expect of a civilization-wide analysis, the conception of the contemporary industrial crisis and the critique of industrialism are culturally pervasive. Both affect all aspects of industrial social life to some degree but the political, economic, psychological, and ecological manifestations of this crisis are especially important. The last aspect—the ecological dimension of the industrial crisis—is new in the use of rigorous scientific methods, updated scientific knowledge, and the latest technologies unavailable to earlier industrial social critics. Contained within this ecological component of the limits-to-growth critique of postindustrial society and its alleged crisis is the reappearance of Malthus's conjecture about the finiteness of the earth restricting population growth applied to other environmental concerns such as types of environmental pollution endangering all forms of life and the availability of renewable and nonrenewable natural resources; hence, the labelling of this limits-to-growth viewpoint as "neo-Malthusian."

The best-selling and widely quoted Club of Rome report, *The Limits to Growth*, might be considered the founding document of the contemporary industrial crisis and its public and scholarly awareness. Since the time of its first publication in 1972, it has been translated into many languages and has sold millions of copies. The great influence of this report could be attributed, partially anyway, to the fact that "15,000 copies [had] been dispatched to political and social leaders throughout the world."[37]

One profound element of this important document was the report's authors' strong emphasis upon the interaction between various claimed crises. This interaction constituted the multifaceted crisis of industrial society, called by the Club members "world problematique," leading to the title of their first project: "The Predicament of Mankind."[38] The Club's emphasis upon the claim that the varied problems facing advanced industrial societies formed a complex whole requiring consideration and corrective action on the holistic or global level of analysis led the report's authors to rely upon the global models of systems engineer Jar Forrester.[39] This global level of inquiry has characterized several subsequent Club of Rome reports.[40]

The Club of Rome's strong contention that the challenges confronting industrial culture are interrelated synergistically and therefore must be studied in the aggregate on the global level has been an important contribution to the contemporary industrial crisis literature. While individual subgroups of humans have confronted and been annihilated by environmental threats of all types (including being destroyed by fellow humans), the current crisis is striking in the global scope of the threats and the resulting endangerment of the entire human species and possibly the totality of the Earth's living organisms. Here the earlier point about the interrelatedness and interdependence of all earthly life graphically symbolized by the Chernobyl nuclear cloud is apt. What the industrial crisis claimants fear is not just a local disaster like that produced by an earthquake but the devastation of the entire planet's living population as a product of the all-encompassing nature of the industrial crises illustrated, in part, by the list referred to previously.

The new planetary dimensions of these crises and their probable synergistic interrelationships demand much more of our cognitive skills and creativity in sorting out and treating such an interactive complex of phenomena. These two characteristics of global scope and synergism attributed to the contemporary world problematique have caused even the critics of the limits-to-growth position to appreciate the uniqueness and severity of the current industrial crisis. Opponents such as Beckerman admit that "the case against economic growth has become one of the most widely publicized—and widely accepted—of all indictments of modern society".[41] Even Kahn recognizes:

> Challenges to the concept of progress are not new. What is new is the effectiveness of today's challenge and its broad support by the upper-middle class and professional elites...In the past, challenges to modernity have come from romantics, reactionaries, aristocrats, aesthetes, and various religious and ideological groups. Many of these people, too, have jumped on the Club of Rome bandwagon. However, the basic impetus for the campaign against economic growth still

comes from "modern," "progressive," and "enlightened," individuals and groups with much greater than average education and affluence... As a result, during the last decade the antigrowth syndrome has become dominant among intellectuals and educated elites all over the world, especially in the Affluent countries.[42]

Finally, referring to social issues, pro-growth economist Henry C. Wallich observes, "Except for the preservation of peace, none goes deeper than the limits-to-growth controversy."[43] Jay Forrester sums up the point clearly: "The limits-to-growth debate deals with the most important issue of our time."[44]

In light of Forrester's statement, Wallich's supposed separation and subordination of the limits-to-growth issue to world peace is misleading since even (or should I say "especially"?) world peace is one social goal threatened by interrelated global challenges to industrial civilization; for example, consider possible military conflicts over the control of vital natural resources such as crude oil from the Middle East and the military activities by advanced industrial nations in the Persian Gulf during the recent Iraq-Iran War protecting oil tankers as being the most recent manifestation of this possibility.

Another fundamental and unprecedented characteristic of the industrial crisis is the claim by some of its advocates that the problems of advanced industrial society are caused by this social order's very own successes rather than an inherent deficiency or some external factor. The authors of the second report to the Club of Rome, Mesarovic and Pestel, argue:

> The most important factor, however, that separates the current series of crises from the crises of the past is the character of their causes. In the past, major crises had *negative* origins: they were caused by the evil intentions of aggressive rulers or governments, or by natural disasters regarded as evil according to human values—plagues, floods, earthquakes, and so on. In contrast, many of the crises of the present have *positive* origins: they are the consequences of actions that were, at their genesis, stimulated by man's best intentions.[45]

Two contributors to a volume devoted to discussions of the alternatives to growth explain the idea of the undesirable consequences of industrial society's "success" even more cogently for supporters of the limits-to-growth when they write:

> In contrast to other crises in history, which have been caused by visibly negative factors—such as plague and drought—the "cause" of the

current crisis—material growth—is generally considered "good." It is obviously difficult to obtain the same cooperation and commitment in fighting something "good."[46]

Other than Marx's emphasis upon the internal contradictions of capitalism, one of the most well-known formulations of the internally caused crisis of industrial (capitalist) society is Joseph Schumpeter's conclusion regarding capitalism's eventual demise because of its successes:

...the actual and prospective performance of the capitalist system is such as to negative [sic] the idea of its breaking down under the weight of economic failure, but that its very success undermines the social institutions which protect it, and "inevitably" creates conditions in which it will not be able to live....[47]

This "self-destructive" thesis of Schumpeter's was ignored by economists and economic growth-based political thinkers during the years between its first publication in 1942 and the 1970s because of the sustained economic growth and prosperity that marked the post-World War II period in the West.[48] The great confidence—even boastfulness—about the economic future during the high-flying years of the 1960s is reflected in the following statements. The first is by President Lyndon Johnson:

No longer do we view our economic life as a relentless tide of ups and downs. No longer do we fear that automation and technical progress will rob workers of jobs rather than help us to achieve greater abundance. No longer do we consider poverty and unemployment landmarks in our economic scene.[49]

The second statement is one by Max Ways about "the great rediscovery of the postwar period" that

capitalism is *not* subject to a ceiling of diminishing returns; innovation is *not* a self-exhausting process; the era of radical change we now experience is *not* headed toward a new "point of rest"; all the buffalo on the plains of progress have *not* been shot—indeed, they are breeding faster and faster.[50]

We should note the stark contrast between the progrowth optimism of the early 1960s within postindustrial thought and the current pessimism. This is true because the enthusiasm and confidence of the early 1960s evaporated as economic historian Hirschman informs us:

But the sense of pervasive crisis which has characterized the 1930s and 1940s reappeared in the 1970s, in part as an aftereffect of the still poorly understood mass movements of the late 1960s and in part as an immediate reaction to the contemporary shocks and disarray.[51]

Whether the self-destructive orientation of industrial capitalism is based upon its harming the very values it requires to exist, as Schumpeter and other social theorists argue,[52] or upon the unanticipated bad outcomes of good intentions such as increased life span creating an overpopulation problem with all of its ecological consequences, as Pirages and Ehrlich assert,[53] is less important than one other vital point: each of these diverse self-destructive theses refers to what were once heralded as the "strengths" of the industrial social order and will therefore incur substantial resistance to both their criticism and proposals for their revision.

One of the distinguishing aspects of the current industrial crisis is its involvement of the very values and institutions realized so successfully by the industrial revolution and its ensuing culture. For the moment, we need not examine in detail the various analyses of the self-destruction of the industrial society and its ultimate replacement. *What I wish to emphasize here is the unique normative aspect of the contemporary crisis as the product of previously accepted—and in some instances, like economic growth, largely still adhered to—values gone sour.*

In conclusion, the thesis of the self-destructive nature of industrial society, if accurate, makes analysis of the crisis difficult and its remedies complicated because of its challenge to industrial civilization's fundamental values and the relationship between the value basis of the crisis and the current distribution of industrial societal power. The crucial social importance of industrial values and the challenge to them by the limits-to-growth advocates will be a major theme in this work.

By now, it should be clear that whether motivated by the concern for the environment, the scarcity of material resources, or from other factors deriving from the "success" of industrial civilization in generating unprecedented material wealth (and waste products to match), the basic values of industrial civilization are at stake in the limits-to-growth controversy. The profound relevance of political philosophical analyses which encompass the examination and assessment of social values should be evident to this debate over industrial values. Yet, surprisingly and disappointingly, there have been few political philosophical treatments of the limits-to-growth attack upon the industrial way of life and thought. I strongly believe that the absence of such analyses creates a serious obstacle to progress in the debate over economic growth and the future of postindustrial society. In my earlier work I wrote:

Examining these discussions, [of the economic growth controversy] one is struck *inter alia* by the absence of political scientists' contributions and of politically sophisticated presentations of the LTG [limits-to-growth] position. Analysis of economic growth—its nature, consequences, advantages, and disadvantages—has been left to members of other disciplines. Economists, systems engineers, and environmentally concerned natural scientists such as ecologists, physicists, demographers, and geologists, dominate the LTG presentations.[54]

With precious few exceptions during the intervening years since their publication, these observations regarding the general neglect of the limits-to-growth controversy and the profound politically relevant issues it raises, by students of politics—especially political philosophers—unfortunately, remain true. One goal of this book is to begin to correct this serious gap by stimulating my fellow students of politics—particularly those of political values—to address the crucial issues, including matters of species life and death, raised within our domain by the industrial crisis. Thoreau perceptively remarked, "There are a thousand hacking at the branches of evil to one who is striking at the root."[55] Pertaining to the study of advanced industrial society, as I shall try to show in the following discussion, there are many scholars "hacking at the branches of evil" instead of at its normative root.

The Political Nature of the Industrial Crisis

Within the study of the scientific method, problem formulation holds a centrally important place. The full understanding of the nature and precise formulation of any problem to be addressed by scientists is essential to the several methodological judgments that the scientist must make throughout the scientific research project. Furthermore, the propriety of subsequent judgments is determined relative to their suitability to the original problem definition. Decisions otherwise acceptable by themselves may be erroneous or disadvantageous if they are inappropriate to the problem raised as it is specifically defined.[56] If human rationality as a whole is problem-based, as the philosopher Karl R. Popper has emphasized in his philosophy of science and theory of knowledge,[57] it is difficult to overstate the importance of carefully attending to the formulation and understanding of the set of problems constituting the crisis characterizing contemporary industrial civilization.

I think it is agreed by most social commentators that the apparent origin and driving force for the current industrial crisis was ecological. The "energy crisis" in 1973 made the scarcity of cheap petroleum for an oil-dependent advanced industrial society obvious to both its public and policymakers. Environmentally devastating oil spills were highly publicized, most recently the *Exxon Valdez*, Alaskan oil spill of March 1989 and the beach pollution on the Atlantic coast beaches during the summer of 1988. All of these graphically demonstrated the human-caused pollution of our natural environment. Such ecological crises have forced many citizens and leaders of advanced industrial societies to question their post-World War II growth-fed optimism about the future of their culture as well as the premise of unlimited economic growth and the continued economic "progress" implied by the industrial worldview and value system.[58]

It is because of dramatic ecological events that most analysts consider the crisis of industrialism to have begun in the late 1960s or early 1970s. In addition to the general political turmoil of this period associated with the war in Vietnam, critical reactions to it, and worldwide student protests on this and other issues, the environmental movement and greater public consciousness of the importance of ecology to the survival of the human species began to surface. Of course, the shock of the quadrupling of the price of oil by the OPEC nations in 1973 and its global ramifications served as reinforcement of the previous few years' heightened ecological sensitivity and concern.[59] Also, the immense significance of the publication of *The Limits to Growth* must be mentioned here as well.

Many of the policymakers and citizens who were roused from their ecological ignorance by the calamitous events of this period came to appreciate both the scope and severity of these ecological threats. The effects of the newly comprehended ecological problems were interpreted as touching all aspects of the industrial way of life and threatening its very foundation to the extent that the future of the entire human species, nay, the entire planet's survival, was considered jeopardized. A definitive history of the rise of the recent environmental consciousness and its movement within advanced industrial societies has yet to be written and, furthermore, this movement remains ongoing and perhaps even more intensified as threats such has global warming or the depletion of stratospheric ozone worsen. Nonetheless, the nature and the role of contemporary public concern over ecological issues and threats within the broader context of the crisis of the industrial social order should be examined. In so doing, the essential political nature of the current industrial crisis will be clarified.

One of the most important contributions made by biologist Garrett Hardin in his influential and widely reprinted article, "The Tragedy of the Commons,"[60] is his emphasis upon understanding the human population problem which is just one component of the complex set of ecological problems confronting us today. Hardin refers to two students of the nuclear arms race who claim that the problem of building up military hardware between enemy nations to achieve greater security has "no technical solution,"[61] and then goes on to apply their idea about the nature of military competition to the overpopulation problem.

Hardin defines a "technical solution" as one that requires change in the technique of the natural sciences, demanding little or nothing in the way of change in human values or ideas of morality."[62] With this conception in mind, the thrust of Hardin's discussion is that the problem of too many people inhabiting the earth is not open to techncial solution; that is, it will not be solved by a mere "change only in the techniques of the natural sciences" without any "changes in human values or ideas of morality." In short, Hardin argues that what was then (and, alas, still is) conceived as a scientific-technical problem is essentially a value-based, normative-moral one.

Here we see a prime example of the importance of problem formulation and understanding. If Hardin is correct (as I think he is), searching exclusively for technical changes (such as more effective birth control devices) will not solve the overpopulation problem; an examination of the underlying values regarding the social problem and a prescription for appropriate value changes are needed.[63] This is quintessentially a political philosophical process.

Along with the practical political process of obtaining social agreement to accept new values and implement the prescribed value changes, political philosophical analysis may be applied to the broad range of ecological issues in addition to the one—human overpopulation—Hardin focuses upon. *One major aim of both this section and of the entire work is to show the basic normative political nature of the contemporary industrial crisis, encouraging others to think systematically about prescribing value changes and corresponding alternative social institutions; in short, to design a new social order created to avoid the various threatened calamities and thereby end the industrial crisis by transforming advanced industrial society.*

The historian Fritz Stern has remarked: "Capitalism is too serious a subject to be left to the economic historian alone," and then adds: "Such is also the case with industrialism."[64] I agree with both statements. Indeed, I would go on to suggest that although the industrial crisis has received much scholarly attention as well as popular media coverage, consideration of the crisis has been inappropriately dominated by either technical, scientific, ecological analyses or technical, economic analyses. Few, if any, political—especially normatively political—and/or moral discussions have been attempted.

It should be noted that in addition to the paucity of political analyses of the industrial crisis, the various divisions between scholarly disciplines hindered (and continue to hinder) the studies of the truly multidisciplinary and transdisciplinary problems the industrial crisis presents. Unfortunately, these multiple academic divisions act as barriers to communication and insight and are harmful to a comprehensive understanding of advanced industrial society. On the one hand, there is the split between economics and political science (to be discussed in part 2) further compounded by the isolation between these social sciences and the natural scientific environmental studies; on the other hand, these scientific environmental studies and the scientific-aspiring social sciences are separated from the normative criticism of growth-based postindustrial society.

In fact, the limits-to-growth critics of the industrial social order who have strongly argued for recognizing the ecological aspects of the industrial crisis have themselves been largely responsible for much of the misconceptions and neglect of the normative political nature of the problems facing industrialism. Too many natural scientists discussing the biophysical limits to economic growth end their studies prematurely without considering the political ramifications of their argument.[65] Understanding the dual nature of the industrial crisis and the limits-to-growth critique of industrial society—including both scientific and normative components—will explain the serious gaps that characterize the existing literature on the economic growth controversy. This understanding will also inform future endeavors that attempt to address the complex questions associated with the nature and viability of industrial civilization.

To be sure, the amount of lead that can be absorbed safely by the human body; the amount of sulphur dioxide in the air before serious adverse consequences to human life occurs; the amount of mercury in fish; and like questions, all present biophysical limits and problems for human existence. Nonetheless, and this is crucial to my argument, the *way* in which postindustrial society responds to these limits and problems (including comprehension of how and why industrial values and processes cause these problems by pushing closer to the biophysical limits) will involve, unavoidably, human values including political and moral ones. We must keep in mind that the basic social problems constituting the contemporary industrial crisis have no technical solutions but instead require scientific and value political analysis as well as political creativity regarding the nature of a sustainable, desirable society and how to construct it.

I contend that the industrial crisis and the main issues of the desirability and feasibility of one of industrialism's central tenets, continuous and unlimited economic growth, form too serious a subject to be left to natural scientists of various fields and economists who, by and large, seek technical solutions alone. The problems facing industrial civilization, as presented by the limits-to-growth advocates, require normative analysis—including political, moral, and perhaps even aesthetic and theological analyses (to complete the components of normative discourse).

With a few notable exceptions, the overwhelming portion of the immense literature on the limits-to-growth problems of industrial society has omitted political issues and values and contains very few systematic, politically sophisticated analyses despite the obvious fundamental political relevance of this research—to be expected, I suppose, from trained natural scientists and contemporary economists who usually seek to avoid political discourse. Normative discourse which emphasizes value assessment of the status quo and the possible prescription of value changes in response to the crisis within industrialism has also been missing. Again, this is understandable given the general acceptance of value noncognitivism within postindustrial society; that is, the belief by most natural and social scientists, especially economists (and the public as well), that value questions are not open to reasonable debate and resolution. But more on this point in part 2.

Therefore, the discussion that follows will consist of a normative political examination of: the nature of the industrial crisis; the eventual demise of industrial society; and the creation of not only a "post-postindustrial" social order in the vague, temporal sense made popular by Daniel Bell,[66] but a *transindustrial* society founded on an alternative set of values that go beyond the industrial ones presently under challenge and in crisis (and may include some preindustrial ones). I hope thereby to set an example for political philosophers by addressing the profound problems of evaluating industrial values, assessing their need for change, and recommending and defending superior substitute values. If, as I shall argue, advanced industrial society has been repoliticized as a result of its contemporary crisis, so must the theory of such a society!

The End of Industrial Civilization
Does Not Mean the End of the World

If one approaches the political philosophical elements of the industrial crisis, then, and only then, will one have the proper understanding of the total meaning of this set of threats to industrial civilization. Having asserted this, however, necessitates examination of the skeptic's or critic's appropriate query about evidence for this claim: is the prevailing "doom and gloom" reaction to the contemporary crisis of industrialism warranted? What evidence can be supplied to support this viewpoint?

I would like to suggest that the pessimism characterizing contemporary industrial thought (here Vonnegut's expression, "utterly terminal pessimism," may be sadly appropriate if my analysis of the death of industrial civilization is sound) is itself a product of a fundamental, if only implicit, set of normative judgments that ought to be made explicit by the progrowth defenders of the existing industrial social order and the desirability of its values. Moreover, if these latter judgments are rejected and replaced by an alternative transindustrial set of values, the depressing quality of the writing about the challenges to industrial culture in the form of the limits to economic growth need not occur and can be exchanged for encouragement about the future of humanity. This objective may not be completely possible, but, to borrow a word from the historian L. S. Stavrianos' revealing title: *The Promise of the Coming Dark Age*,[67] with a change in values humanity may be able to look to the future with "promise." According to Stavrianos:

> This is an exhilarating moment in human history. Far from being an Age of Trouble, or Alienation, or Anxiety, this is rather the age in which man for the first time can turn from his age-old struggle for survival to a new struggle for self-fulfillment that will enable him to realize his humanity.[68]

I understand that the Chinese equivalent for the English word "crisis" means roughly: "a dangerous opportunity to improve matters." Biologists Paul Ehrlich and Anne Ehrlich refer to the same Chinese concept when they quote a Chinese proverb as the epigraph to their volume: "a calamity is time of great opportunity."[69] If we consider this Chinese aphorism that crises present both opportunities for betterment as well as risks in relation to the industrial social crisis, let us ask: risks to what in this case? Here the risks pertain to the ongoing existence of the industrial social status quo, including its values, institutions, and including, of course, its distribution of wealth and power. Impending changes in this social structure need not be assessed negatively; indeed, they may be evaluated positively depending upon one's judgment of the current social circumstances and the possible opportunities for change made manifest by the crisis. In this way, the dread inherent in the ordinary understanding in English of crisis may be overcome.

On the concept of crisis the economist Andre Gunder Frank also notes its positive component tied to social transformation:

> Crisis does not mean end. On the contrary, "crisis" refers to the critical time during which the end will be avoided through new adaptations if possible, only failing these, the end becomes unavoidable. *The Concise Oxford English Dictionary* defines crisis as: "Turning point; especially of disease. Moment of danger or suspense in politics, etc. as cabinet, financial. From Greek *krisis*, decision." The crisis is a period in which a diseased social, economic, and political body or

system cannot live on as before and is obliged, on pain of death, to undergo transformations that will give it a new lease on life. Therefore, this period of crisis is a historical moment of danger and suspense during which the crucial decisions and transformations are made, which will determine the future development of the system if any and its new social, economic, and political basis.[70]

This deeper understanding of the meaning of crisis, emphasizing the time for change of the entity experiencing the crisis, whether an individual medical patient or an entire civilization,[71] and the opportunity for the impending change in the entity to produce an improvement, is crucial to our discussion. Rather than view the current industrial crisis apocalyptically, as the end of the world, it is of the first importance, I think, to recognize that this crisis—or "moment of decision" in Greek, or "moment of great opportunity" in Chinese—may instead mean that the contemporary industrial world, its values, and social structure are irreversibly flawed ("diseased") and declining as a result of these flaws. Admitting the crisis, we shall discover that these values and social institutions cannot be revived and survive *in their present* form, and, furthermore, that this decisive time could be the opportunity to create a superior social order.

I believe that this sense of crisis characterizes current industrial civilization. Residents of our social order are confronted with crucial decisions and judgments of value which will transform their social and individual lives. No wonder technical solutions have not worked! Once the aforementioned point about the nature of the crisis experienced in industrial civilization is recognized, the doom and gloom of much of postindustrial thought in reaction to its crisis may be seen to consist of a profound sweeping value judgment supporting the current advanced industrial order—a judgment that must be stated explicitly and defended thoroughly and not merely assumed while expressing one's despair and dread about the uncertain future.

To reinforce this chapter's argument for the significance of problem formulation and understanding (in this instance, the meaning of the industrial crisis), I would like to refer to a remark by the political philosopher Herbert Marcuse about the relation between liberation and slavery: "All liberation [Marcuse wrote] depends on the consciousness of servitude."[72] In addition, the social theorist Philip Slater expresses a similar point more generally when he says: "For me real hope begins with the recognition and identification of dilemmas."[73]

Both Marcuse and Slater assert the positive values of recognizing conditions of negativity as a necessary prerequisite to improving these circumstances. Some of the difficulty humanity faces in the last decade of the twentieth century in being liberated from the negative conditions of industrial civilization so vividly described by the limits-to-growth critics is our general failure to concede the existence and fundamental normative nature of the industrial crisis and this society's various ills. The crisis pertains not only to the biophysical limits receiving so much attention (called "outer limits" by United Nations' agencies)[74] for which a technical solution alone (or a "high technology" panacea, as some hope room temperature fusion would be) is not likely to be sufficient, but to a society requiring a change of basic values (the "inner limits") and social transformation in order to mitigate, if not resolve, the various social problems caused by the inner limits and their implementing institutions within industrial society such as those listed by Sale. One goal of this volume is to elucidate the nature and meaning of this crisis as a necessary first step to just such an amelioration.

In his reflections on advanced industrial society, Slater explains why the industrial crisis may be misapprehended or even why its recognition, once achieved, is suppressed. Furthermore, he discusses how even the most dismal formulation of the crisis need not lead to despair at all; indeed, he illustrates how such depressing descriptions of social reality can contribute to the end of despair and the achievement of a more desirable state by eliciting the painful but necessary action required for our lives to be improved.

He begins his discussion with a curious epigraph from psychologist Alexander Lowen: "The path to joy leads through despair," and then proceeds to explain that according to Lowen:

> despair is the only cure for illusion. Without despair we cannot transfer our allegiance to reality—it is a kind of mourning period for our fantasies. Some people do not survive this despair, but no major change within a person can occur without it. People get trapped in despair when this despair is incomplete—when some thread of illusory hope is still retained.[75]

I think that this psychological analysis provides insight into much of the predicament of contemporary industrial citizens and their culture. The illusion of unlimited economic growth that forms the bedrock of industrial civilization, the dream of limitless economic growth with prosperity for everyone, and the social value of "unlimited progress" has been challenged effectively by recent developments. These include: biophysical limits asserted by the limits-to-growth advocates and recent shocking environmental, economic and political events. Even the steadfast defenders of industrialism find themselves either denying that a crisis exists at all and going on to counterattack the limits-to-growth critics of industrial society (as exemplified by the progrowth literature and defenders of industrial culture such as the contributors to the Simon and Kahn volume) or suffering the pains of being trapped in their incomplete despair because they still hold on to the idea that industrial culture can somehow be salvaged with its basic values intact, including unlimited economic growth.

These industrial diehards, from scholars like Beckerman, Kahn and Julian L. Simon, to virtually all policymakers like former president Ronald Reagan down to the county and municipal leaders (but see rise of antigrowth movement in American West),[76] hang on to, instead of mourn for, their illusory unlimited growth conception that deserves to be laid to rest. Ridding ourselves of that concept and recognizing its futility as well as undesirability would free industrial inhabitants to create a new and more satisfying social order for all of its members. This could occur despite the temporary grief associated with the mourning period for our fantasies that would surely characterize the transitional period. "So long as we imagine things are getting better we will never reexamine basic assumptions."[77]

Combining these ideas of Marcuse, Slater, and Lowen, one can conclude that positive social change depends upon the recognition of the undesirable and impossible beliefs constituting our present social values as well as the capacity to withstand the sadness accompanying such recognition of our mistaken values and illusory dreams destined to go unfulfilled. We must despair totally of industrial values like unlimited economic growth and its attendant social policies before we are able to discard them and choose better ones; we can indeed achieve joy, but only through the temporary despair associated with the rejection of values that delude us.

From this viewpoint, the current despair within advanced industrial civilization must be made complete. We must not be trapped into maintaining the current flawed social values by only partially jettisoning them. If the thrust of this section is understood, the following statement will be accepted with all of its profound social consequences:

Indeed, we are confronted not with the end of the world, although it will surely be the end of the world as we have known it, but with a grand opportunity to share in the creation of a new and potentially higher, more humane form of post[trans] industrial civilization.[78]

Death of a civilization need not only involve grief for the lost values and institutions, its way of life, although this grief is both understandable and, as Lowen and Slater suggest, necessary for social improvement. It may also include an encouraging and inspiring view toward the new opportunities that are presented to create a better social order in its place as a result of our new insight.

To conclude this chapter about how the industrial social crisis and demise need not result in overwhelming despair, let us consider remarks by the popular observer of social change, Alvin Toffler:

> One can look at the economic death agonies of industrial civilization as unequivocally bad. Most of us reading this are products of that civilization and have large stakes in its survival: jobs, careers, power, egos. To read that it is in its twilight casts a *Gotterdammerung* gloom about us.
>
> Yet one might also look upon the coming years of trauma as the long-needed opportunity to set some old problems straight... in short, to undertake an awesome but exhilarating task that few generations in human history have ever faced: the design of a new civilization.[79]

Following a more detailed examination of the crisis of industrial civilization in later chapters, I shall outline (in the final part) some prescriptions for the design of a new transindustrial social order. To my mind, no more significant problem exists for political philosophy than a careful, defensible interpretation of the value-based nature of the current crisis of industrial culture followed by the thoughtful presentation and defense of the "design of a new civilization." We have decreasing time available for these urgent tasks because of the recent "last gasps" of industrialism's preoccupation with economic growth as seen in Reaganism and ever-worsening ecological conditions: for example, increasing deforestation, population growth and declining food stocks per capita, untreated toxic waste sites, ocean pollution, global warming, acid rain, soil erosion, stratospheric ozone depletion, etc. Great amounts of collective thought and action will be required if these vital goals of postindustrial social transformation are to be achieved in time.

What should be reassuring to those unfamiliar with the history of political philosophy is that this critical social role is not new for this mode of discourse. The repoliticization of advanced industrial society should awaken public recognition of the practical importance of political philosophy and a full discussion of the fundamental social values for public policy-making. This is especially important during dangerous times of social crises with the concomitant opportunity for social change. These are the times when political philosophy is most needed and—encouragingly—when it has been most active and most insightful, from its origins in the crisis within the ancient Greek *polis* to the present.

2

The Death of Industrial Illusions

> One needs to destroy illusions in order to create the conditions that make illusions unnecessary.
>
> —Erich Fromm[1]

The Liberating Aspects of the Death of Social Illusions

Fromm analyzes the differences between the "having" and "being" modes of existence and their influence upon the characters of both individuals and societies. He addresses the nature of knowing according to such "being" mode thinkers as: the Buddha, the Hebrew prophets, Jesus, Master Eckhart, Freud and Marx.[2] He then concludes that a common point within all these thinkers' messages was that they all believed the accepted view of reality during their lives to be false. They claimed that genuine knowledge could only begin with the shattering of these illusory beliefs.

I shall discuss later the significance of Fromm's distinction between "having" and "being" in detail, largely for its implications concerning the "having" mode's dominance within materialist industrial society (where the nature of the industrial value of materialism will be addressed as well). At this point in the discussion, however, let us understand that before industrial citizens will be able to know which social values are worthy of acceptance, the illusory goals within the industrial worldview, such as unlimited economic growth and material prosperity and success available for all, must be eliminated no matter how painful the disillusionment process may be.

The importance of knowledge of a better social life through removal of illusions about social reality as well as the liberating consequences of such knowledge in order to achieve a more fulfilling individual and collective existence may be clarified by drawing an analogy to Karl Popper's fallibilist theory of knowledge.

The heart of Popper's theory is the rejection of absolute, perfect and certain knowledge so long and avidly sought by man as both humanly and logically impossible: humanly impossible owing to man's fallibility and logically impossible because the foundation of human knowledge implied by this quest for the ultimate sources of absolute certain knowledge is misconceived.[3]

This age-old futile search for perfect knowledge and its sources has resulted in harmful theoretical consequences according to Popper. It has trapped us in the false but historically important dilemma between infinite regression leading to skepticism and dogmatic absolutism implying irrationalism.[4]

It was one of Popper's major achievements to have realized that much of traditional Western philosophy was suffering from the ill effects of an important goal that was illusory. Popper's own theory of knowledge, known as "critical rationalism," recognized and rejected this long-standing, fatal misconception of Western thought and offered an alternative account shorn of this infallibilist, delusory conception. In it, all knowledge claims are examined and considered vulnerable to refutation; therefore, none can obtain the status of perfection.[5]

The major benefit of Popper's insight is that it frees humans from the two undesirable conclusions about human knowledge by eliminating the false dilemma caused by the illusory goal of absolute certain knowledge: skepticism or dogmatism. This accomplishment is achieved by virtue of a theory of knowledge that exposes the erroneous nature of the fundamental goal that produced these two negative conclusions. The illusion of absolute certain knowledge needed to be destroyed.[6] Popper's fallibilist theory describes how to avoid both skepticism and dogmatism making the illusion of certainty unnecessary.

Just as Popper's fallibilist theory of critical rationalism demonstrated the wrongheadedness of the once basic aim of Western philosophy, infallible knowledge, the contemporary industrial citizen must recognize the wrongheadedness of the fundamental value of industrial civilization: unlimited economic growth. Both of these basic conceptions constitute impossible and misconceived human goals; they are illusions. We must recognize them for what they are and reject them so that the genuine and solvable problems can emerge and be pursued.

Popper's theory of knowledge poses the question: What alternative philosophical goals should replace the infallibilist theory's certain knowledge? Similarly, limits-to-growth critics of industrialism should ask: What social values should replace industrial civilization's limitless economic growth? Moreover, how do we implement the radical social changes implied by this disillusionment process? These two questions concerning advanced industrial social values and institutions are essentially political and should be the subject of systematic political, philosophical, and scientific inquiry. I hope to begin such an inquiry in this book.

I wish to make a final point before we leave this topic. The environmental critique of industrialism based on the biophysical limits to growth is not, strictly speaking, a normative critique of industrial values. It is possible to accept with great regret the existence of such limits to growth, making limitless economic growth impossible, while continuing to uphold the desirability of industrial values.

Even if we accept that ecology is essentially nonnormative in nature, we can nevertheless agree that the environmental social movement may have dramatically increased the industrial public's consciousness of the limits of economic growth. By attacking the various sources of the different forms of pollution, the dangers of nuclear power or noting and protecting the limited quantities of vital, nonrenewable energy resources, minerals, animals and plants, the environmental movement addressed the significance of unlimited economic growth as a foundation of industrial culture, and publicized the many damaging social consequences resulting from this basic industrial value.

Thus, the environmental movement started the painful but necessary industrial disillusionment process. It has shown that scientifically detectable problems caused by ecological scarcity can have—and have had—profound normative implications similar to the announcement of a fire to residents of a building: the prescription of a quick exit is implied!

The biophysical, environmental, limits-to-growth critique of industrialism and the normative critique of industrial values are philosophically different in theoretical status and type of evidence suitable to each but are related in their implications for social action. On the relation between values and the environment the following statement by two students of the limits to growth is useful:

> ...If it can be shown that the continuation of current growth trends leads to an inhuman society, even with clean air and water [then] under such conditions, the quality of life deteriorates whether or not acceptable biophysical environmental quality can be achieved. Therefore, investigations of limits to growth must consider not only the quality of the biophysical environment, but the comprehensive quality of human life for all members of society.[7]

Therefore, as I have argued, biophysical environmental analyses are insufficient unless accompanied by what is essentially a political philosophical study: the inquiry into "the comprehensive quality of human life for all members of society" wherein I take "comprehensive quality" to refer to not only to clean air, water, etc., but to a social order that creates a just and self-fulfilling life "for all members of society." I believe ecological analyses require consideration of social value choices and their defense to be complete. Unfortunately, few contributors to the limits-to-growth literature meet this normative requirement. Thus, human justice, freedom and self-fulfillment (and other political values) should be deemed important enough to be considered along with the biophysical requirements for survival.

Resisting Disillusionment about the Industrial Value of Unlimited Economic Growth

While the point about the positive effects of human disillusionment seems psychologically sound, it nonetheless is vulnerable to an objection mentioned by the economist Albert Hirschman who argues for the importance of human disappointment in social life.[8] Hirschman describes Leon Festinger's well-known research in psychology on cognitive dissonance as follows: the findings of Festinger reveal that people avoid dissonant information and only seek data that can be used to confirm the merits of their previous judgments.

Contrary to Festinger's view that human disappointment is suppressed and thus is not an important aspect of social life, Hirschman interprets his finding as evidence of just how powerful the human fear of recognizing our errors and experiencing disappointment with our judgments and actions can be.[9] Along with our anxiety reduction, humans seem to be disappointment-reducing and disappointment-suppressing organisms as well!

Hirschman's interpretation of the human reaction to disappointment and its importance as a "driving force in human affairs" is noteworthy for its emphasis upon how far people will go to reconstruct (or misperceive) reality in order to deny the disappointment experience or to admit error as the cause of the disappointment:

...the denial of reality that is practiced testifies to the *power* and *vitality* of the disappointment experience. We engage in all kinds of ingenious ruses and delaying actions before admitting to ourselves that we *are* disappointed, in part surely because we know that disappointment may compel us to a painful reassessment of our preferences and priorities.[10]

By denying disappointment, Hirschman argues, we not only avoid the admission of past failures of judgment and the unhappy results such admissions may involve, but, in addition, we prevent the pain of the "reassessment of our preferences and priorities"—the examination and possible change of our values.

Let us assume that Hirschman's account of the role of disappointment in human experience is accurate (since a detailed discussion of this psychological claim is beyond the scope of this work). An objection to my earlier claim about the importance and positive value of the disillusionment process might take this form: if such a process invariably results in disappointment, including recognition of error and disenchantment with one's previous values leading to a painful reassessment and possible replacement of these values, and, furthermore, if most people do not want these results and will strongly resist them, is not the claimed beneficial social significance of the disillusionment process seriously undermined?

Despite the fact that industrial civilization has brought so much dissatisfaction and danger to human survival, most of its inhabitants and policymakers deny the existence of an industrial crisis in the fundamental normative sense discussed earlier, wherein the admission of such a crisis would entail a change in basic values, such as limitless economic growth. Instead, we continue to avidly maintain industrialism's central value tenets including, of course, unlimited economic growth. This is demonstrated by the continuation of the universal policy objective of economic growth by policymakers in virtually all existing social orders as well as transnational public support for the social value of economic growth by most of the world's populace. "Grow or die" seems to be the watchword of industrial values setting up a grim alternative to limitless growth that both leads to industrial pessimism and (disappointment- and disillusionment avoiding) denial of the challenge presented by the limits-to-growth position.

Those who refuse to admit that industrialism is currently undergoing a crisis and who defend the industrial values advocate the progrowth view. They have generated the large number of writings in rejoinder to industrial civilization's deprecators within the economic growth debate, thereby avoiding the radical implications of the disturbing reassessment of industrial preferences and priorities. By denying the existence of the crisis and the resulting disappointment, they negate the need for any normative reassessment of the industrial social order's present so-called advanced stage.

"Disappointment [Hirschman writes] frequently will have to pass a certain threshold before it is consciously avowed—but then, just because of the earlier delaying actions, it may well be experienced 'with a vengeance.' "[11] This assertion is important for our discussion in two respects. First, it may explain the paralyzing and overwhelming despair of terminal pessimism associated with the industrial crisis. Second, it may explain the limits-to-growth advocates' urgent (and sometimes understandably extreme) efforts to achieve a greater public awareness about the nature and severity of the industrial crisis. These advocates fear that we might easily reach the threshold limit where public recognition of the existing limits to growth would be too late to spur the necessary value reassessments and social changes: the damage incurred would then be irreversible. In that event, disabling despair for the entire human species and all of the planet's living creatures would be appropriate because it would indeed be too late to do anything useful about our misguided priorities; "the fatal plunge into the abyss" would be at hand. We would be left with Woody Allen's unhappy choice between hopelessness and extinction.

Hopefully—and all social inquiry, especially political philosophy, may be considered to be an optimistic enterprise presupposing that the diagnosis of social ills will have some beneficial social impact—the current industrial crisis will rouse people and policymakers from their disappointment-denying deceptions and delays in acting before it is too lake. Moreover, it may inspire political philosophical examination and transformation of the values and thereby along with the other components of social transformation (like social movements) fundamentally change the way of life of industrial society.

The strong resistance by defenders of the postindustrial status quo and advocates of progrowth values to claims of the existence of the industrial crisis and to pleas for a reassessment of industrial values by the limits-to-growth advocates tends to support Hirschman's "avoidance" explanation. From this perspective, Ronald Reagan's and other progrowth proponents' electoral successes throughout postindustrial society and the public enthusiasm for their message of ceaseless, unlimited economic growth for all may be viewed as part of this disappointment-denying phenomenon. It was so much more comforting to hear the message of the resurgence of America and the coming limitless prosperity—"the morning in America"—then to admit that at its foundation was a fantasy and that a change in our values and social order were necessary!

Nevertheless, considering the reluctance of mankind to experience disappointment and admit errors—and our tendency to deny reality in order to accomplish these objectives—the fact that the apocalyptic limits-to-growth literature and critical environmental movement exist at all, especially as extensively and influentially as they do in the multidisciplinary scholarly community, the public media, and slowly but significantly within the public at large,[12] provides evidence that the phenomenon of human denial is breaking down as social conditions worsen and the undesirable consequences of industrial values are experienced directly by more advanced industrial citizens.

Not only for the cogency of this argument, but for the present and future well-being of humanity, we must hope that the denial limit of disappointment or disillusionment—the limit beyond which man's denial capacities will end resulting in consciousness of reality—occurs before the actual ecological and social limits endanger all earthly life. Furthermore, once the denial limit is crossed we must hope that sufficient resources of time, materials, human energy, creativity, and will remain to replace the old misguided values and social order built upon them with new and more satisfying ones for the "comprehensive quality of life for all members of society." If some of the industrial crisis advocates and limits-to-growth critics of industrialism have been guilty of extremism—as most of their opponents charge—we need to keep in mind that the necessary and radical social change that these critics so passionately prescribe is powerfully thwarted by the psychologically-based denials of their claimed threats to industrial values and civilization. Furthermore, the immense importance of what is at stake must be recognized as well as the extreme resistance and ruling power by those who benefit most from the current economic growth-based, industrial values and social order: the postindustrial elite.

The writer Jeremy Rifkin informs his readers of the old French proverb, *"Les gens heureux n'ont pas d'histoire"* ("Happy people don't make history"), and then adds:

> When you and I are feeling really happy and content with the way our life is going, we rarely if ever entertain the idea of a radical change in the way we go about things. Why should we? As the saying goes, "Don't knock a good thing."[13]

As students of contemporary industrial society and its crisis, we must concentrate our attention on the overwhelming majority of the human population—industrialized or not—who are not happy. As psychologist and social theorist Fromm observes about the citizens of the richest advanced industrial society: "We [Americans] are a society of notoriously unhappy people: lonely, anxious, depressed, destructive, dependent, people who are glad when we have killed the time we are trying so hard to save."[14] It is these people—both inside and outside advanced industrial society—who *should* be disappointed with their lot in life and who are thus, at least, potentially open to reassessing and changing their values and society. These are the people prepared to "make history" rather than the relatively miniscule number of individuals who are sufficiently satisfied to engage in disappointment- and disillusionment-denial of the industrial crisis and who thereby oppose such a value reassessment and social transformation process.

It is true that the few affluent and satisfied people—members of the postindustrial elite—who so strongly defend and prescribe this same postindustrial value structure for all humanity have been overwhelmingly effective in achieving its almost universal adoption, but not in the realization of its impossible and illusory promises. Most of the remainder of the earth's unhappy and deprived people do, in fact, aspire futilely to join the industrial elite instead of recognizing this social order's crisis. As a result, they do not change their value priorities and thus fail to transform their social institutions and practices. Thus, these industrial elite-aspirants are destined to be denied genuine human fulfillment by a pernicious, competitive, industrial value system in which few are permitted to win despite the endless struggle of most competitors.

Camus's *Philosophie Des Limites* and Its Relevance to Advanced Industrial Society

Humanity's denial of central elements of the human condition such as: the denial of disappointment and of our goals being illusory (or the limits to human satisfaction); the denial of our mortality (or the limits to life); the denial of our fallibility (or the limits to human knowledge); the denial of the need for conservation and pursuing less than the maximum material productivity (or the limits to economic growth); or, the denial of limits in general, are all part of man's unique nature.

As the French novelist and social thinker Albert Camus has emphasized in his *"philosophie des limites"*, "Man is the only creature who refuses to be what he is"[15]—a limited being confronting a limited world. Refusal to recognize limits or the complete denial of them (Camus terms it: "escaping" from them)[16], and the profound consequences of these choices characterize modern (industrial) man, according to Camus. This, along with the recommendation to fully recognize our limits, is the central component of Camus's worldview. Within it is Camus's essential concept of "absurdity" whose definition most pertinent to our discussion is: "lucid reasoning noting its limits"[17] or "that divorce between the mind that desires and the world that disappoints."[18]

Now, one might think that a philosophy such as Camus's which takes as its driving force the idea of man's limits and the absurd relation between man and a world which also contains limits would be unrelievedly pessimistic. Indeed, casual readers of Camus may get that impression. However, it is essential to note that absurdity or the recognition of the limits to the human condition is not the conclusion of Camus's thinking but its starting point.[19] Because of the absurdity that characterizes humanity, man must become aware of the limits to our being and the world's. Within these limits, Camus advises, we must live with as much lucidity as possible. If this aim is achieved then we will fulfill the goal of Pindar used by Camus for the epigraph of *The Myth of Sisyphus:*

"O my soul, do not aspire to immortal life, but exhaust the limits of the possible."[20]

Camus concentrated his political writings on modern man's "metaphysical rebellion" leading to the historical, unlimited, and violent revolutions of the nineteenth and twentieth centuries which embodied contemporary man's protest against his absurd—limited—condition.[21] In my view, Camus's philosophy of limits would be a good antidote to industrial civilization's current denial of or escape from the limits that characterize our human condition by resorting to illusory conceptions such as unlimited economic growth.

Camus attacks the denial of the limited nature of man—mainly our mortality and fallibility—and the limited nature of the world inherent in the historic manifestations of metaphysical rebellion. These manifestations take the form of modern revolutions since the French Revolution. I propose to focus in a similar way upon the unrealistic or escapist nature and the resulting significant social consequences of the founding illusion of modern industrial civilization: limitless economic growth.

The basic traits of industrial society must be perceived and changed if we are to avoid the calamities projected by the limits-to-growth advocates (some early indications of which are already present; for example, human starvation and environmental pollution and its adverse effects upon human—and other—life) and forecasted by Camus who witnessed the already fully developed, mind-boggling excesses of twentieth century violence.[22] Once the modern escape from man's limited social reality—in all its myriad forms—is ended, then we may construct a social order consistent with these unavoidable limits and "exhaust the limits of the possible," seeking to go no further. As the mythical Sisyphus was punished by the Gods to eternally roll a boulder up a mountain only to have it fall back down again, it is only by recognizing the limits of the human condition that humanity can achieve the only happiness possible.

Referring to Sisyphus and his consciousness of his "unspeakable penalty in which the whole being is exerted toward accomplishing nothing." Camus says:

> The lucidity that was to constitute his torture at the same time crowns his victory..."I conclude that all is well," says Oedipus, and that remark is sacred. It echoes in the wild and limited universe of man ...I leave Sisyphus at the foot of the mountain...He too concludes that all is well...The struggle itself toward the heights is enough to fill a man's heart. One must imagine Sisyphus happy.[23]

Other students of modernity have noted its major characteristic of the denial of limits; for example, Daniel Bell:

> The deepest nature of man, the secret of his soul as revealed by the modern metaphysic, is that he seeks to reach out beyond himself; knowing that negativity—death—is finite, he refuses to accept it. Behind the chiliasm of modern man is the megalomania of self-

infinitization. In consequence, the modern hubris is refusal to accept limits.... [24]

The renowned student of industrialism, Lewis Mumford, explains the sense of limitlessness that characterized the industrial worldview from its earliest stages:

The desire for life without limits was part of the general lifting of limits which the first great assemblage of power by means of the megamachine [the mechanized, industrial, social order] brought about. Human weaknesses, above all the weaknesses of mortality, were both contested and defied... From the standpoint of human life, indeed of all organic existence, this assertion of absolute power was a confession of psychological immaturity—a radical failure to understand the natural processes of birth and growth, of maturation and death.[25]

This denial of limits and the megalomania of industrial humanity takes several forms: the political violence resulting from political absolutism and the escape from absurdity or limits that Camus focuses upon; the fascination with absolute power, mechanization, speed, and militarism that Mumford focuses upon;[26] and the addiction to economic growth resulting from the illusion of unlimited economic growth and universal prosperity that the limits-to-growth advocates focus upon.

The example of industrial humanity's refusal to be what it is and refusal to recognize the limits to our social lives whether imposed from internal sources—humanity itself—or from the world we find ourselves in (keeping in mind Camus's notion that absurdity or man's limited condition is a relationship between humanity and its world and not a characteristic of humanity alone) reinforces the fundamental social vision of industrial civilization: ceaseless economic growth. Ceaseless economic growth is an illusory economic vision: Mumford would term it as "myth"; Slater would express it as "fantasy"; Camus would call it "escape"; and Hirschman would say "denial." The concept is so crucial to industrial civilization that recognizing it as illusory rivals the anxiety experienced when other existential limits such as mortality and fallibility are confronted.

The Political Profundity of the
Limitless-Economic-Growth Illusion for Industrial Society

Political philosophers going back to their beginning with Plato have always recognized not only the philosophical import of a social order's underlying values but, in addition, the practical importance of these social values for the survival of the particular social order under examination. This is better known as the problem of legitimacy. Perhaps the eighteenth century French political philosopher Jean Jacques Rousseau put it most clearly when he wrote:

> The strongest is never strong enough to be always the master, unless he transforms strength into right, and obedience into duty.... Let us then admit that force does not create right, and that we are obliged to obey only legitimate powers.[27]

What a ruling elite within a society wishes to accomplish is to establish acceptance of its values and the social structure predicated upon these values as legitimate by the overwhelming majority of its citizens in order to "transform strength into right, and obedience into duty." Therefore, every dominant elite's rulership and the social arrangements included within its social order presuppose a legitimizing principle or set of principles upon which their right to rule is based.

Obviously, the industrial elite is not the first elite nor is it the first ruling group to resort to a set of legitimizing ideas—ideology, to use Marx's concept—for the social order it created. What is new about the ideology of industrial civilization is that our civilization places its primary legitimizing value not upon religion or monarchy but upon unlimited economic growth. Any challenge to this value challenges the very foundation of the industrial social order. This is why the limits-to-growth proponents, in conjunction with the events of the last twenty years, have jointly precipitated an industrial crisis.

Fromm discusses industrialism's "Great Promise of Unlimited Progress" and the new religion called "Progress" characterizing the industrial age:

> The Great Promise of Unlimited Progress [was] the promise of domination of nature, of material abundance, of the greatest happiness of the greatest number, and of unimpeded personal freedom... With industrial progress, from the substitution of mechanical and then nuclear energy for animal and human energy to the substitution of the computer for the human mind, we could feel that we were on our way to unlimited production and, hence, unlimited consumption.... [and] the trinity of unlimited production, absolute freedom, and unrestricted happiness formed the nucleus of a new religion, Progress.... [28]

What makes this industrial promise and civic religion of unlimited progress and consumption politically important is its role with regard to the legitimacy of the industrial (capitalist) culture. A student of capitalism relates an important point for our discussion regarding political legitimacy and unlimited economic growth for the capitalist social order:

This social justification [of profits for the few capitalists] places the capitalist in contrast to the feudal lord, the ancient slaveowner, or the eastern potentate, all of whom controlled the production process as firmly as the capitalist does today. However, these earlier dominant classes rested their ideological superiority and their right to rule on claims other than economic prowess. Some classes had religious claims (the Hebrew priests, the medieval church, "divinely" appointed kings); others had military claims (medieval lords, Roman emperors, Indian war chiefs); still others had political, cultural, or other claims. Only the capitalist class bases its claim to dominance on privilege directly on its ability to make profits by selling goods in the market.[29]

Another student of industrial values makes the same point but, significantly for our discussion, does not restrict his comments to capitalism; he applies them to industrial societies as a whole:

Modern society represents the first large-scale attempt to found stability and authority not upon earlier patterns of inherited privilege or traditional associations, but rather directly on the achievement of economic production and the satisfaction of needs. . . . In concrete terms, the well-being of every individual is thought to be identical with the steady rise of the Gross National Product. . . . *The principle of legitimacy for modern society . . . now consists in a permanently rising level of consumption.* This principle is today at work not only in government-managed capitalist societies (North American and Western Europe) but also in the industrialized socialist nations (Eastern Europe and the Soviet Union).[30]

This remarkable point will be elaborated upon later, but it should be noted here that this claim about the unique economic basis of the legitimacy of industrial society includes the assertion of industrial values transcending the capitalism/socialism conflict around which most of the contemporary political rhetoric and action depend. *To my mind, it is the commitment of virtually all of the elites of the world's nation-states today to industrial values, namely, continuous, maximum, unlimited economic growth—the new religion of Progress and Unlimited Prosperity—that is of the utmost political importance; not the varying individual cultural manifestations of this commitment or the different technical means to accomplish these industrial goals.*

Borrowing the term from John Kenneth Galbraith,[31] we may call this claim the "industrial convergence thesis," to convey the idea that despite ideological and institutional differences, the industrialized capitalist and socialist societies have much more in common on a deep normative level than their political institutional differences would imply. From this view, whether one's economy is capitalist market-oriented or socialist state-commanded is less important than both systems' seeking unlimited material abundance and consumption. (Of course, the socialist economies are at a distinct disadvantage in reaching this goal since none of them are fully advanced industrial nations. Therefore, much of the argument to follow does not apply to them—yet.)

If contemporary political thinkers, policymakers, and the public as a whole insist upon viewing the current political world in terms of left/right ideology or superpower conflict, then many of the underlying bases for the dynamics of contemporary social life and its ills will be overlooked. This important point is expressed in the question: "If there is no commitment to economic growth, what can the Soviet Union—or Japan or the United States—hold out as a social goal for its people?"[32]

Ecological scarcity and threats know no national borders or economic means once the fundamental, unlimited, growth-based goals are accepted.

In brief, the imperatives of the industrial production system common to East and West have brought a convergence of environmental ills that call into question the basic premise of the industrial system— and therefore of many features of the political institutions rooted in that system, whether those institutions are nominally capitalist or communist.[33]

The significance of the industrial convergence thesis emphasizing similar industrial values as the grounds for the legitimacy of both industrial capitalist and socialist societies is a "reduction" in the best sense of that controversial, scientific, methodological term: a more fundamental, and therefore more penetrating, level of explanation is being claimed than what was relied upon previously. (In the next part we will refer to this false claim and call it the "fallacy of reductionism.") Furthermore, attention is directed at a more profound cause of the industrial crisis than the typical ideological differences usually cited: the basic industrial values at the foundation of all industrialized social orders, be they capitalist or socialist.

Although most of my illustrations and references in the following discussion shall come from capitalist societies, this should not be taken as a retreat from or contradiction of the industrial convergence thesis. I omit discussion of contemporary socialist societies because of the limits of space,

my knowledge of such societies, and, most significantly, the fact that contemporary socialist societies are generally not "advanced" industrial societies with regard to providing basic needs as well as luxury goods for their
populations. Therefore, they are less illustrative for my argument than the
materially affluent, capitalist industrial societies. Nonetheless, from this
viewpoint one may certainly view the dramatic, market-oriented changes
occurring in both the People's Republic of China under the post-Mao leadership, and the Soviet Union and Eastern bloc nations under Gorbachev, as
confirmation of the convergence thesis.

The industrial convergence thesis also contains the idea that while
there are considerable dissimilarities between capitalism and its private control of the means of production, and socialism's public control of these
means, these dissimilarities exist largely with respect to the means of
achieving the similar industrial goals of unlimited economic growth and
continuously increasing material wealth and consumption. Both capitalist
and socialist political systems reflect the identical, fundamental, and industrial social values essential to their legitimacy: unlimited economic growth
and the Great Promise of Unlimited Progress!

The Japanese Matsushita (Panasonic) Company anthem clearly expresses the industrial commitment to economic growth:

For the building of a new Japan
Let's put our strength and minds together
Doing our best to promote production
Sending our goods to the people of the world
Endlessly and continuously
Like a water gushing from a fountain
GROW INDUSTRY, Grow, Grow, Grow.[34]

The role played by the value of limitless economic growth in industrial social life and its legitimacy is crucial here. It explains the preoccupation with economic growth as a public policy issue within all industrial
societies—and even in most nonindustrialized societies where the elites,
if not the masses, have adopted the industrial value structure. Economic growth today is, according to one student of contemporary politics:
"the overriding objective and supreme justification of [industrial] social
organization."[35]

Before concluding this chapter and beginning a fuller discussion of the
limits to economic growth and their implications for advanced industrial
society, I think some additional clarification of the fatal industrial flaw of
the addiction to unlimited economic growth is in order.

On the Industrial Value of Unlimited Economic Growth

The maverick antigrowth economist Herman Daly explains the essential industrial characteristic of unlimited economic growth as follows:

"Growthmania" is an insufficiently pejorative term for the paradigm or mind-set that always puts growth in the first place—the attitude that there is no such thing as enough, that cannot conceive of too much of a good thing.... The way to have your cake and eat it too is to make it grow.

Growthmania is the attitude in economic theory that begins with the theological assumption of infinite wants and then with infinite hubris goes on to presume that the original sin of infinite wants has its redemption vouchsafed by the omnipotent savior of technology, and that the first commandment is to produce more and more goods for more and more people, world without end. And that this is not only possible, but desirable.[36]

Daly and his fellow supporters of the limits-to-growth critique of industrial civilization's foundation value of economic growth seek to convince us that the necessary environmental conditions for the achievement of the social goal of "producing more and more goods for more and more people, world without end," do not now and can *never* exist!

By recognizing ecological scarcity, we expose the reality that there are absolute, unavoidable environmental limits restricting continuous economic growth, even if these limits are currently unknown or are the subject of controversy among scientists. A sophisticated understanding of post-industrial society informed by a political philosophical viewpoint contains this central idea: all human needs and wants are not infinite, nor are they capable of satisfaction by economic growth alone. The important distinction between needs and wants has been stressed throughout Western political thought.[37] This distinction reveals the existence of alternative values, and the limits based on these values, which are necessary to counteract the desirability of unlimited economic growth.

In the context of analyzing our addiction to economic growth, contributors to the limits-to-growth literature may be divided into two groups: first, those critics of the industrial social order who focus upon the *impossibility* of unlimited economic growth because of ecological limits manifested by environmental pollution and the scarcity of resources; and, second, industrial critics who emphasize the *undesirability* of endless economic growth based upon their conception of the human condition with regard to wants and needs, our ideals, and their value assessment of the type of society produced by the single-minded commitment to unlimited economic growth.

An extreme devotion to endless economic growth is held by virtually all national elites (regardless of culture, political ideology, political system, or economic structure) as both a possibility and as a social value incorporating presuppositions about the nature of humanity and its environmental condition. Actually, limits-to-growth critics of the industrial value of economic growth could effectively rebut their progrowth opponents by asking: who are the real extremists in this debate?

One profound consequence of the industrial crisis is that the progrowth addiction forming the foundation of industrial civilization has become a prominent social issue. Although it is new to the American agenda, the issue has been in the foreground of public policy discussions in other advanced industrial nations, especially in Western Europe. As a result, the social effects of accepting the presupposition of endless growth have been challenged and fundamentally clarified by the limits-to-growth critics of the postindustrial order.

For the last two decades, when our civilization has perceived the negative consequences of growth addiction and become aware of the limits to growth, our response has been similar to Slater's image of a man running with increasing speed to obtain more oxygen in an air-sealed tunnel. Rather than slowing down and examining the bases of our plight while polluting less and conserving energy and natural resources, we have redoubled our efforts and commitment of resources to the very source of our difficulties—the social goal of unlimited economic growth—with the same suicidal result!

Let us examine the ideal of economic "growth" itself. Daly informs his readers that the first dictionary meaning of the verb "to grow" is: "to spring up and develop to *maturity*."[38] The dictionary that I consulted provides the following for its first meaning of "to grow": "to increase by natural development, as any living organism. . . ."[39] By combining these two definitions, we obtain the idea that growth is both limited (to the point of maturity only) and natural.

> Mammals, including man, grow in their childhood and youth, after which they stop growing. In no phase of normal development does exponential [unlimited, ever-increasing, continuous] growth take place.[40]

The conception that growth be limited on the model of human growth, continuing only until the point or limit of maturity is reached, is applicable to our discussion of the industrial social value of economic growth. We do not look at a fifty year-old person and consider it a deficiency that she or he is no longer growing taller. If, *per impossible*, a human (or any living organism for that matter) were to grow continuously and unlimitedly, it would be disastrous—its very health and survival would be endangered.[41]

Given this understanding of natural growth being limited and the nature of the set of pathologies most frequently found in advanced industrial societies under the general rubric of "cancer" (or exceeding the limit of the healthy growth of cells with respect to speed and number), it should not be surprising that the environmental critics of industrial society have coined the condemnatory slogan: "Growth for the sake of growth is the ideology of the cancer cell."[42]

The critics of industrial civilization charge that just as ceaseless unlimited growth is not desirable for individual human development, so this excessive—escape from limits—concept of growth as a fundamental social value is undesirable for industrial civilization as a whole. At this point in the debate between the anti- and progrowth advocates, those who defend the industrial value of unlimited growth and other industrial values (such as Herman Kahn or Julian Simon) might retort by saying: "Aggregate economic growth on the societal level is not analogous to natural, individual-based, limited growth. Therefore, the value of unlimited, aggregate economic growth is untouched by its critics' attacks based upon their supposed, but false, analogy to the individual." Such defenders of industrial growth would charge their opponents with the logical fallacy of composition: falsely assuming that what is true of the individual is also true of the whole.

Of course, in such an argument the progrowth advocates must support their claim that the value of unlimited economic growth on the aggregate societal level is neither relevant to, nor conditioned by, the limited nature of individual human beings—the ultimate beneficiaries of such a social order. Thus, one may ask: Is unlimited societal growth inhuman? Is the collectivist argument made by the supporter of unlimited economic growth vulnerable to the typical individualist countercharge that a collectivist chimera or illusion is being used to the detriment of individual, flesh and blood, human beings?

The essentially metaphysical individualist-holist dispute may be put aside by this effective rejoinder: the holist argument about the possibility and desirability of unlimited economic growth on the aggregate level is open to the potent criticism that such an imagined societal level growth is not beneficial to *all* individuals (utilizing the very wedge driven between the individual and holist levels by the progrowth defender); some people in society benefit while others pay the costs for such economic policies and have few gains to show for it. Furthermore, if individuals are not permitted harmless trespass of ecological limits, then neither are collectives. Indeed, the individual (or local) crossing of ecological limits is much less likely to trigger harmful global or widespread consequences than infringements by larger societal groups!

Another significant aspect of the concept of growth is the distinction that Mesarovic and Pestel draw between "undifferentiated" and "organic" growth.[43] The former type of growth, according to these authors, consists of mere replication of cells by cellular division, usually exponentially, with an increase in quantity alone. The latter type of growth

> involves a process of differentiation, which means that various groups of cells begin to differ in structure and function.... During and after differentiation the number of cells can still increase, and the organs grow in size, but while some organs grow, others might decline.[44]

Mesarovic and Pestel believe that most of the world's current crises are the product of undifferentiated growth or mere increase in numbers—the proliferation of "advanced" industrial consumer goods such as: computers, luxury automobiles, digital watches, instant cameras, video cassette recorders, microwave ovens, electric toothbrushes, cordless telephones, car telephones, compact disc players, projection color televisions, etc.; "more and more goods for more and more people"—or higher Gross National Product. They argue in favor of the organic conception of differentiated growth, including its component of decline for some portions of the organism and its applicability to the larger unit of analysis. A vision of the whole organism, rather than just one cell, is needed to replace the simpler but dangerously misleading idea of undifferentiated or quantitative growth.[45]

The crucial implication of this distinction for public policy involving the desirability of continuous economic growth is that while acceptance of the limits to growth should lead to a de-emphasis upon economic growth as the central value of industrial societies, it need not lead to a universal anti-growth policy for all nation-states, rich or poor. The idea of differentiated growth can highlight the fact that for most of the world's desperately impoverished populations whose absolute biophysical needs are not being met, achieving economic growth and realizing greater productivity of material necessities still remain a matter of life and death for millions of people.

Defenders of the ideology of unlimited economic growth charge the limits-to-growth advocates with elitism, claiming that economic growth is necessary to reduce poverty. Thereby, they hope to legitimize all progrowth public policies.[46] However, if the idea of differentiated growth is adopted, as most limits-to-growth proponents suggest, elitism does not follow from their position. Poor Third World populations and their leaders need not fear that the industrial crisis and the limits-to-growth challenge to unlimited economic growth will engender an all-inclusive, global antigrowth policy producing death and misery for millions. Once the concept of differentiated growth is recognized by Third World leaders their reluctance to support the limits-to-growth position and its policy implications should end. They can then support this view knowing that their own economic growth for the basic needs of their populations remains consistent with it. Global justice can and must be compatible with the limits-to-growth position!

This essential point was made by the Executive Committee of the Club of Rome in its "Commentary" to their famous first report. It has been overlooked by the defenders of limitless growth ideology who rely heavily upon the charge of elitism in their effort to discredit this critique of industrialism. These members of the Club of Rome wrote:

We unequivocally support the contention that a brake imposed on world demographic and economic growth spirals must not lead to a freezing of the *status quo* of economic development of the world's nations. If such a proposal were advanced by the rich nations, it would be taken as a final act of neocolonialism. . . . The greatest leadership will be demanded from the economically developed countries, for the first step toward such a goal would be for them to encourage a deceleration in the growth of their own material output while, at the same time, assisting the developing nations in their efforts to advance their economies more rapidly.[47]

This is the concept of differentiated growth wherein negative growth in some nations of the world occurs (where it is needed less) while others retain the more urgent need and right to grow economically. Whenever economic growth is necessary to pull preindustrial societies out of devastating poverty and misery, this social goal should and must be the aim of public policy augmented by all of the assistance that the world's relatively rich, advanced industrial nations can provide. The truly needy of the world—including those *within* the advanced industrial societies—have a stronger moral and political claim upon the material goods and global natural resources than the already affluent since their lives are at stake and their miseries and deaths are preventable. The obligation to save humans from preventable deaths and suffering would seem, *prima facie*, morally and politically overriding of all other goals for the postindustrial rich, including all that this obligation entails with regard to industrial social values and their change.[48]

The strength of the concept of differentiated organic growth is that it is both limited and differentiated. The entire product need not grow for a component (in this case, the poor nations) to grow and satisfy their populations' basic needs. Improvement of the material quality of life, desperately required for about one quarter of all of humanity, would still occur.

At the same time, given a truly differentiated growth process and the adoption of alternative nonindustrial, nongrowth values, some nations—the comparatively and absolutely affluent, advanced industrial ones—would actually experience *economic* or *material* maintenance or decline (but not necessarily nonmaterial decline with, for example, an increase in leisure time and activities). These value changes would prevent overdeveloped, advanced industrial societies from threatening the environment and suffering the pathological consequences of industrial growth extremism. Most importantly, this would lead to an increase in justice, domestically and worldwide.

In order for this result to be achieved, we must address a key, normative political issue: the nature and manner of achieving a just, global redistribution of wealth. To this quintessential political problem, its role within the limits-to-growth controversy, and the consequences of the failure to realize social justice through the doctrine of unlimited economic growth, I devote part 2.

Part II
Modern Economics as the Reductionism of Politics

3

The Modern Rise of Economics and the Demise of Politics

...do not let us overestimate the importance of the economic problem, or sacrifice to its supposed necessities other matters of greater and permanent significance. It should be a matter for specialists—like dentistry. If economists could manage to get themselves thought of as humble, competent people, on a level with dentists, that would be splendid!

—John Maynard Keynes[1]

The problem is, of course, that not only is economics bankrupt but it has always been nothing more than politics in disguise... economics is a form of brain damage.

—Hazel Henderson[2]

The Meaning and Significance of the Absence of Political Studies of Economic Growth

As I have discussed, the limits-to-economic-growth writings are vast, both in number and in multidisciplinary scope, yet anyone who is the least politically sensitive would be impressed, as I was, by the absence of contributions by political scientists (including political theorists), and, moreover, by the lack of politically informed presentations of this position or responses to it.[3] As we have seen in chapter 1, the study of economic growth and the controversy surrounding it involving its nature, environmental consequences, and desirability have been left to the members of other disciplines, mostly natural scientists and economists.

This gap in the inquiry into the political dimensions of the economic growth issue despite its immense significance to the future of the entire planet, particularly to the advanced industrial societies suffering from growth addiction, not only provides a *raison d'être* for my work examining the political implications of the limits-to-growth controversy, but, in addition, reveals a crucial component of my argument.

This component concerns the current widespread belief in the almost total separation of the modern discipline of economics from both politics and political science. Economics, the newer field, seems to have eclipsed political science by garnishing most of the respect of the professional social scientific community as well as the public's. It is considered the most scientifically developed of the social sciences and therefore the most practically important for policymaking. The existence of the American Council of Economic Advisers (when no such official body of political scientists exists) and the Nobel Prize for Economics[4] (when, again, there is no such prize for political science or any other of the social sciences), is sufficient evidence for the inequality in the perceived scientific and social significance of these two disciplines.

This separation between modern economics and political science explains the paucity of political writings on *economic* growth and the small impact the limits-to-growth research has had upon students of politics because this subject, by its very nature, appears to fall squarely within the bailiwick of economics. One essential claim of my argument derives from this separation: the divorce of modern economics from political life and thought is revealing of a profound characteristic of modern industrial society itself. Here I refer to modernity's high esteem for economics as a discipline (reflected and reinforced by the Nobel Prize's misleading pretense) and the preeminence for modern citizens of its subject matter of economic behavior and values: the acquisition and accumulation of economic wealth and the goods it can buy. Simultaneously, modern civilization's equally important degradation of political science's domain of political action—"politics" in the ordinary pejorative sense—degrades the field of study that focuses upon it as well.

One aim of this chapter is to understand how modern economics and economic values came to be viewed as the reductionist[5] replacement for politics and political values producing the depoliticization of modern society. In addition, I hope to address how one of the distinguishing characteristics of modernity—the social goal of unlimited economic growth—came to be used as an ideologically-laden substitute for the political redistribution of wealth and income. In order to achieve these aims I suggest that we examine the rise of modern economics. Such an examination, I believe, should include: the dependency of modern economics upon the "free" market considered as a nonpolitical means of allocating social goods and bads; the ascendency and later supremacy of economic values in modern and contemporary advanced industrial society foremost of which is the value of economic growth; and, finally, the consequences of these developments for both political science and political action. When we understand the role of economics, economic values, and action within advanced industrial society we shall understand much about the industrial values as a whole and in that sense the discussion contained within this part provides a good introduction to the next part which shall examine the nature of those values.

When one considers the origin of Western thought, its contrast to modern thought is perhaps most sharp with respect to the significance attributed to economic activities within society. What today would be considered important economic problems and behavior were assigned in classical civilization to the realm of the private household and were distinguished from and subordinated to the all-important study of politics and participation in the public life of the *polis*. For the ancient Greeks the economic sphere was determined by the needs of human survival while the political sphere was the domain of free, and quintessentially higher, human endeavors. Hannah Arendt expresses this characteristic quality of classical life as follows:

Natural community in the household [the unit of ancient economics] therefore was born of necessity, and necessity ruled all activities performed in it.

The realm of the *polis*, on the contrary, was the sphere of freedom, and if there was a relationship between these two spheres, it was a matter of course that the mastering of the necessities of the life of the household was the condition for the freedom of the *polis*.[6]

It is difficult for modern citizens socialized to the primacy of economic behavior, economic values, economics as an analytical category within modern society, and the first ranking of the discipline of economics among the social sciences, to comprehend the depreciation of economic phenomena and their examination by classical society. Furthermore, classical thinkers considered these economic topics as manifestly inferior in significance to classical political thought and action.

No activity that served only the purpose of making a living, of sustaining only the life process, was permitted to enter the political realm... As far as the members of the *polis* are concerned, household life [the management of which was the original meaning of the Greek word *oikonomia*] exists for the sake of the "good life" [i.e., the aim of the political process] in the *polis*.[7]

Perhaps there is no better source on the classical Greek view of the relation between economics and politics than Aristotle's *Politics* and no better commentator on this work than Ernest Barker. Referring to Aristotle's assertions on economics in the first book of the *politics*. Barker writes:

Such economic theory, subordinated as it is to political theory, which in turn is subordinated to (or, perhaps one should say, is the crown of) ethics, admits of no isolation of the economic motive, and of no abstraction of economic facts as a separate branch of inquiry. It is a theory of the ways in which households and cities can properly use the means at their disposal for the better living of a good life. *Wealth, on this basis, is a means to a moral end, as such a means, it is necessarily limited by the end, and it must not be greater—as equally it must not be less—than what the end requires.*[8]

Thus, in Aristotle's thought, subordination of economic action and values (especially what has become our modern preoccupation with the accumulation of wealth) to noneconomic ends, specifically to the normative political concept of the "good life," is made clear by Barker. In the perspective of Greek antiquity, to lead a life dominated by concern for private household affairs (or "economics" in modern terminology) was denoted by its derogatory use of "private," meaning "to be deprived of something"— that something being the public life of the community or political "crown." Moreover, such a private life dominated by economic concerns was "idiotic" and not fully human in the Greek view.[9]

Obviously, the modern worldview has reversed this classical evaluation of politics as supreme and economics as subordinate to *both* politics and ethics. With the rise of modern economics, continuing into the post-industrial world of today, economics has supplanted both of these older branches of human knowledge in social significance and public esteem. Nonetheless, one underlying theme of this discussion is to prescribe and offer support for the reexamination of this premodern paramount assessment of political science and its subject matter (including political philosophy) as well as moral values over economic action and values and its study. The result will be to grant economic thought and action comparatively less social value; enough only to instrumentally facilitate the attainment of the higher political and ethical ends (perhaps along the lines suggested by Keynes in the epigraph, but more on this later).

In addition to Aristotle's point about wealth being only a means to ethical values, it may be necessary to heed Keynes's counsel and not "overestimate the importance of the economic problem, or sacrifice to its supposed necessities other matters of greater and more permanent significance." Economists, like dentists, may be socially required but their importance to society is such that their subject matter, economic behavior and values, ought not be the preoccupation of human existence governing all that we think and do. Such is the case in postindustrial society wherein because of the general material affluence and the fact that acquiring the survival level of wealth and requisite goods themselves is possible for all of its members—perhaps for the first time in history—the economic problem of acquiring even more assets is "overestimated."

In the contemporary world, even in those societies which are not industrially developed, it seems as if the "good life" is exclusively defined in economic terms. Whether economic aspirations are achieved or not they appear universal in scope. What current society does not have economic growth as one of its most important values and objectives for public policy?

The modern demise of social esteem for the political might appear to parallel the classical inferior view of economics except that even the ancient Greeks could not "drop out" completely from the economic domain—or the realm of necessity—however subordinated it might be assessed relative to the revered public and political life. As Arendt pointed out in the passage quoted earlier, economics was the realm of necessity because it addressed the necessary preconditions for the higher life of politics. Actually, the dissimilarity within ancient thought between the social value of politics and economics must appear stark to the modern viewer. Political activity is not only accorded decreasing respect within modern thought and social life but this social order's subsequent advanced industrial stage is characterized by the complete abandonment of intentional political action by many of its citizens.[10]

I wish to argue that this modern reversal of the classical belief about the primacy of political thought and action over economic thought and action, with the latter set dominating postindustrial society, has many undesirable consequences. This revolutionary value change associated with industrialism should, to my mind, be reexamined and itself reversed to reestablish the *status quo ante* whereby the study of economics and its subject matter are of only instrumental value and are therefore subordinate to the noneconomic ends of human experience including politics and morals. The modern attempt to depoliticize society is specious. Only when we understand how and why this desired but erroneous modern depoliticization based on economic reductionism has been achieved—albeit temporarily—can we in the advanced industrial era be able to take action to remedy the resulting social ills. We must, I contend, properly repoliticize our contemporary social order and make the necessary value and institutional changes.

Economism and the Limits-to-Growth Challenge

The current hegemony of the economic perspective and the devaluation of politics are essential elements of advanced industrial civilization. It is the adoption of these new social values that constitutes, among other developments, the rise of industrialism and modernity. Importantly, however, what these modern value changes represent is being seriously challenged by the limits-to-growth position. Therefore, this position may be construed as generally implying, and occasionally making publicly explicit, the faults of the economics-over-politics presupposition of the industrial worldview. One fundamental assertion of this discussion is that when the value implications of the limits to economic growth and modern economics' hegemony are recognized fully by both the contemporary elites and the general public—and perhaps even before—a full-fledged repoliticization will occur as part of a revolution (or counterrevolution) in values.

This projected repoliticization (some aspects of which we are already experiencing in the contemporary industrial crisis) may not return the inhabitants of advanced industrial civilization to the classical glorification of politics. Instead, it may lead to a social order where the modern dominance by economic values, economic action, and their disciplined inquiry over political values, political action, and their study—political philosophy and political science—can be upset. If this were to occur, then the attempted and temporarily successful modern reduction of politics to economics would come to an end.

Not only do I believe that this repoliticization process has begun presently in advanced industrial societies experiencing the limits-to-growth crisis (like the United States) but that, furthermore, it *must* occur if life in postindustrial civilization is to improve—some limits-to-growth advocates would say "survive." For a culture preoccupied with the "new" and its claimed superiority over what preceded it, this view that old values may not necessarily be wrong or inferior—indeed, that they may be rationally preferable to the contemporary ones—will be difficult to accept especially given the universality of the industrial value of unlimited economic growth and what we may term "economism," or the excessive commitment to and valuation of economic values and behavior in social life.

Therefore, the postindustrial individual would do well to examine and reconsider her or his values. Indeed, the limits-to-growth controversy may be the sufficient stimulus for this disturbing normative analysis to begin the reexamination and possible adoption of some of the values upheld by preindustrial society. Especially important are those values concerning the high regard for politics and noneconomic ends of life, such as ethics. These can serve as limits to economic goals and behavior such as occurred in classical and medieval society. To paraphrase Barker on Aristotle: Economics, on this basis, is a means to normative ends; as such a means, it is necessarily limited by these ends, and it must not be greater than what the ends require.

The proper place for the social categories of the political and the economic within the social order and their relative valuation are essential issues for all students of society, especially students of contemporary postindustrial society. Yet these issues, as we have seen, are largely neglected because of the economism and economic reductionism of politics that characterize the latter. Let us begin to fill this gap by analyzing the political implications of the limits to economic growth.

Modern Economics and Modern Society

The creation of modern economics is traditionally credited to Adam Smith and his work, *An Inquiry into the Nature and Causes of the Wealth of Nations*, first published in 1776. Although Smith's volume was pathbreaking for the modern study of economics, economic historians are quick to add the importance of two prior schools of economic thinkers before Smith: the Physiocrats and the Mercantilists.[11] Despite general agreement among intellectual historians on the continuity of economic thought from Smith's precursors to modern economic thought, for the purposes of this discussion the differences between the Physiocrats and Mercantilists on the one hand, and Smith on the other, are fundamental and involve the politics-economics relation.

> ...the writers called "mercantilists" of the seventeenth and eighteenth centuries mingled the phenomena we classify into *economics* and *politics*. They considered economic phenomena from the point of view of the polity...with Quesnay [a prominent member of the Physiocrats], economics is not made radically independent from politics, nor is it severed from morality.[12]

Despite Smith's having held a chair in moral philosophy at the University of Glasgow and having written a work in this field, *The Theory of Moral Sentiments*,[13] we begin to see with his work the development of modern economic thought characterized by its declared autonomy from both politics and ethics, and accorded greater social significance than either of these two older fields of study. While Smith, the moral philosopher, did not yet separate economics from morals (a development that would occur later in post-Smithian or postclassical thought, commonly termed "neoclassical" economic thought),[14] he did originate the division between economics and politics that would eventually lead to the reversal of their respective appraisals in modern society. Note the following passage from *The Wealth of Nations*:

> The natural effort of every individual to better his own condition, when suffered to exert itself with freedom and security, is so powerful a principle, that it is alone, and without any assistance, not only capable of carrying on the society to wealth and prosperity, but of

surmounting a hundred impertinent obstructions with which the folly of human laws too often encumbers its operations.[15]

Hirschman comments upon this statement by Smith as follows:

> Smith affirms here that economics can go it alone: within wide limits of tolerance, political progress is not needed to be a consequence of economic advance.... In this view ... politics is the province of the "folly of men" while Candide's garden can be cultivated with success provided such folly does not exceed some fairly ample and flexible limits.[16]

We see here in Smith, following Hirschman's interpretation, the early formulations of the independence of economics as a domain of human inquiry as well as the devaluation of politics as the "province of the 'folly of men,'" destined to become one of the distinguishing components of modern economic thought and modern thought in general. It is important to note that this rise of modern economics, begun by Smith and other classical economists including David Ricardo, Thomas Robert Malthus, and John Stuart Mill,[17] occurred simultaneously with the rise of modern society. Furthermore, depending upon one's conception of modernity, the origin of modern economics and its dominance within industrial society may be viewed as consisting of the revolution in values that modernity represented by overturning the medieval value and social structure.

Arendt's characterization of economics as: "until the modern age a not too important part of ethics and politics ... "[18] is a good starting point for our examination of the origins and development of modern economics and what they reveal about contemporary society. The first point that should be noted about the birth of modern economics is its rather late emergence as a discipline of inquiry and social category in the history of Western civilization. This was so because of: (1) the absorption of economic phenomena by the prior existing field of study of political science and my oral philosophy in both the ancient and medieval periods;[19] and, (2) the dependence of modern economics upon the free market as a means of social allocation of goods and bads. This means of social allocation essential to modern economics did not prominently enter Western society until the nineteenth century.[20] We shall take up these points in turn.

Dumont says:

> The modern era has witnessed the emergence of a new mode of consideration of human phenomena and the carving out of a separate domain, which are currently evoked for us by the words *economics*,

the economy. How has this new category appeared, a category that constitutes at one and the same time s separate compartment in the modern mind and a continent delivered to a scientific discipline and that, moreover, embodies a more or less paramount value of the modern world?[21]

I, too, would like to address Dumont's question regarding the origin of the independent domain of economics, its supreme social position and what it reveals about modern society, particularly its politics.

We have seen how classical thought emphasized the submersion and subordination of both the economics category and economic behavior to political thought and action. Furthermore, because the classical view of politics was essentially about the creation and maintenance of the "good life" and hence normatively oriented, economics was a part of and inferior to ethics in classical society as well.

Moving beyond the classical period, medieval thought continued this engulfed (some economists would probably wish to say "reductionist") conception of economics as a "not too important part of ethics and politics." Medieval thinking, like its classical predecessor, held up economic action to ethical and religious scrutiny and it was from the latter perspective that medieval standards of conduct were generated and applied to the crucial social questions of the period: the nature of the just price of goods and the defensibility of usury.[22]

The major economic premises of medieval thought were:

that economic interests are subordinate to the real business of life, which is salvation, and that economic conduct is one aspect of personal conduct upon which, as on other parts of it, the rules of morality are binding.[23]

We may thus conclude that for the entire premodern era of Western civilization the economic category barely existed. To the extent that such phenomena within the domain-defining concept were recognized as such they were deemed components of the larger, more significant ("higher"), and determinative fields of politics and ethics with no independent status. Both the autonomy and preeminence of the economics discipline and subject matter would have to await the rise of modern society.

As suggested earlier, some economists may say that until the modern era and the rise of an autonomous field of economics their domain was itself reduced erroneously to politics and ethics—they conceive of economics as more than Keynes's humble, specialized enterprise similar to dentistry. Perhaps it was a reaction (critics of the domination of economics and its values within industrial and postindustrial society would say "overreaction") to the long-standing, historical absence of economics as a legitimate, independent domain with its own explanations that provided the motivation to create modern economics. Certainly, important value differences between premodern and modern civilization are disclosed by this variation in the hierarchy of the social value of economics, politics, and ethics. Commenting upon the consequences of the nineteenth-century social revolution to a market society in England, the economic historian Karl Polanyi captures this important point:

> A self-regulating market demands nothing less than the institutional separation of society into an economic and political sphere. Such a dichotomy is, in effect, merely the restatement, from the point of view of society as a whole, of the existence of a self-regulating market. It might be argued that the separateness of the two spheres obtains in every type of society at all times. Such an inference, however, would be based on a fallacy. True, no society can exist without a system of some kind which ensures order in the production and distribution of goods. But that does not imply the existence of separate economic institutions; normally, the economic order is merely a function of the social, in which it is contained. Neither under tribal, nor feudal, nor mercantile conditions was there, as we have shown, a separate economic system in society. Nineteenth century society, in which economic activity was isolated and imputed to a distinctive economic motive, was, indeed, a singular departure.[24]

The establishment of the modern, industrial, secular, mass social order—commonly referred to as the "industrial revolution"—is less often recognized as a "revolution in values"[25] or a "moral crisis" or "spiritual revolution,"[26] wherein traditional values were rejected and new ones substituted; perhaps the foremost being the quintessentially modern birth of the autonomous social category of economics and its primacy within the modern value structure and as an independent academic discipline. This modern revolution in values transformed the historical politics-economics relation whereby the political was superior and in its stead provided the glorification of economic goals and conduct both for society as a whole and the individual actor. In addition, the corresponding depreciation of political action approached the point of threatening the elimination of politics as a highly rated social category and social value. Politics within industrial society fell into disrepute and eventually both ethics and religion were relegated to purported unreasonableness and declined dramatically in social value because of value noncognitivism.

Mumford provides a notable formulation of the vast extent of this startling, modern revolution in values when he writes about capitalism (or what I prefer to term "modern industrialism"):

...the new capitalist spirit challenged the basic Christian ethics... The capitalist scheme of values in fact transformed five of the seven deadly sins of Christianity—pride, envy, greed, avarice and lust—into positive social virtues, treating them as necessary incentives to all economic enterprise; while the cardinal virtues, beginning with love and humility, were rejected as "bad for business"....[27]

This transformation to an independent and much-honored discipline of modern economics as well as the upward reevaluation in social esteem placed upon economic activities did not occur all at once (as if any such general, social revolutionary change could). Furthermore, this new perspective upon the portion of human behavior once severely restricted by political and ethical values freed economics, to be sure, but also probably engendered the contemporary addiction to unlimited economic growth.

Turning to another prominent classical economist, Thomas Malthus, we find (in what Daly calls "the first textbook of political economy") Malthus's following assertion:

It has been said, and perhaps with truth that the conclusions of Political Economy partake more of the stricter sciences than those of most of the other branches of human knowledge.... There are in Political Economy great general principles... [but] we shall be compelled to acknowledge that the science of Political Economy bears a nearer resemblance to the science of morals and politics than to that of mathematics.[28]

Thus, even at the time of the classical economists when their study was known as "political economy" (it was not termed "economics" until Alfred Marshall's text, *Principles of Economics*, was published in 1890),[29] the legacy of the past political and moral supercession of their field remained. If economics was ever to become fully independent as a discipline of inquiry and its subject matter accorded legitimacy as a distinct social category of human behavior—let alone the dominant perspective that it was to achieve within modern society—its further separation from politics and ethics was required in addition to reversing the traditional relationship between these older fields and economics.

Given the primacy of the economic view in the modern world, the hypothesis is that this view must be deeply rooted in the mental constitution of modern man... [I]f a separate domain was to be carved out of the political domain: the economic point of view demanded to be emancipated from the political. Subsequent history tells us that there was another side to this "emancipation": economics had to emancipate itself from morality.[30]

This necessary "emancipation" of economics from politics and morality did not completely occur until the development of the immediate successor to classical economic thought: neoclassical economics. It is beyond the scope of this discussion to provide a thorough analysis of this still-influential school of economic thought whose leaders wrote in the last quarter of the nineteenth century and which still informs much of contemporary economic thinking. To many contemporary economists the foundations of their discipline are still contained within neoclassicism.[31]

Nevertheless, some of the main tenets of neoclassical economics which remain influential and are pertinent to our subject deserve note. First and foremost, is the neoclassical effort to make economic inquiry into a strict natural science, or what Paul and Anne Ehrlich call "suffering from an advanced case of 'physics envy.'"[32] The effort to be scientific led neoclassical economists to reject the normative tradition in economics. Dobb reports that in response to this normative tradition in economics, begun by the preclassical and classical economists,

positivists [those who reject normative discourse as unreasonable] have tended to eschew [it] as an alien element and an intrusion into economic theory *qua* scientific discipline, concerned (it is said) with positive statements about what *is* and not with what *ought* to be.[33]

And, on the theme of "Ideology in Economics," an economist admits that:

economists are generally uncomfortable with the question of ideology... for the problem challenges professional identity and belief in the discipline's collection of tools, concepts, research procedures, and analyses. Given the economists' desire for status as "scientists" the very notion of ideology is threatening.[34]

We can say that these logical positivists' scientific orientation eschewing value judgments and upholding of value noncognitivism all began in economics with neoclassicism.

Neoclassical economists also changed the level of the units of economic analysis relied upon by classical economists. The classical economists' broad societal-wide questions, such as the social distribution of wealth, considered by one leader of classical economics, David Ricardo, as the "principal problem in Political Economy,"[35] were replaced by analyses of the economic behavior of smaller decisionmakers—households, firms, and industries—constituting the birth of the neoclassical subfield of microeconomics. "One commentator has described this shift in emphasis as a displacement of the key classical questions of growth and distribution by such little ones as 'why does an egg cost more than a cup of tea?' "[36] Another economist reflects upon the change in research problems for neoclassical economists especially regarding the downgrading of distribution and writes: "Of we adhere sedulously to the injunction to treat microtheory one term, and macrotheory the next, then the only proper time to teach distribution theory is between terms, in the Christmas recess!"[37]

In addition to the discovery by neoclassical economists of the idea of marginal increments of utility whereby the consumer's subjective perception of expected utility was viewed as the key to economic activity—what Dobb terms the "Jevonian Revolution"—the neoclassicists were enamored with the logical positivist interpretation of the natural scientific method. They attempted to emulate this method of knowing in their economic studies wherein they identified economics and economic problems with the operations of the free market. What is perhaps most important for our discussion here is that neoclassical economists reflected the diminution in significance of the previously central economic issue of their predecessors within classical economics: the distribution of wealth and income, shown in the remark by Weintraub.

The focus of classical economics upon noneconomic, causal factors determining the distribution of social goods and bads, such as the political and social institutions of property ownership and class relations involving political power, was shifted by the neoclassicists to the purely economic factor of economic conditions of exchange within the market which were considered independent of political aspects of property and class relations.[38] This difference in focus between classical and neoclassical economics bears importantly upon the politics-economics relationship and the possibility of reconstituting political economy. A political scientist writing on the prospects for a restructured field of political economy using neoclassical economics notes a major obstacle:

...the central metaphors of [market-dominated, neoclassical] economics and political science are markets and power, two concepts that... do not mix well. If markets are operating smoothly, the exercise of power is not possible. This is hardly a favorable starting point for theoretical integration.[39]

As a result of these traits of neoclassical economics, political science and economics grew almost totally apart with their practitioners conducting their respective research in isolation from each other. The autonomy of economics was fully established when the separation from politics partially begun by Smith was completed by the neoclassical economists utilizing their positivist rejection of normative discourse. On the specific issue of the distribution of economic goods, the shift to neoclassicism primarily included the important change in the casual explanation of this previously central (classical) economic problem. The focus of analysis of distribution was moved from sociopolitical causes to "purely economic," internal market causes of relations of exchange. Such fundamental reductionism necessarily involved the (largely implicit) elimination of politically crucial power relations as a major cause of the distributional pattern. One point to keep in mind is that as industrial economies have developed and competitive capitalism has evolved into the corporate capitalism of advanced industrial society, the politically reductive market argument is no longer applicable (if it ever was). If, indeed, political power was once absent in the market society of the nineteenth century—which I would deny—it certainly returned with a vengeance with the rise of the market-dominating, multinational, corporate oligopolies of contemporary capitalism.[40]

The Ideological Implications of a Politically Independent Economics

The motivations for disciplinary autonomy associated with modern economics and its "emancipation" from both politics and ethics should be understandable to the current generation of students of science heavily influenced by the work of Thomas S. Kuhn on the significant theoretical and nontheoretical benefits to its members of independent disciplinary status.[41] The advantages of an independent existence for a scientific community is particularly profound for economics not only in their shared paradigmatic perspective making communication among other disciplinary members easier, but also, like any other community, in distributing the community's goods. Thus, it is a situation of economists (who lead all social scientists in being employed outside the academy) actually serving in positions within the very economy they are supposed to study.[42]

On what may be termed the "captive economic scientist" problem reflecting the role of ideology or normative judgments in economics, the prominent economist Gunnar Myrdal writes the following about the "interests and prejudices" of economists: "most important are, of course, the forces in society at large that put pressure on economists to so direct their work that they come to conclusions in line with dominant interests and prejudices."[43] Antigrowth theorist Hazel Henderson writes on this issue of the captive economist by interpreting economist John Kenneth Galbraith: "Economists, Galbraith claims, have too often become advocates and apologists for the existing arrangements that sustain and employ them." She then goes on to offer the following illustration of this phenomenon: "Often, the proponents of private or public works projects such as downtown redevelopments, highways, and sports arenas employ economists to prepare cost/benefit analyses that inevitably tend to justify their plans."[44]

From the work of Kuhn and those of his followers who emphasize the impact of sociological and psychological factors upon the conduct of scientists' research and these comments by economists, we see the importance of external, noncognitive influences upon a discipline's members and their research problems, methodology, and conclusions. Indeed, even the definition of the discipline's field of inquiry itself, that is, the particular definition of domain-defining concepts such as "economics" and "politics," may be affected by outside factors: "The disciplinary split between economics and political science has tribal, organizational, sociological, and intellectual components."[45]

Here I agree but would have preferred the explicit inclusion of "ideological" or normative components (unless "tribal" or "sociological" mean "ideological"). As we have seen, the scope of the definitions of these key concepts is especially significant and *value-laden* in the cases of economics and politics. What we may have in the rise of an independent and politically separate economics is an instance of what Neuhaus calls in his critique of some portions of the environmental movement, "the worst kind of politics: the politics that refuses to see itself as politics."[46] In turn, modern economics may be seen misleadingly presenting itself as nonpolitical to the postindustrial citizen who views anything "political" pejoratively; this false nonpolitical image of economics thereby enhances the public respect for it.

A suppressed but unavoidable political element within a discourse or worldview usually is suspect as a "disguise" (to use Henderson's term in the epigraph to this chapter) of the real political phenomena involved, usually for ideological or class-interest purposes. Perhaps this false but popular nonpolitical image of modern economics is what Henderson wishes to convey when she terms economics as a "form of brain damage." This cognitive pathology may be said to consist of an inability to conceive and perceive the irreducible political component within modern economic relations with its cause being economism or the economic reductionism of modern politics.

The broader, premodern concept of the domain of politics encompassing economic matters as one of its essential elements and constituting for the latter its normative goals, indicated one set of values with regard to the following issues: public life over private concerns; nonmaterial aims (spiritual or moral) over aims requiring acquisition of material objects; a larger responsibility and range of state involvement in the lives of its citizens; and, the rationality of normative discourse. The much narrower, separate, exclusively scientific, value-neutral, and reductionist modern conception of the field of economics emancipated from what is conceived to be politics, with its claim of superior rationality and social value to both political science and politics, indicated the converse value rankings on these same issues: private life over a public one; materialism over pursuing nonmaterial values; much smaller responsibility and scope of state activities; and, the nonrationality of normative discourse.

The value changes implied in the establishment of an autonomous economic science separate from its once superior fields of politics and morals—with the latter two domains now held in disrepute and considered irrelevant—reflects the nature of much of the change in our modern value structure. The ancient and medieval philosophers, and even the early preclassical Mercantilists and Physiocrats, all considered economics and economic behavior as a means to such noneconomic values as: political power, moral goodness, religious salvation, and so on.[47] Speaking of the Mercantilists, Henderson writes, "The theoreticians of these practices did not call themselves economists but were politicians and merchants who were trying to explain and justify their policies and actions."[48]

In all previous civilizations man's economic activity and relations were submerged in, justified, and limited by noneconomic aspects of human existence and their respective values such as politics and morals. This is one of Polanyi's main assertions in his important work. He refers to a simple, historical fact that all residents of advanced industrial societies should consider:

> All types of societies are limited by economic factors. Nineteenth century civilization alone was economic in a different and distinctive sense, for it chose to base itself on a motive only rarely acknowledged as valid in the history of human societies, and certainly never before raised to the level a justification of action and behavior in everyday life, namely gain.[49]

Therefore, once the autonomy of the branch of knowledge known as economics was established and legitimized, these noneconomic ends could no longer serve as justifications for economic behavior. Indeed, if accepted, they would constitute limits to economic action. Thus, purely economic goals were required to give meaning and justification to unlimited economic goals and behavior. Deprived of noneconomic ends—largely political and moral values—and compounded by a value-neutral, scientific status along with value noncognitivism, the exclusively instrumental, economic means of premodernity were transformed into intrinsic ends because means without ends are irrational.

It is ironic that the discipline of modern economics, eschewing any choice among values by its claimed independence from and rejection of values, eventually transforms chosen economic means into self-justifying, intrinsic goals such as economic growth in contemporary growth-addicted societies. *The reductionist component within modern economics is this elimination of the traditional social ends of economic means leaving only economic means themselves to constitute what was once the whole subject.*

When we realize that modernity consists of a revolution in values involving the rejection of traditional, premodern, social ends which were derived largely from politics, ethics, and theology, we may more fully appreciate the radical shift in human perspective that occurred with the creation of modern industrial civilization. The expansion of trade and the rise of new economic classes to political power only partially explain the advent of the dominance of economic values and economics within Western culture; a dominance which constituted modernity and the rise of the ideology of unlimited economic growth.[50] In addition, the secularization of society; the attempted removal of values from the study of politics as well as from economics[51] (or what industrial crisis theorist Murray Bookchin terms the "denormatization of politics");[52] and the accompanying denigration of the political process were all important factors in this change of world-views from medieval to modern.

One does not have to be a Marxist to see both the problem facing the nineteenth century capitalist elite and how it came to be solved. Deprived of political, ethical, and religious values for the legitimation of their society's unequal distribution of wealth and income, and to justify further the expansion of the economy, the beneficiaries of the new social order required a new set of social categories and values (Marx would say "ideology") to fill the void created by the rejection of the traditional modes of legitimation. The German sociologist Hans Peter Dreitzel writes on the industrial crisis of legitimation:

... the bourgeois classes found the solution to the problem of secularized legitimacy in the economic basis of its rule. During the era of market capitalism, the main legitimation of bourgeois rule was the idea that everybody would have an equal chance in the market... But since the development of monopoly capitalism and state intervention, *the domination of the ruling bourgeois and the persisting inequality has been effectively legitimized by a steady augmentation of per capita income* [i.e., economic growth]. While the unequal distribution of wealth and income has remained a persistent feature of all industrialized societies, the continuous growth of the economic output guaranteed an absolute rise of the standard of living which even in the lower classes provided each generation with a level of material gratification which far surpassed the experience of the preceding one.[53]

The rise of modern autonomous economics and adoption of its *implied but denied* values (foremost of which was unlimited growth, despite its claimed value neutrality and its mechanism of the self-regulating market) filled this legitimation or ideological void satisfactorily. With this in mind, we may better understand Dumont's previously quoted assertion about economics being a category that is "deeply rooted in the mental constitution of modern man."

This politically crucial legitimizing or ideological role of endless economic growth is fundamentally threatened by the limits to economic growth as well as by the transformational social movements of postindustrial society and their alternative values associated with the recognition of these limits. This explains the profound political impact of these limits and those who emphasize their existence and the corresponding need to cease the universal policy goal of unlimited economic growth for affluent, advanced industrial societies in addition to the adoption of nongrowth-based values and social institutions.

One important illustration of the transformation of values connected with modernity concerns the meaning and purpose of human labor. Because modern society lacked the traditional patriarchal or feudal obligations to work, some new reason for continuous labor beyond biological survival was required. Here the role of unlimited individual accumulation of wealth—so essential to the ideology of unlimited economic growth and postindustrial society founded upon it—was decisive. A political student of this period writes:

All these limits [traditional limits to accumulation] had to go, and there was no reason to think up other limits. Indeed, any other limit would presumably have to be justified in terms of some moral principle which would encroach on the market system, whereas the whole point was to get away from moral as well as traditional limits....[54]

Of course, when the premodern, noneconomic values which also acted as limits to economic accumulation (for example, the prohibition against usury) were discarded, a civilization was established based upon the primacy of unlimited economic growth and the unlimited economic activity to achieve this normative objective: endless consumption.[55]

4

Industrial Economic Reductionism: Depoliticization through the Addiction to Unlimited Growth

Growth is a substitute for equality of income. So long as there is growth, there is hope, and that makes large income differentials tolerable.
—Henry C. Wallich[1]

We are addicted to growth because we are addicted to large inequalities in income and wealth. To paraphrase Marie Antoinette: Let them eat growth. Better yet, let the poor hope to eat growth in the future.
—Herman E. Daly[2]

Why Economists Fear and Suppress Politics, Especially Redistribution

Modern economists not only separated themselves from politics but actually devalued political phenomena and even regarded them as dangerous. While disciplinary distinctions may be made without invidious comparisons with previously existing modes of thought, creating any such disciplinary autonomy may produce a reductionist result. This result is mistaking a part for its whole as in the fields of politics, economics, and morality, once combined but now being ignored or viewed as superseded by a newly created mode of thinking: modern thought, and in particular, modern economic thought.

Certainly, classical and medieval thinkers who conceived of economics as a means to achieve or apply moral principles and values would look askance at a completely autonomous, modern economics—an end unto itself—cut off from moral and political restraints or limits. This absence of limits upon modern economic behavior will be discussed subsequently, but what should be made clear here is that this issue about the nature and limits of economics is not a scientific or narrow methodological one; it is essentially a normative issue having to do with the values served by each conception. I suggest that to distinguish economics from politics and morality need not—and should not—lead to a total separation from these two prior disciplines; a cross-disciplinary field of normative political economy encompassing the overlapping aspects of all three disciplines is needed.

The doctrine of limitless economic growth, so prominent within contemporary economies, was—and still is—the economic means to avoid negatively-considered politics, especially the politically explicit redistribution process. As an illustration, in an essay on economic development, Hirschman takes the unusual and revealing position for an economist—that of claiming that economic development will not be achieved in poorer countries by economic factors alone (note the usual pejorative characterization of politics by an economist); "dismal politics" is necessary! He writes, "If that effort [to achieve economic development] is to fulfill its promise, the challenge posed by dismal politics must be met rather than avoided or evaded. By now it has become quite clear that this cannot be done by economics alone."[3]

The progrowth economists look upon a no-growth society—advocated by many limits-to-growth critics of the current policy of unlimited growth—with fear and loathing because of its necessary increase in *visible* political processes particularly revolving around the redistribution of wealth and income in order to create greater social justice. The increase in political consciousness of the members of a society without economic growth is the result of the destruction of the socially—especially politically—profound "growth illusion"; or, the distraction of "people's attention from the fact that although their incomes command more in the way of goods and services, their relative shares have not changed."[4] Such an illusion as a result of ceaseless economic growth is crucial to our discussion of the normative political implications of the limits to economic growth because of its great political impact. One political analyst formulates this point much more bluntly than most economists:

The viability of current political arrangements hinges on the ability of the [United States] economy to turn our attention away from the objective fact, to cloud that reality, by directing our strivings toward growth and its promises...by diverting the attention of materially deprived groups away from disruptive political activity.[5]

We could call this function of economic growth the "growth diversion" or, to borrow another politically inspired label: "the great conservative idea of growth", used as a "surrogate for redistribution".[6]

Daly expresses this core idea of the political usefulness of the economic concept of unlimited growth as an alleged but illusory substitute for redistribution to achieve greater social equality when he says:

Let there be more for everyone year after year so that we need never face up to sharing a fixed total. Unequal distribution can be justified as for saving, incentive, and hence, growth...one purpose of economic theory is to make those who *are* comfortable *feel* comfortable...we are told: "Don't worry about today's inequities, but anxiously fix your attention on tomorrow's larger total income."[7]

We should keep in mind our earlier discussion in the previous part about social illusions and the role of crises and despair in getting rid of them. This illusory, industrial social value of endless economic growth has two essential political aims: (1) to avoid redistribution which harm the rich; and (2) to help the poor increase—absolutely only—their own income without taking assets away from the rich; and, thereby maintain the rich's higher rank in society by avoiding implementing a policy of genuine redistribution which would necessarily include the closing of the gap between rich and poor. The immense political importance of this illusory doctrine is made evident by the fears expressed by progrowth economists concerning prescriptions for the curtailment of economic growth and the resulting destruction of the growth delusion and diversion.

Walter Heller is typical of economists who view with dismay what they consider to be the dangerous zero-sum (or "winner-take-all-loser-give-up-everything")[8] political conflict inherent in the redistributive process which could sever the social fabric when the (illusory) benefits (for the nonelite) of economic growth are no longer available. This would occur either because the limits to growth finally terminate growth or because the illusory nature of such growth, for purposes of achieving social equality, is eventually recognized. Heller writes:

Consider the problem [of correcting social ills] in a no-growth setting: to wrench resources away from one use to transplant them to another, to wrest income from one group for transfer to another, to redeploy federal resources from current to new channels (even assuming that we could pry loose a substantial part of the $70 billion [now a multiple of roughly 5 under the Carter/Reagan budget increases] devoted annually to military expenditures—and to do all this on a sufficient scale to meet the urgent social problems that face us—might well involve us in unbearable social and political tensions. In this context, one rightly views growth as a necessary condition for social advances, for improving the quality of the *total* environment.[9]

Economists' fears of "unbearable social political tensions" associated with redistribution of income, and the claimed avoidance of such tensions through the achievement of economic growth, are central components of modern, antipolitical, reductionist economics. The expectation that politics will be socially disruptive and perhaps even fatal to the social order (remember Smith's view of politics as "the folly of men") is also reflected in some fundamental values affecting the political process in advanced industrial societies, such as the competitive nature of postindustrial social goods (to be discussed later), individualism, and the lack of community. I believe that this point supports one of the main contentions of this discussion: the limits-to-economic-growth controversy reflects essential, normative political issues that should be addressed and discussed among and between political philosophers, policymakers and the public in general. Of course, if these industrial values should change, then the political process and the policy of endlessly seeking economic growth, with the consequences of each, must be viewed differently.

The antipolitical views of modern economists are so pervasive that statements like Heller's could easily be reproduced many times over. However, rather than providing an overlong list of examples, I prefer to cite just one more by the economist Adolph Lowe:

In the regions of industrial maturity, I expected that the very fact of continuing growth, by steadily raising everyone's standard of living in absolute terms, would for an indefinite period stifle socially disruptive demands for a change in the distributional shares.[10]

This use of economic growth as a substitute for the politically explicit, elite-harming, and socially divisive redistributive process is a main ideological weapon of industrial and postindustrial elites. As discussed earlier, for the crucial legitimizing function within their social order industrial elites rejected traditional premodern, political, moral, and theological bases and therefore were obliged to rely upon a new legitimizing ground: economics, and, in particular, unlimited economic growth. Both concepts served this political need of the elites well. Polanyi's claim about the uniqueness of the nineteenth century industrial civilization resting upon economic foundations is compelling in light of these considerations.

Environmental movement critic Richard Neuhaus worries about enthusiastic supporters of this social movement in the United States replacing genuine politics with another concept—nature—that is claimed to transcend political life. He also mentions other politically transcendent concepts such as "God" and "historical necessity."[11] It is possible to view such concepts essentially as attempts to reduce politics because of the disesteem politics has suffered in modern times.

On the basis of our discussion thus far, I would add one more politically reductionist concept to Neuhaus's list: limitless economic growth. Clearly, if one fears a social process such as politics and its consequences, then one would welcome such reductionist efforts. The political philosophical components of economists' fears of politics shall be addressed shortly. But first, one of the few values that antinormative, value noncognitivist, scientific economists do maintain explicitly, Pareto optimality, requires analysis.

Economic Reductionism of Politics and the
Economic Goal of Pareto Optimality

In connection with the ideological role of modern economics, especially its doctrine of endless growth, attention should be turned to the central normative concept tolerated within positivist economics: "Pareto optimality." Pareto optimal circumstances—so revered in economics—occur when "some people will be better off without anyone being worse off";[12] that is, the Pareto optimum exists when some people gain absolutely and no one loses absolutely, which implies that members of the latter group who do not gain anything (or as much as the first group of gainers) become *relatively* worse off but *not* as worse off as they could be if some of their previously held assets were taken from them producing an absolute as well as relative loss. (We should note the absence of discussion by mainstream economists of relative wealth within this key economic concept, but much more shall be said subsequently about this crucial postindustrial value of relative wealth.) This important, normative economic concept of Pareto optimality operates to maintain the current distributional structure. How so?

A conservative outcome occurs because Pareto optimality ignores the issue of the equality of the preexisting distribution implying the politically significant rejection of the redistribution of wealth and income for the purpose of greater social equality. Redistribution to achieve greater social equality sometimes requires that some people (the rich) are made worse off relatively, even perhaps absolutely, to speed the equalizing process along: the typical transfer policy of postindustrial welfare states that Heller feared so much. Such a Pareto optimal, redistributive policy is consistent with the rich still receiving absolute gains, just lesser ones than the nonrich!

However, the Pareto optimum standard also permits the possibility of some who do gain absolutely, like the poor in an unlimited growth-oriented economy, to be *relatively* worse off, and increasingly so, compared to the rich, because of this public policy of continuous economic growth. As long as everyone gains absolutely, including the poor, and nobody loses absolutely (previous assets taken away), the existing unequal distribution will remain unmitigated. In fact, this distributive inequality will likely increase wherein members of the rich group typically gain more from growth than the nonrich because of the competitive advantages economic wealth confers upon the former and the nature of economic growth in advanced industrial society.

Limits-to-growth critics emphasize the selectivity of economic growth according to whom it benefits (the rich)—while actually harming the already poor and deprived.[13] Although these critics point out that the post–World War II, spectacular economic growth in industrially advanced societies has not achieved the promised elimination of poverty within these societies, one does not need to be an economist to know that despite—or perhaps because of—economic growth, extreme poverty, even destitution, has continued or even worsened during the Reagan years of the 1980s! This deplorable development has been shockingly visible by the rise of the problem of homelessness in America during this period.[14]

Thus, the concept of Pareto optimality and its silence about and diversion from the key postindustrial economic value of relative wealth (which is not only accepted by most economists but unwittingly by the postindustrial public as well) has decisive political consequences in such a society preoccupied by the relative definition of wealth such as occurs in advanced industrial societies.

Concerning the point of the multiplier effects of economic wealth, the economist Fred Hirsch notes the greater vagueness and elusiveness of achieving economic equality compared to political, legal, and social equality.[15] One possible explanation is that redistributive efforts at achieving greater economic equality unavoidably hurt the elite if they are really redistributive in aim and nature; that is, they seek to close the gap between the rich and poor by raising the latter's economic status relative to the former. In contrast, the other forms of equality (i.e., political, legal, and social equality) do not harm the elite as long as inequality of economic wealth exists. This is the case because the elite can use their economic superiority to advantage in noneconomic areas, thus destroying genuine equality in these areas despite its nominal existence—with great ideological benefit to the elite. For example, consider the purported equality in the American legal system and contrast it to the reality of tremendous inequality.

It is common for progrowth economists to label limits-to-growth advocates as elitist because the latter wish to halt economic growth. To the defenders of unlimited economic growth and victims of the addiction to this social value, growth is the only means to improve the quality of life for the poor.[16] However, limits-to-growth advocates have always been selective in their attack upon the industrial value of unlimited economic growth. (See the following discussion on these advocates' recommendation of selective economic growth where needed in poor countries, and my presentation in chapter 1 of differentiated growth. Also, it should be recalled that the Club of Rome opposed the freezing of the global *status quo* with all of its inequality, to be replaced by a dynamic, global equilibrium model.)

In opposition to the defenders of unlimited economic growth, I would argue that it is they who are the real elitists. They argue in favor of economic growth as the only policy to improve absolutely but *not* relatively (which would hurt the rich's comparative standing), the gains of the poor. This is predicated upon the omission or even suppression of the alternative policy of redistribution. An alternative policy, of course, would harm the elite members (probably in both absolute and relative senses).

Furthermore, the social policy of solving the problem of poverty through economic growth actually helps the rich increase their advantages as indicated by distribution data in both advanced and developing industrial countries.[17] It must be concluded that the growth delusion has been quite effective historically—until challenged recently by confronting the anxiety and miseries raised by the limits to growth, their advocacy literature, and the social movement for postindustrial social transformation. This could explain the heated, critical response to advocates of such limits; the limits-to-growth position threatens to destroy the economic growth illusion to the serious detriment of the elites!

Pareto optimality is consistent with economists' antipolitical orientation in that if an economy is growing and no one is losing assets or income (that is when Pareto optimality is achieved), the need for explicit political decisions regarding the crucial distributional issues of justice and equality appear to be nonexistent since the "optimal" situation has been realized. Achievement of the economic goal of Pareto optimality also obviates the need to make comparative (political) judgments about the gains that different segments of the population receive, reflecting another important characteristic of economics: its skepticism about interpersonal comparisons of value or utility which are viewed as ethical matters beyond the domain of scientific (positivist) economics.[18]

The concept of Pareto optimality reinforces the ideology of unlimited economic growth in that the only way to achieve one's increase in wealth or income without taking from another is through economic growth or enlarging the social pie. Since the fundamental significance of relative wealth in advanced industrial societies and its mortal threat to the policy of ceaseless economic growth will be discussed subsequently, I shall not consider this aspect regarding Pareto optimality here, except to note economist Amartya

K. Sen's criticism of this (self-contradictory) value for positivist economists who self-proclaim their avoidance of such value judgments and this value's suboptimal consequences for a just distribution of social goods:

> There is a danger in being exclusively concerned with Pareto-optimality. An economy can be optimal in this sense when some people are rolling in luxury and others are near starvation as long as the starvers cannot be made better off without cutting into the pleasures of the rich.... In short, a society or an economy can be Pareto-optimal and still be perfectly disgusting.[19]

One other comment I would like to make concerning the relativity of economic values, Pareto optimality, and my main point about the ideological use of economics or the "politics-in-disguise" characteristic of the doctrine of unlimited economic growth, involves the marginalist revolution in economics. "What the marginalists did was to make *relative* price and *relative* scarcity the fulcrums of economic analysis."[20] This school of economics also emphasized the famous Decreasing Marginal Utility Law,[21] whereby increasing the supply of a good decreases its added utility. Thus, the added utility of the thirty-ninth ice cream soda is less than the first and its price should reflect this decreased utility. (It should be noted here that the Decreasing Marginal Utility Law implies an eventual extreme point beyond which no utility would be derived: the saturation point. The unlimited nature of industrial growth ideology violates this basic tenet of marginalist economics.)[22]

Given this emphasis upon relative prices and scarcity it seems quite surprising to me that the concept and postindustrial social role of relative wealth should be ignored or underemployed by economists who stress Pareto optimality which in practice highlights only absolute improvements for the poor, no matter what effect—usually detrimental—achieving this economic goal might have on the poor's *relative* standing to the rich. This inconsistency by economists who first introduced the relativist Decreasing Marginal Utility Law and then ignore the crucial relativist aspects of wealth and goods within advanced industrial society as well as the beneficial consequences of this oversight for the elite, appear to suggest an ideological purpose being served.

This ideological use of economic growth as an alleged substitute for redistribution is the political heart and soul of the so-called "economic" doctrine of continuous and unlimited growth. Actually, it is a *political* ideology masquerading as a scientific, nonpolitical view. Here modern reductionist economics does indeed seem "nothing more than politics in disguise" and "a form of brain damage"! Moreover, because of these traits it appears as Neuhaus put it: the "worst kind of politics: the politics that refuses to see itself as politics."

In my previous work on the political underpinnings of the limits-to-growth issue, I emphasized this key point:

It is in this politically self-interested desire for an apparent nonpolitical redistribution as a means to achieve political stability by increasing (absolutely only) the poor's income in an acceptable and nondamaging manner to the nonpoor that economic growth may be viewed as an attempted substitute for politics.[23]

In this analysis of the ideological use and defense of the doctrine of unlimited economic growth, mention should be made of the corresponding economists' critique of no-growth policies which is the inverse of their defense of a growth-oriented society. If economic growth is to avoid political redistribution and the expected attendant political conflict between classes, a no-growth society would be one in which all the undesirable political traits purported by antipolitical economists would be magnified. Adam Smith's negative pronouncement of this stage of national economy has been followed faithfully by most later economists: "The progressive state is, in reality, the cheerful and the hearty state to all the different orders of society. The stationary is dull; the declining melancholy."[24]

Other examples abound of antipolitical, progrowth economists attacking a society not characterized by economic growth.[25] Indeed, the currently dreaded economic "recession" is defined as "no growth for two consecutive calendar quarters." It is central to my argument that the primary reason why the progrowth advocates judge the no-growth society as undesirable is that they tenaciously cling to their addictive growth values; it should be no surprise that they therefore find a recommendation of a no-growth society highly unattractive, even dangerous (perhaps unwittingly realizing the implied fatal threat of this policy and the values that underlie it to their growth-based social order).

One signal of the failure of economists to realize that, at bottom, the essential disputes within the limits-to-growth controversy are over political values is that very often progrowth economists will point to the negative characteristics of a period of no-growth. They offer the example of a recession and proceed to argue that no-growth has been tried and only produces social misery. What such economists overlook is that a recession is not a no-growth society in the same sense meant by limits-to-growth critics of postindustrial growth-dependent society. A recessionary period is a *failed growth* period with progrowth values intact and unsuccessfully realized. No wonder such a period seems so dismal to economists! And indeed it is dismal, given their values based upon the supremacy of unlimited economic growth.

The point I wish to make is also one that rarely appears in the limits-to-growth literature: the critics of unlimited, economic growth-fixated society who stress the existence of the limits to such growth are ultimately arguing for changing political values so that the lack of economic growth will *not* constitute a serious social failure. In my view, the most important issue raised by the economic growth debate and limits-to-growth controversy is the choice of political values. This is why the potential contribution of this controversy is marred in addition to the interests of advanced industrial citizens disserved by not having an adequate, political philosophical analysis of these basic value conflicts.

The political importance of the ideological use of the unlimited economic growth doctrine—or postindustrial distributive politics in disguise—is illustrated when one of this economic system's distinguishing traits is made explicit: "Privilege under capitalism is much less 'visible,' especially to the favored groups, than privilege under other systems."[26] This important aspect of industrial capitalism is expressed by the contemporary, German political philosopher Jürgen Habermas as "a depoliticization of the class relationship and an anonymization of class domination."[27]

Using Habermas's formulation here, *one of the most important elements of my argument concerns the doctrine of continuous and unlimited economic growth, and its use as a substitute for redistribution serving as a main weapon in the elite's arsenal with the aim (or effect, if not intended) of depoliticizing class relationships and anonymizing class domination.* The profound consequences of this doctrine upon class structure and conflict cannot be ignored by any student of contemporary society unless she or he is a reductionist economist who self-servingly and erroneously attempts to evade this issue and argument by critics of the industrial worldview by claiming that they are "extra-economic," and thus can simply be dismissed as outside their domain of inquiry.

For an historical account of how economic reductionism via economic growth as a replacement for genuine redistribution occurred in one post-industrial society. I refer the reader to Alan Wolfe's analysis of post–World War II America: *America's Impasse: The Rise and Fall of the Politics of Growth.*[28] The heart of his discussion focuses upon the crucial year of 1946 wherein he found much supporting historical evidence for an explanation of the normative politics of growth addiction similar to the theoretical one presented here.

Instead of making a political choice [Wolfe writes], America opted for an economic surrogate. A bipartisan coalition was formed to pursue economic expansion, at home through growth and overseas through empire. Once the rationale of the political system became the enhancement of growth, everything changed, including the role of political parties, the structure of political ideology, the nature of public policy, and the meaning of dissent. America embarked on a massive experiment. Politics would concern itself with the means— growth—and the ends, or purpose, of social life would take care of themselves.

Unlike political choice, economic growth offered a smooth and potentially harmonious future—instead of divisive, possible ugly, and certainly disruptive struggles over redistributional issues...Growth, in other words, was transpolitical[!][29]

Of course, we know that the purported "transpolitical" claim of economic growth as a substitute for redistribution is the result of an illusion (economic brain damage) brought on by the ideology of economic reductionist doctrine of unlimited economic growth and the elites whose interests this ideology serves. This illusion is rapidly being exposed by the disguise-lifting, consciousness-creating and consciousness-raising, limits to growth and their consequences. Once the doctrine of the limitlessness of economic growth is questioned as being either impossible to achieve and/or undesirable in itself, its resulting ideological manipulation will be recognized by its victims and thereafter challenged by them. Thus, this recognition will destroy this illusion's political effectiveness just as the awareness of any illusion produces its own self-destruction. Hence the need for political disillusionment when the illusions are as damaging as this one. The path to joy is, indeed, through the despair of the mourning period for our fantasies. When the fantasy of unlimited economic growth is recognized as such we may then proceed to create a social order whose conditions for existence do not require such delusions or its detrimental effects. No wonder the rhetoric of both sides of the limits-to-growth controversy is impassioned—so much is at stake!

5

Liberalism and the Economic Reductionism of Politics

Few would contest the proposition that today Western societies exhibit little in the way of a widespread political consciousness among its members and fewer still would doubt that political things are mostly held in disrepute by the members of these societies...[over the past 150 years] the main trends in political thought, irrespective of national or ideological variations, have worked towards the same end: the erosion of the distinctively political.
—Sheldon S. Wolin[1]

Liberalism's Attempt at Suppressing Politics and
Disguising Domination Out of Fear of Downward Mobility

Whenever modern economics or modern society in general is considered, the political philosophy of liberalism must be addressed. Its role in both the use of the modern discipline of economics and in the modern social order is essential because of the economistic nature of this type of society. I shall not assume the burden of a full-fledged discussion of the vast subject of liberalism and the immense primary and secondary literature it has spawned (which would be beyond the scope and purpose of this work). Instead, I would like to refer to the analysis of liberalism provided by Wolin. It illustrates the fundamental connection between liberal political philosophy, the addiction to unlimited economic growth as the ideology of industrialism, and the reductionism of politics. In this manner, the essential political significance of the limits-to-growth controversy will become clear.

Using the writings of John Locke, Wolin attempts to show how within Locke's seventeenth century political philosophy both the scope and social significance of the category of the political decreased and politics came to be identified with the necessary, but coercive and therefore feared, government alone.[2] The liberal view of politics and government as fundamentally coercive and a necessary evil to protect property and maintain law and order, is important because of this view's relation to the liberal economic reduction of politics.[3] The classical liberal economist emphasized the absence of physical compulsion—and thus the absence of the heart of politics as the liberal conceived it—in their ideal society.

It was...the relative absence of coercion in economic transactions, that tinted the economists' model of society with antipolitical tones and ultimately made it an alternative to the older conception of a politically directed system.[4]

Wolin's aim here is to support his characterization of liberalism as a "philosophy of sobriety, born in fear, nourished by disenchantment, and prone to believe that the human condition was, and was likely to remain, one of pain and anxiety."[5] The contrast between this pessimistic, antipolitical liberalism and classical thought is great, particularly regarding the value of politics, economics, and the possibility of normative knowledge.

What drove the liberal to such a despairing view of the human social condition? The brief answer is insecurity about losing one's property and declining in social status. The threat of downward mobility or the loss of elite advantages was a fate "worse than death" according to one of liberalism's and modern economics' founding thinkers, Adam Smith. He said that, "man's suffering was more intense... 'when we fall from a better to a worse situation than we ever enjoy when we rise from a worse to a better'."[6]

Wolin provides insight into the "fear of falling" and the antiegalitarianism of liberalism (and modern society relying upon liberal doctrines) when he writes about the liberal man:

Liberal man moved in a world where pain and deprivation threatened him from all sides. His fears were compressed into a single demand: social and political arrangements must ease his anxieties by securing property and status against all threats excepting those posed by the competitive chase itself. His aversion to pain defined that demand even more closely; to be secure was to able to "count on things," to be able to act with the comforting knowledge that one's property would not be snatched away....It followed that equality must give place to security of possession, because the psychological malaise attendant upon social levelling would be felt more deeply, that is, produce more pain, than the pleasures experienced by those whose lot would be somewhat improved. As Smith had put it earlier, "a very considerable degree of inequality is not near so great an evil as a very small degree of uncertainty."[7]

It is not surprising, therefore, to understand why the modern liberal accepts "a very considerable degree of inequality" (as Smith put it), fearing, as she or he does, the attempt to reduce inequality by painful redistribution. In the latter's place, the liberal endorses the ideology of limited economic growth as a means to avoid this redistributive attempt at increasing equality. Understanding this crucial point about unlimited growth doctrine as a surrogate for redistribution, the standard charge by progrowth advocates that economic growth is needed to help the poor and that the limits-to-growth critics of unlimited growth are really elitists trying to protect their newly-acquired goods from the upwardly mobile masses is turned upon itself. Thus, the liberal defenders of limitless economic growth are, wittingly or unwittingly, prescribing a policy that benefits the elite in their ceaseless efforts to "ease their anxieties" about their "property being snatched away."

The historical background of continual social and political crises during Locke's lifetime served as the context for his influential restricted conception of man's cognitive capabilities.[8] This theory of Locke's regarding man's limited ability to achieve knowledge had a profound effect on later liberal thinkers. Locke writes in his *Essay Concerning Human Understanding*: "Our minds are not made as large as truth nor suited to the whole extent of things."[9] Wolin adds that Locke's epistemological pessimism, "worked to erode confidence in the possibility of political philosophy's providing the knowledge for dramatic advance...Political knowledge, Locke pointed out, is...undemonstrable."[10]

Relying upon this skepticism about the possibility of political knowledge, political liberals, and their economic counterparts, the classical and neoclassical economists, emphasized that "action meant first and foremost economic action."[11] This reductionist move was made when the classical economists of the eighteenth century made the assumption that the body of economic knowledge that they were producing was identical to knowledge of social life *in toto*, including, of course, politics.[12]

This raises the important issue of the meaning of politics and its significance—a question rarely raised in discussion of the controversy over economic growth (not surprisingly, given the dominance of economists in this debate and their antipolitical view). It is important to comprehend that the process of defining politics is self-reflexive. All definitions of this term are themselves political in the sense of affecting the social distribution of goods and bads even if a particular method of value allocation claims to be nonpolitical or politically transcendent by being dependent upon some narrower (reductionist) concept of politics. This is so because of the social use of this definition: setting the boundaries of legitimate public or state action.

A prominent example of this phenomenon would be the ideal of the allegedly nonpolitical "free" market within liberal thought, and economic growth as a substitute for redistribution—as I have tried to show. What the authors of an introductory textbook in political science assert is helpful here: "All definitions of politics are political acts...Any political system always defines some people in and some people out...The problem is to define yourself into politics."[13]

Contemporary political philosophers and members of the public must beware of attempts to make it appear as if politics is being diminished or reduced entirely in order to depoliticize advanced industrial society to great advantage of the already powerful groups. The use of the doctrine of unlimited economic growth as a replacement for and prevention of politicizing redistribution seems to be just such an attempt at misleading depoliticization: a deception that benefits the elite. It is this economic reductionism of postindustrial politics that is currently under severe challenge by the limits-to-growth and the social transformation movements that have grown up based upon them. Within the academy, such limits-to-growth, industrial critics consist mostly of natural scientists who have acknowledged the existence of barriers to ceaseless economic growth for an increasing world population of over five billion people and the need for transforming postindustrial society (however, they rarely provide the details of the nature of the new society or how it is to be achieved).

To the defenders of the economic growth delusion, or economic reductionism, it appears as if an endlessly growing market economy could make the political value choices implied by the allocative decisions unnecessary and with them politics as well. It is this mistaken claim that endears the doctrine of unlimited economic growth and liberalism to antipolitical economic growth advocates and underlies their attempted economic reduction of politics.

What differs between the unlimited and no-growth or balanced growth perspectives are the methods employed and the beneficiaries of the required allocative process. In one method, explicitly political, public bodies and publicly accountable officials make the decisions which, strictly speaking, should be made in the public interest. In the other, politically reductionist method—not nonpolitically, for we now see that the total avoidance of politics is chimeral—what may also be termed the covertly political, suppressive, or reductionist method, the private self-interests of a relatively small but powerful elite group are protected under the delusory doctrine of substituting absolute gains for the nonelite to be achieved through constant economic growth instead of gains in their relative share of the social wealth: unlimited economic growth instead of redistribution.

I contend that we should be enthusiastic about these realizations brought about by the limits to growth, especially if increasing public participation in the political process and political education accompany repoliticization. Because the limits of growth "blew the cover" of the disguise of the ideology of unlimited economic growth, we now have the first opportunity since industrialism began to assert not only the irreducibility of the political allocative process but, moreover, to insist that this process should not be obscured to protect one social group's distinct advantages—even if that process cannot be eliminated in substance. Political consciousness inspired by the limits to growth should lead to confronting the necessary allocative process by the society as a whole: explicitly, thoughtfully, and confidently. This goal can only be accomplished within a participatory democratic polity.

Repoliticization of advanced industrial society should create a resurgence in the appreciation of the social value of politics understood in the classical, normative sense. The broader the conception of politics within postindustrial society with its concept of citizenship more open than the Greek *polis*, the easier it will be to define oneself into this conception. The skills to participate in political discussions and decisions necessarily involve the careful consideration and selection of desirable political values. Therefore, an additionally advantageous consequence of the limits-to-growth critique of industrial civilization should be the heightened public valuation and appreciation of political philosophy which specifically addresses this crucial social allocative process.

Environmentalist Lester R. Brown expresses the importance of these normative issues and discourse within the context of the demise of the unlimited growth-based worldview:

> The principal dynamic that has shaped society since the beginning of the Industrial Revolution has been the growth ethic. If material growth as we have know it cannot continue indefinitely, then a new ethic... will take its place. Although the changes originate in the physical realm, they ultimately manifest themselves in new values. Soedjatmoko, former Indonesian ambassador to the United States, points out that "once growth ceases to be our reason for being then we have to ask basic questions about the purpose and meaning of life."[14]

The radical, depoliticizing aspect of liberalism and modern economic thought was fueled by its rejection of the traditional sources of political authority and legitimacy, such as the church and inherited social status. Moreover, the need for political authority and, specifically, political legitimacy, was similarly downgraded since their social role was usurped by the advent of the self-regulating market.[15]

The "free" in the "free market" meant free of government's interference, privileges of status, and other institutional restraints such as religion.[16] Wolin comments upon the unprecedented removal of a distinctively political authority—as opposed to its claimed liberal economic replacement of the market—within liberal society as follows: "Hence, what was truly radical in liberalism was its conception of society as a network of activities carried on by actors who knew no principle of authority."[17] The central distributive decisionmaking for the entire society, under the pain of punishment if disobeyed, was deemed unnecessary by the liberal owing to the establishment of the free market. This made the quintessential political issue of making, justifying, and enforcing such political decisions to *appear* to be dissolved (reduced) and thereby ending the need to study such political processes as well. Hence, we can chart the decline of the political and its systematic study (including political thought) in a liberal, market-based and growth-addicted society.

Crucial for our discussion is Wolin's conclusion regarding liberalism's approach to the issue of distribution: "The age-old function of distributing goods according to some standard of justice was transferred [erroneously reduced] from the political sphere and assigned to the impersonal judgment of the market mechanism."[18] As a result of this transferrence, Wolin sees politics and political philosophy "usurped"[19] by economics and the idea of the self-regulating, free market. To Macpherson, politics and political philosophy became "penetrated"[20] by economics. In my work, I have chosen the scientific concept of "reductionism" to express the same phenomenon of the inappropriate claim of the replacement of political processes and values by economic ones. The ideology of unlimited economic growth was the "vent," "safety valve," "social lubricant," and "solvent" for politics.[21] As such, it was the prime agent for the depoliticization of industrial and postindustrial society.

The attempt by liberals to replace political phenomena with the institution of the market—alleged to be purely economic and nonpolitical— was driven, in part, by their view of the superiority of the free market over the typical institutionalization of political authority and power. When this liberal judgment of the desirability of the market over politics is made clear other liberal values are revealed as well. First, the liberals devalued political authority and power because they appeared explicitly to be wielded by identifiable individuals and to be based upon physical threats. In contrast, the market, they claimed, is characterized by neither personal rule nor physical threats.

Liberals [writes Wolin] proved to be unconcerned about the compulsions arising from a system of property because the pressures seemed to be impersonal and lacking in physical duress. On the other hand, liberals would become agitated over political power because it combined both a personal and a physical element... The identification of government with coercion became part of the liberal outlook....[22]

Second, liberalism's advocacy of the desirability of impersonal decisionmaking has been a main reason for its social order's ability to disguise its actual power structure from even its own elite beneficiaries as well as from the victims of this power structure: the masses. This liberal emphasis upon impersonal political power, the obscuring of politics (through economic reductionism), and the social order's inequality through the disguise of economic growth ideology, all enabled liberalism to achieve its "depoliticization of the class relationship and an anonymization of class domination" as Habermas put it—now threatened by the limits to growth!

> It is part of the genius of capitalist exploitation that, by contrast with exploitation which proceeds by "extra-economic coercion," it does not require the unfreedom of specified individuals. There is an ideologically valuable anonymity in *both* sides of the relationship [between capitalist and worker] of exploitation.[23]

Let us not underestimate the benefits for the elite of this anonymization or disguising of political power accomplished through the reductionism of the liberal doctrine of unlimited economic growth. The ideological or legitimation benefits are huge when the exploited within liberal society have only an impersonal market to confront and blame for their deprivations. Because of this anonymization of liberal power within such a social order, such victims usually blame themselves rather than the social order. To illustrate how the dispersal and hiding of responsibility can protect the real power holders within liberal society, consider a recent discussion of the ecological phenomenon of acid rain:

> A century ago, the smokestack in town was known to be the source of bad smells and to kill flowers and trees. To escape criticism, plant designers built taller stacks to spread the output more thinly over the countryside. So it should not surprise us too greatly that we cannot today attribute the acid in a particular raindrop to just one smokestack—this anonymity of power plants was just what the designers had in mind.[24]

Once again we return to what was undesirable to liberals and economists about political life: the explicitness or visibility of the political process with clear individual responsibility and the physical basis of political power both producing increasing conflict and the vulnerability of the ruling elite to criticism, attack, and possible removal by the nonelite. What is important to emphasize here is that the advantages of this depoliticization did not and does not benefit all citizens equally. As I have tried to show, the existing elite gain disproportionately.

Wolin summarizes his view of liberalism as follows:

> In many ways the political thought of the two centuries after Locke constituted one long commentary on the three themes just discussed: the equating of government with physical coercion, the emergence of [market-dominated] society as a self-subsistent entity [replacing politics], and the willingness to accept compulsion from an impersonal source.[25]

Questions may be posed here in reaction to this presentation of some of the essential components of liberalism: Why is coercion that is anonymously or collectively wielded morally superior to coercion wielded by identifiable individuals? Are not the victims of both types of coercion similarly harmed? One difference that we have discussed is that the former (liberal) type of coercion produces more security for the wielders of coercion owing to the disguise or anonymization of their rule which thwarts any possible challenges—but how is this fact morally relevant? Is liberalism's point here sound? Is there a normatively significant difference between a slave losing her or his freedom to one or more masters whom she or he can identify and attack, and a worker being coerced by an anonymous impersonal market wherein the identity of her or his oppressors is masked? Is the latter type of coercion really morally preferable?

The attraction of the liberal market as a replacement for (explicit) politics is based on economic reductionism. As we have seen, at the foundation of the liberals' rejection of politics is a pessimism about the possibility of achieving political knowledge. In the next section I would like to pursue this basic component of liberalism as it pertains to a specific problem vital to political inquiry: the possibility of achieving knowledge of human (political) values or normative (political) knowledge.

Value Noncognitivism and the Economic Reductionism of Politics

Beginning with Locke, liberalism contained a general skepticism about the capability of humans to achieve knowledge of reality and, in turn, this skepticism excluded the possibility of knowledge of human values. This rejection of such normative knowledge as beyond human cognition and the resulting eschewing of normative issues and discourse as nonrational or even irrational has been termed "value noncognitivism," and is a major element of the worldview of modernity, especially given the dominance of natural science in the latter.

Daniel Bell expresses this important point simply: "The real problem of *modernity* is the problem of [normative] belief."[26] Bell also notes that a major difficulty for modern society is its lack of "a political philosophy that justifies the normative rules of priorities and allocations of the society."[27] This vacuum exists because of value noncognitivism; until it is rejected, we have little chance to create a political philosophical alternative to an economic theory and social order based on the illusion of continuous and unlimited economic growth.

Weisskopf discusses the "repression of the normative dimensions" involving the reduction of human reason to technical, instrumental, means-ends rationality and the elimination of the normative dimension from modern life and thought.[28] Bookchin introduced the term "denormatization of politics" to refer to the shift from classical to modern political thought which can be generalized for all modern thought and life as the "denormatization of modernity" as a whole.

Part of the rejection of political philosophy, morality, and theology by liberalism in favor of some automatic, quantitative, nonnormative mechanism such as the market, must have presupposed value noncognitivism and its attendant dismissal of normative discourse as nonrational (or even irrational). Daly writes of the shift in economic thought to denormatization as well as the political consequences of economic reductionism:

> Chemistry has outgrown alchemy, and astronomy has emerged from the chrysalis of astrology, but the moral science of political economy has degenerated into the amoral game of political economics. Political economy was concerned with scarcity and the resolution of the social conflicts engendered by scarcity. Politic economics tries to buy off social conflicts by abolishing scarcity—by promising more things for more people, with less for no one [i.e., Pareto optimality], forever and ever [i.e., progrowth ideology]....[29]

The widely accepted value within economics—Pareto optimality—was discussed earlier, but this exception to the pervasive value noncognitivism in economic thought should be addressed in this context as well. "Changes that better the lot of some at the expense of others are thought [by economists] to be products of arbitrary value judgments and therefore ethically invalid."[30]

The influence of the antinormative element within positivist economics now understood as value noncognitivism is evident here. As I have emphasized, with neoclassical economics, the economics discipline moved from a normative, primarily political and moral inquiry, to a scientific inquiry specifically, and erroneously, eschewing both political and ethical judgments.

I would like to note the following consequences of the dominance of this skeptical, antinormative view within economics which I claim is based upon a false position about the possibility of normative knowledge. First, economists reject any comparative value judgments of a person's or a group's *needs* as more important, desirable, or valuable than others.[31] This implies that *everyone's* improvement (including the rich) is the only justifiable public policy and dismisses redistributive policies which would entail some people (the rich) doing worse; the latter policy requiring value judgments to be made subordinating some people's needs to those of others. Such a social objective of constant and universal gain requires a policy of endless growth. When the limits to growth are approached (as they are today) this fundamental legitimation of the unequal social structure will be destroyed by its own political ramifications and the collapse of its own illusory and undesirable political presuppositions.

Second, this ceaseless, unlimited growth view of more and more things for everyone reflects the "pig principle": "that if you like something, more is better".[32] This preoccupation of antinormative economics with maximization is of fundamental significance. It overlooks the profound distinction between the ideas of maximum and optimum. The maximization orientation is a major component of unlimited growth ideology. If we accept the progrowth economists' premises: that some (or all) people will want—in contrast to need—more of something considered valuable, and that there are no recognized limits to economic growth, then it follows that we *should* grow endlessly to satisfy people's wants. From this deduction the immensely important, industrial social value of ceaseless and unlimited economic growth is derived.

Keynes's distinction between relative needs and absolute needs provides a good conclusion to this chapter and a transition to the next chapter's treatment of the underpinning of the industrial addiction to unlimited economic growth by the social limit to growth of relative wealth. This very concept of relative wealth will also be the undermining of unlimited growth-based ideology because of the political consequences of this normative limit. On these two types of human needs Keynes wrote:

> Now it is true that the needs of human beings may seem to be insatiable. But they fall into two classes—those needs which are absolute in the sense that we feel them whatever the situation of our fellow human beings may be, and those which are relative in the sense that we feel them only if their satisfaction lifts us above, makes us feel superior to, our fellows. Needs of the second class, those which satisfy the desire for superiority, may indeed be insatiable; for the higher the general level, the higher still are they. But this is not so true of the absolute needs. . . .[33]

In this distinction between relative needs that are insatiable and abso-lute needs that are not we confront the fatal error of growth-addiction in advanced industrial societies and one that shall be discussed in the following chapter as a nonbiophysical or social limit to growth: the nature of the social goods within materially affluent industrial societies becomes domi-nated by relative or competitive goods to the extent that the desire for them *cannot—by definition*—be satisfied by economic growth.

This revolutionary development in the history of humanity wherein the primary goods of society are essentially relative or competitive as a result of the absolute or biophysical needs of most of the industrial population having been satisfied explains why economic growth producing absolute gains exclusively does *not* help the nonrich. Furthermore, it explains why the nonrich's economic position relative to the rich has improved so little—if at all—despite the great amount of economic growth in the post–World War II period (especially in the United States). I would like to further pursue this point about relative wealth in advanced industrial society in the next chapter.

6

The Concept of "Relative Wealth": A Social Limit to Growth that Destroys the Addiction to Growth and Spurs Repoliticization

In reality, the source of all these differences [between the savage and the social civilized man], is that the savage lives within himself, while social man lives constantly outside himself, and only knows how to live in the opinion of others, so that he seems to receive the consciousness of his own existence merely from the judgment of others concerning him.

—Jean Jacques Rousseau[1]

The structural characteristic [of advanced industrial society] in question is that as the level of average consumption rises, an increasing portion of consumption takes on a social as well as individual aspect. That is to say, the satisfaction that individuals desire from goods and services depends in increasing measure not only on their own consumption but on consumption by others as well.

To a hungry man, the satisfaction derived from a square meal is unaffected by the meals other people eat or, if he is hungry enough, by anything else they do. His meal is an entirely individual affair...At the other extreme, the quality of the air that the modern citizen breathes in the centre of the city depends almost entirely on what his fellow citizens contribute toward countering pollution, whether directly by public expenditure or indirectly through public regulation...The value to me of my education [or any other social or relative good] depends not only on how much I have but also on how much the man ahead of me on the job line has.

—Fred Hirsch[2]

As we have seen, most of the limits-to-growth literature has concentrated on the biophysical limits contained within ecology: population, natural resources, and the environment. I would like to discuss a nonbiophysical limit that is more germane to this part's subject of modern economics and its core value of unlimited economic growth: the definition of economic wealth—and goods in general—within advanced industrial societies.

Because of the historically unprecedented material affluence of these societies as a whole whereby most of their citizens' biological needs are no longer problematic, an individual's wealth, the definition of social goods, and the individual's satisfaction upon acquiring these socially defined goods all become comparative in nature or relative to how successful others are within the society in acquiring these goods. More goods have therefore become relative in nature because of this competitive factor in their enjoyment by individual possessors and this accounts for the prominence of competitive success as a primary value in such a society. As America's largest bank's (Citicorp) recent advertising slogan reads: "Citicorp, because Americans want to succeed, not just survive!"

Among the large segment of the population within affluent industrial societies which has its absolute or biological needs met, relative goods are of primary importance. As we have discussed regarding Keynes's distinction between absolute and relative needs, the former are limited, satiable, and refer only to individuals while the latter are unlimited, insatiable, and social in that they refer, in theory, to all other fellow citizens.[3]

Hirsch's distinction between a hungry man attempting to satisfy his private, absolute, biological need and the contemporary job-seeker whose satisfaction of a social or relative good like education is dependent upon how much of this good is possessed by fellow citizens (one can criticize Hirsch here for implying that the *total* value of education is social), is similar to the distinction between preindustrial society wherein the satisfaction of basic, absolute, biological needs was a ceaseless preoccupation for most of its members, and materially affluent postindustrial societies wherein the achievement of the satisfaction of satiable, biological needs leads to an important shift to the attempted satisfaction of relative or socially dependent needs (or, to be more accurate, "wants").

When one is hungry or lacking in any of the basic human needs for survival, one's thoughts and actions are dominated by efforts to remove this deficiency and the resulting pain and suffering; thus, one in such an unhappy situation is not easily dissuaded or diverted from the drive to meet one's absolute needs. The growth illusion or the misleading promises of unlimited growth ideology for the nonelite would have little appeal if the nonelite were absolutely destitute; that is, unable to satisfy their biological or absolute needs, instead of being, for the most part, poor relative only to the elite.[4]

Galbraith, too, makes this same point to show the increasingly profound significance of advertising in advanced industrial society: "No hungry man who is sober can be persuaded to use his last dollar for anything but food. But a well-fed, well-clad, well-sheltered, and otherwise well-tended person can be persuaded as between an electric razor and an electric toothbrush."[5] Thus, when all human survival needs are met (as they are for the overwhelming majority in advanced industrial society), not only do people become vulnerable to persuasion and diversion from aspects of social reality by manipulative advertising but, moreover, the nature and scope of goods change as does the potential for acquiring them and the satisfaction derived from them once possessed. The definition of economic wealth changes, too.

Once our meals, adequate shelter, and fulfillment of our other physical needs are assured and we become an "otherwise well-tended" person, ways to distinguish ourselves from other, similarly well-tended people become important; our consciousness of and susceptibility to social goods and competitiveness increase. Rousseau, one of the first and most penetrating analysts of modernity, emphasized this drive for public esteem or social distinction and its relation to social inequality as one of the defining characteristics of modern society.

His attempt to address the subject in his *Discourse on the Origin of Inequality*, provides his readers with a hypothetical but instructive account of how inequality began and evolved. One of the critical junctures of this evolving process of inequality was the change in humanity's environment from one of isolation to one of much greater social interaction with one's fellow humans. With this increase in socializing came a new desire and evil according to Rousseau:

> Each one began to consider the rest, and to wish to be considered in turn; and thus a value came to be attached to public esteem. Whoever sang or danced the best, whoever was the handsomest, the strongest, the most dexterous, or the most eloquent, came to be of most consideration; and this was the first step towards inequality, and at the same time towards vice. From these first distinctions arose on the one side vanity and contempt and on the other shame and envy; and the fermentation caused by these new leavens ended by producing combinations fatal to innocence and happiness.[6]

My primary aim in this chapter is to show that because of the increasing social significance of the idea and value of relative wealth to the point of dominating postindustrial society, the doctrine of unlimited economic growth and its ideological role are destroyed and along with it the foundation of industrial civilization. This occurs by definition of, or by the very meaning of, this civilization's most important value: competitive success at acquiring relative wealth. In its comparative or competitive aspect, the modern industrial social value of relative wealth necessitates that not everyone can improve their economic lot relative to everyone else—no matter

how much growth occurs or for how long, *per impossible, ad infinitum*!
Postindustrial society is a zero-sum society wherein *absolute* increases in
economic wealth for everyone produced by aggregate economic growth will
do nothing to increase one's competitive standing relative to one's fellow
citizens or competitors. This important point deserves further elaboration.

Every person cannot be among the top ten percent of income earners
or own a valuable etching that was produced in limited numbers or score in
the 98th percentile on the Scholastic Aptitude Test or, in general, succeed
where "success" is defined competitively (as is manifest in the example of
standardized tests where the percentile score is usually considered more
important than the raw absolute score). The "luxurious," socially scarce,
fashionable, status-conferring goods, available to only a relatively few
people because of their inherently limited accessibility or exclusive social
definition, are made to constitute the foremost desires of people within
advanced industrial civilization whose absolute needs are currently being
met and appear secure for the future.

Dominance by such competitive goods and values in affluent postindustrial societies means more failure than success in citizens acquiring
them or else these competitive goods, when widely distributed, would lose
their distinctive competitive social value or social cachet. A competitive,
rarely attained good is restricted to comparatively few persons and is
thereby relatively valuable; while an extensively dispersed good involves a
decrease in relative or competitive value of that good in a society dominated
by relative wealth. This is the case because the good is now achieved or
possessed by most people and therefore is no longer relatively or competitively distinguishing.

The obvious significance of relative goods and wealth in post-industrial society defeats the main claim of the advocates of limitless economic
growth: such growth is the only means (that is, politically acceptable to the
elite—a point usually omitted) available to help the poor of a particular
society or the impoverished of the entire world. This progrowth position
also implies the dismissal of non-Pareto optimal redistribution because of
elitist, liberal, antipolitical, economic reductionism and the objections following therefrom.[7]

Speaking about the "poor" seems to require some clarification regarding the definition of this social group. Certainly, it will be pointed out by
critics of this discussion that there is a world of difference between someone
who lives in substandard housing, is unemployed, lives on governmental
assistance, and is lacking in basic biological necessities (what Gorz calls
"destitution"), and someone earning $50,000 annually in America and
living in a suburban home full of electronic conveniences (who might consider himself or herself "relatively poor" in Gorz' language).

Nevertheless, in such competitive societies it is still possible that the latter person feels impoverished relative to the much higher income earners living the media-projected, competitively successful, luxurious life of the rich. All along the wealth and income scales of such a society people can— and often do—feel deprived relative to the top group despite their rather considerable material possessions objectively considered.

This might explain, at least partially, the well-known phenomenon in America of virtually all Americans defining themselves among the middle class (especially for the objectively-defined upper class who so classify themselves erroneously), because everyone has their eye on the richer group above them—even the objectively-defined wealthy. Thus, the social category of "poor" in such competitive societies is more significant than the relatively small number of destitute would imply. *The fatal error committed by progrowth supporters that I wish to highlight is their overlooking the fact that economic growth has not, will not, and cannot help the poor and middle class (objectively defined) who lack relative goods because by the time the postindustrial political economy makes such goods available to these people the goods have lost, by this very "trickle down" process, their competitive—or relative—value.*

This antieconomic growth argument against the possibility of it being useful concerning relative goods does not apply to the largely preindustrial, objectively poor countries, most of whose population are destitute and require provision of absolute goods for survival. Here, economic growth *will* indeed help these destitute people because of the lesser significance of the comparability or relativity of wealth in these societies (as with the hungry man in both Hirsch's and Galbraith's illustrations quoted earlier). This recognition of the appropriateness of economic growth within destitute societies protects the critics of growth-based, industrial civilizations from the charge of elitism and of denying the deprived of the world their due.

Needless to say, a redistributive dynamic equilibrium on the global level as recommended by the Meadows group would require fundamental changes in values throughout the world. These authors, to their credit, recognized the crucial role of values, as was pointed out earlier, as did the Executive Committee of the Club of Rome, although both groups did not discuss this critical point at length and, as a result, it was lost amidst the reaction to their shocking computer projections about environmental pollution and resource shortages. (In all the many commentaries generated by this seminal study few, if any, have taken note of this primary normative component to this original limits-to-growth position. What I have argued and attempted to demonstrate throughout my discussion is that the ultimate issue in the economic growth controversy is normative in nature and not biophysical.)

Let me try to clarify this important point about the futility of unlimited economic growth as an ideologically-based promise of help to the post-industrially deprived by referring to the well-known "trickle effect" or "trickle down theory" whereby the poor of a society would have the (false) impression of economic advancement by acquiring goods and services previously affordable only by the rich. This trickle effect is similarly used by its proponents to the economic reductionist doctrine of limitless economic growth: to give the nonelites a false consciousness which benefits the elite. (This theory was obvious in the policy objectives of the 1981 Reagan tax cut. Administration officials were explicit in proclaiming the need for rich individuals and corporations to reap benefits so that these might "trickle down"—although this phrase was rarely, if ever, used—to the rest of society in the form of higher wages and new jobs.)

We can see the use of the trickle down theory by the social theorist Marion J. Levy, Jr. who claims that this trickle effect enables members of advanced industrial societies to "find integration in the appearance if not the actual achievement of social mobility" and thereby to produce stability within such societies. Levy goes on to offer the following analysis of this economic (*cum* political) theory:

> In the context of relatively modernized societies new goods and services are frequently first produced at relatively high prices and in relatively small quantities. When these new goods and services become available, they tend to be identified with the elite members of the society. One of the reasons for this is that during their early appearance they tend to be relatively more expensive since many of the economies of mass production which will characterize them if they are popular are not possible when they are originally introduced. Therefore, during their early appearances they tend to be available to the members of the society with the larger incomes at their disposal ... if the goods continue to trickle down in the scale of social prestige as it were, those who acquire them have something of the *feeling* of upward mobility. ...[8]

The political consequences of such a trickle effect are both obvious and important. The stability of a society with an effective trickle down process will have its existing class structure maintained by having nonelites accept this structure and believe that they are gaining according to its principles of distribution. Several comments are in order here. First, note should be taken of the candid admission—without elaboration or discussion—by Levy of the illusory quality of this conservative and elitist trickle effect. The poor get the "feeling" or "appearance" of upward mobility—which, if genuine, would necessarily mean relative losses or downward mobility for the rich above them—when in actuality they are *not* moving up or gaining relative to the members of the rich elite who have already gone on to enjoy other inaccessibly expensive goods and services (as an historical review of income and wealth distribution in the United States would confirm). These latter goods might be available to the nonelite and poor considerably later but then minus the competitive gain and social esteem involved in *initially* acquiring these goods. *The importance of timing within the postindustrial consumption and status-conferring process is hereby revealed.*

Second, the parallel between the doctrines of the trickle effect and unlimited growth with regard to their illusory components for the poor should not be overlooked. It appears that if the social stability and legitimation—and therefore protection—of the elite's advantages are to be achieved in advanced industrial society, it is by the means of tricking the poor through false and misleading policies whether based upon the ideology of unlimited economic growth or the trickle effect. As Tawney points out, industrial social life is a "disguised social war"[9] where the rich are not likely to give in voluntarily to their enemy, their fellow social competitors. Furthermore, like the industrial social value, unlimited economic growth, the trickle down policy comes a cropper because of the relativity of wealth and goods.

Third, Levy's analysis of the trickle effect holds for a society dominated by relative goods *except* with regard to the promised stabilizing or conservative illusion on the part of the poor. Looking at mass-marketed television sets, instant cameras, hand-held calculators, personal computers, and hundreds of other goods each year, the trickle down thesis, as interpreted by Levy, seems to be confirmed—to a point! New consumer items are indeed continuously introduced and considered status-conferring *because* their initial cost is prohibitive for the masses of nonelites. Thus, these goods take on luxurious qualities owing to the fact that they are capable of being acquired by the successful elite only; they bring their owners social honor because of their exclusivity. With mass production, made necessary by the saturation of the luxury market and the reduction in price, such goods become accessible to the middle and even lower class *after a considerable time has elapsed*—as with the television set, one of which, at least, is owned by virtually every household in America (and presumably this analysis suggests the same trickle down process can be expected to apply to the large-screen projection television sets *in due time*).

But herein lies the demise of the political effects of the trickle down theory. By the time the nonelites obtain the desired competitive goods—desired precisely because they were not available to all—these goods have lost their competitive appeal, value, and status-conferring qualities. The crucial point here is that the nonelite can never keep up or even catch up with the elite who always acquire the desired goods *before* the former can. How many people will proudly announce as a mark of distinction that they have just acquired a new nineteen-inch television set (or any other such commodity) once the status-conferring article is mass produced and priced for mass consumption?

The competitive element within advanced industrial societies and the great importance of relative wealth harshly sets up the nonelites for continual disappointment and frustration because of their inability to obtain impossible but nonetheless promised, socially praised, and advertised competitive rewards; *impossible* as a result of the competitive and limited nature of the desired social goods.

Because the nonelites erroneously expect the same utility or satisfaction when *they* acquire the competitive goods as if, *per impossible*, economically and materially, they acquired the goods when only the rich could afford them, they are destined for unavoidable disappointment and dissatisfaction. The nonelites acquire the competitive goods too late in the distributive process to achieve genuine upward mobility or even the illusion of it because they too are seeking relative success ("success, not survival," as the Citicorp advertisement says) which they *cannot* achieve by obtaining these goods at the time they do—last! Indeed, by the time the nonelites can acquire these once but no longer competitive, postindustrial goods, other new competitive goods are on the market—for the rich—that tantalize these victimized classes; competitive goods which they currently cannot afford, once again. To keep to our example of television sets, an example of such a good would be a large-projection television costing $2,500.

The last point, I believe, clarifies several important aspects of advanced industrial society. The first is the unlimited or insatiable nature of human wants in a society which ceaselessly produces new items that are most socially desirable just when they are economically beyond the reach of most consumers. Insatiability of wants is one of the central tenets of liberalism[10] as well as modern economics despite its assumption of diminishing marginal utility. Utility per good is satiable but the liberal reply to this claimed law of human behavior is that it only applies to a particular good—like ice cream sodas—and not to wants in general whereby the consumer can shift from a satiated want to an unsatiated want *ad infinitum* (*ad nauseum?*).

This, in turn, reveals the curious implication of the liberal, economic worldview of individuals never experiencing full satisfaction. The consumer in such a society is always made to seek unsatisfied wants, yet even after acquiring material goods which are supposed to satisfy these wants the consumer only experiences the disappointment of (competitive) expectations unfulfilled which triggers the whole nasty, endless process again. The average consumer in advanced industrial society is in a similar position to the humorist Groucho Marx who did not wish to join a private club that would accept the likes of himself: if a nonelite consumer can afford a good then it probably is not (competitively) worth owning!

The competition is so fierce in a society dominated by the desire for relative wealth and status that, as Mishan claims, "At some point, a man would prefer a 5 per cent *reduction* of his income accompanied by, say a 10 per cent reduction in the income of others, to a 10 per cent increase in his income along with a 10 per cent increase in the incomes of others."[11] The fact that such an absurdity appears rational to us should indicate that something is amiss in this type of social order.

There is another illusion-destroying aspect to a social order emphasizing competitive goods as stressed by two critics of growth-based industrial civilization, Mishan and Hirsch. When such goods do finally trickle down, their social value is considerably diminished by social congestion or crowding produced by the *eventual* mass distribution of nonluxurious goods in advanced industrial societies. Mishan uses the example of international, mass tourist travel to "fashionable" that is, "apparently competitive, status-conferring, previously exclusive, luxurious and expensive" resorts where the pressure is to "enjoy it before the crowds get there" and

As swarms of holiday-makers arrive by air, sea and land, by coach, train, and private car, hot in pursuit of recreation; as concrete is poured over the earth; as hotels, caravans, casinos, night-clubs. chalets, and blocks of sun-flats crowd into the area and retreat into the hinterland, local life and industry shrivel, hospitality vanishes, and indigenous populations drift into a quasi-parasitic way of life catering with contemptuous servility to the unsophisticated multitude...As in so many other things—what a few may enjoy in freedom the crowd necessarily destroys for itself.[12]

That which makes the relative good desirable—definition of a relative or competitive good—cannot be achieved when it is obtained by most, if not all, people. Thus, the very success of the political economy in widely distributing such goods could ruin them and the enjoyment of their acquirers just as in Mishan's illustration of vacation resort areas. Competitive goods' social value purchased and enjoyed by a rich few are *necessarily* destroyed by the mass production and mass distribution processes because it is exclusivity itself that is really being prized. Both unlimited economic growth ideology and the trickle down theory not only deny this essential point about advanced industrial society but actually help to suppress it.

Levy and all of the other advocates of economic growth (consisting of virtually all of the existing policymakers) who admire the trickle effect as the only way the poor will be helped, endorse the view of the progrowth advocates and economists Peter Passell and Leonard Ross: "Quite simply, growth is the only way America will ever reduce poverty."[13] Unfortunately, for such unlimited growth-based thinkers (and fortunately for the prospects of industrial social transformation) few members of the poor will be duped by the trickle effect or the progrowth doctrine when competitive or relative goods are the issue—as is increasingly being indicated by the crisis within advanced industrial society. This is the case because both the lack of exclusive, restricted ownership and the presence of overcrowding destroy the elite-desired illusions of the trickle effect and growth ideology wherein economic growth is claimed to be the only means by which the poor will gain and move upward from their lowly station in postindustrial life.

The illusory and manipulative doctrines of the trickle down theory and unlimited economic growth—and the social policies based upon them—cannot produce their desired consequences because of the relative or competitive nature of goods in advanced industrial societies. Of course, naturally scarce resources, like beautiful oceanfront property, cannot be widely distributed so that the central premise of the ideology of growth cannot be applied to them even in a credible illusion! Disappointment is inevitable because such limited goods—whether because of natural limits or socially-imposed limits, like a few numbered artistic prints—will *always* be priced out of the economic realm of the possible for the nonelite.

In the remainder of this chapter I would like to concentrate upon how relative wealth acts as a social—or normative (having to do with values)—as opposed to biophysical, limit to growth. The social science literature on "relative deprivation" is large[14] and the recognition of the comparability or relativity—thus the social nature—of postindustrial, postaffluent goods goes back to the beginning of modernity and the rise of modern society. (This is not to say that there were no elites or relative goods in premodern society, only that because so many inhabitants of the preindustrial populations were destitute and lacking in absolute requirements for survival, absolute goods took precedence.) We have Rousseau's view of modern man living "constantly outside himself" and "only knowing how to live in the opinion of others"; Hobbes's notion (whose work will be examined in more detail in part 3) of a supremely competitive society inhabited by intensely competitive individuals, all seeking power and glory therein: "Virtue generally, in all sorts of subjects, is somewhat [sic] that is valued for eminence; and consisteth in comparison. For if all things were equally in all men, nothing would be prized";[15] and, Thorstein Veblen's analysis of modern "pecuniary emulation" whereby:

the end sought by accumulation is to rank high in comparison with the rest of the community in point of pecuniary strength...since the struggle is substantially a race for reputability on the basis of an invidious comparison, no approach to a definitive attainment is possible.[16]

Although the concept of "relative wealth" has an impressive pedigree of users including the likes of Rousseau, Hobbes and Veblen, its most recent analyst, Fred Hirsch, makes little or no reference to the rich intellectual history of this concept. (The total omission of any reference to Veblen in particular is surprising by an economist.) A thorough account here of Hirsch's penetrating analyses would take us far from our purposes, so I would like, instead, to focus upon Hirsch's main themes of the reasons why ceaseless economic growth will not achieve the stabilizing and satisfying results its advocates claim.

Hirsch's discussion confirms my earlier position that economic growth actually worsens and does not improve the quality of life perceived by the nonelite because it increases the desire—without possible realization—for previously competitive, luxurious (elite) goods. Since these socially scarce goods—primarily valued because they are scarce and owned by comparatively few people—are restricted to the people on the top of the distributive ladder, the nonelite's heightened expectations that *cannot* be fulfilled produce disappointment and resentment when economic growth fails to give everybody what only a few can have and enjoy with the resulting ceaseless "rat race" produced for most people.[17]

This necessary frustration is caused by the inability of economic growth to satisfy the nonelite's competitive quest for what Hirsch calls "positional goods" (emphasizing position relative to others) increases the likelihood of repoliticization: the nonelite erroneously demand from the public sector the satisfaction it cannot obtain from the private economy which, in turn, puts fiscal strains upon the postindustrial state, as we have seen with America's huge debt increase during the eight years of the Reagan administrations and continuing during the first year of George Bush's administration. This analysis of the inevitable failures of the ideology of unlimited economic growth in a social context of relative wealth or competitive goods is the very reverse of what an unlimited economic growth-oriented society is supposed to be, according to its supporters.

Hirsch emphasizes the mistaken understanding of most citizens in a postindustrial society dominated by relative wealth as follows: "what each of us can achieve, all cannot."[18] He terms this the "adding up" problem or "the fallacy of aggregation."[19] Hirsch explains this key phenomenon which proves fatal for the progrowth contention that economic growth can serve as a superior substitute for politics and redistribution: as a society gets more materially affluent, "an increasing portion of consumption takes on a social as well as an individual aspect. That is to say, the satisfaction that individuals derive from goods and services depends in increasing measure not only on their consumption but on consumption by others as well."[20]

When consumer satisfaction is so socially and competitively defined the fallacy of aggregation occurs whereby:

> Acting alone, each individual seeks to make the best of his or her position. But satisfaction of these individual preferences itself alters the situation that faces others seeking to satisfy similar wants... because the sum of such acts does not correspondingly improve the position of all individuals taken together.[21]

It must be stressed that the politically essential phenomena of the establishment and maintenance of community are virtually impossible to realize in such a competitive society. If genuine political action is related to community feeling, then the depoliticization and decline in the public stature of both politics and political philosophy in modern society seem to be explained, at least in part, by the destruction of community characteristics as a result of this competitively-based society.[22]

Hirsch recognizes and briefly discusses the profound political consequences of his argument for the social limits to growth because of the fundamental role held by the doctrine of unlimited economic growth as a depoliticizing form of legitimation of the existing, postindustrial, unequal social structure. Since such growth cannot fulfill its promise of creating greater equality because only a few—the early rich and the current extreme rich—can obtain what is socially considered valuable, economic growth fails in its critical political function of legitimation. This has been our experience not only during the post–1973 period when growth was significantly slowed within the industrial West, but also during peak growth periods when the drive for greater equality by the nonelite did not abate because growth helps very little with regard to acquiring and deriving satisfaction from exclusive, luxurious, competitive goods. *Indeed, boom periods may even worsen the nonelites' perceived notions of well-being because of greater expectations and congestion!* Thus, the desirable consequences claimed by the advocates of unlimited economic growth are undermined by the characteristic of relative wealth within affluent postindustrial societies; this constitutes the *social* limit to growth which supplements the biophysical ones in their lethal threat to the postindustrial social order.

The upshot of this discussion is that economic growth by itself without redistribution, even if truly unlimited by biophysical factors and therefore capable of continuing endlessly, as progrowth boosters argue, would still be unable to accomplish what its promoters claim. Economic growth cannot serve as a means for political reduction or as an effective substitute for redistribution because of the competitive—and thus *socially* scarce even if not physically scarce—nature of goods in advanced industrial societies. Either scarce goods will be bid up in price so that no matter how many economic absolute gains the nonelite make, they will be unable to afford the ever-increasing costs of certain elite or luxury goods like expensive beachfront property or a Rolls Royce automobile; or, the price of the previous luxury goods will decrease (because of mass production economies and saturation of the luxury, elite market) making them accessible to the nonelite and thereby stripping these goods of their relative or competitive value as well as their ability to satisfy the expectations of this largest group within postindustrial society. Therefore, the nonelites are on a treadmill of frustration and disappointment wherein unlimited economic growth ideology keeps them struggling at their posts endlessly until death or retirement!

Part III
The Values of Industrialism
Unlimited Competitive Materialism
and the Normative Limits to Growth

Beyond the Biophysical Limits to Growth: Assessing Industrial Values

> The Industrial Revolution was merely the beginning of a revolution as extreme and radical as ever inflamed the minds of sectarians, but the new creed was utterly materialistic and believed that all human problems could be resolved given an unlimited amount of material commodities.
>
> —Karl Polanyi[1]

> The people recognize themselves in their commodities; they find their soul in their automobile, hi-fi set, split-level home, kitchen equipment.
>
> —Herbert Marcuse[2]

> ...the rich have feelings, if I can put it this way, in every part of their possessions....
>
> —Jean Jacques Rousseau[3]

> You are what you drive.
>
> —Cadillac automobile advertisement on American television and radio; Fall, 1984

The Historical Uniqueness of Industrial Civilization and Its Materialism

Most limits-to-growth critics (such as the Club of Rome writers), basing their analyses on biophysical research conclude that a transformation of postindustrial civilization is imperative for the survival of our planet. Because this transformation will engender social upheaval rivaling the revolutionary change of medieval into industrial society, critics of the existing postindustrial social order must go beyond the claims of biophysical limits to economic growth. While the scientific establishment of these limits is necessary, it is not sufficient by itself. We must begin to engage in systematic and comprehensive examination of and argumentation about the deeply embedded and (mostly) ignored industrial values that lie at the foundation of our society. This means nothing short of addressing the current human condition and its future.

Three inquiries must be embarked upon: a careful study of industrial civilization's values; an examination of alternative nonindustrial values; and, a reasoned defense of the recommended values with a thorough discussion of how the prescribed transindustrial social order can be politically created. I hope to begin such a normative analysis with the purpose of inspiring other students of our contemporary condition—in *both* its normative and scientific aspects—to do likewise. My goal in this part is to examine a central value of industrial civilization: unlimited competitive materialism. I believe it to be the fundamental driving force behind the dangerous policy of unlimited economic growth. Competitive materialism—to my mind, *the* basic industrial value—is unsatisfiable in principle (even if it were worthy of our acceptance) and undesirable in itself (even if it *could* be satisfied). This value, unless changed, will lead our postindustrial social order to its eventual downfall.

In chapter 1, we discussed the profound political significance for industrial society of its efforts to achieve the goal of unlimited, continuous economic growth: this social order's legitimacy and thus its stability and long-term viability are all primarily dependent upon it. The relationship between the nature of industrial politics, including its vital legitimation process, and the doctrine of materialism was not pursued in that context. Before we address such a relationship, let me clarify what I intend to convey by the weighty and problematic term "materialism."

More analysis will follow, but for the present we may understand this term to signify the supreme (or high-ranking) industrial value held by most of industrial society's inhabitants to acquire the maximum possible amount—in an unlimited, ceaseless manner—of tangible material objects, articles, goods, commodities, and so on, (the latter three terms being economic synonyms for objects purchased through the economic system and thereby having exchange value) with prime social regard given to the production of such goods. This material acquisition goal and the efforts to realize it are conceived within the industrial worldview as endless because of industrialism's tenet of the impossibility of reaching a state of human surfeit. Moreover, material acquisition is considered within industrialism to be the essential means by which man achieves the basic "nonmaterial" objectives of (industrial) life such as happiness, self-esteem, social recognition, self-fulfillment, and so on. (Authors of a textbook on "humanistic"— that is, nonreductionist, nongrowth-based—economics explain the term "nonmaterial": "Our age has been so dominated by materialism that to refer to its opposite we use the negative *nonmaterial*. In this age, the word *spiritual* has been so laden with undesirable connotations that we no longer see it as simply meaning the opposite of material. But it does mean this, and we could just as accurately refer to the material as the *nonspiritual*.")[4]

The industrial revolution, as Polanyi observes in the passage quoted in the epigraph to this chapter, was truly revolutionary in transforming medieval culture and social values to industrial ones. Arendt suggests that the ancient *polis* and its primary value of participation in the political and public life of the community came to an end when man turned to "active engagement in the things of this world." She calls this depoliticization and materialist shift of modernity toward "the things of this world" and away from the political life of the *polis*, "the rise of the social."[5]

This phenomenon occurred within modern society with the rise to primary importance of individual acquisition of material goods and the study of such a process: economics.[6] As we have discussed, the ancient disdain for commercial life and the subordination of the economic social category was continued into the feudal period's value structure. One student of the transformation from feudalism to industrial capitalism expresses this point as follows:

> The values of the feudal system stand in stark, antithetical contrast to those that were shortly to prevail under a capitalist [industrial] system. The desire to maximize monetary gain, accumulate material wealth, and advance oneself socially and economically through acquisitive behavior was to become the dominant motive force in the capitalist system.[7]

It is not as if premodern man did not know of material objects or desire them but rather that uniquely in modern industrial society the traditional premodern relation between human desires and "the things of this world" was radically changed from one of limited necessity for survival and subordinated to relations between people (and God, during the medieval period). Furthermore, from this preindustrial perspective, the desiring of the material objects of the world beyond what was needed could lead, by temptation, to undesirable (medievalists would say, "evil") excess: such temptation must be overcome.

Consider the stark contrast of the modern normative viewpoint toward material objects: in modernity, human desires for material goods are considered limitless, socially predominant, and valuable beyond mere survival needs; indeed, they form the supreme value of society toward which all others are subordinated. For those of us living and acculturated within an advanced industrial society, the 180-degree value reversal that constituted the industrial revolution is difficult to comprehend in all of its profound consequences when our contemporary culture defines this normative reversal as "progress."[8]

A detailed historical account of the revolutionary nature and great significance of the transformation to industrial civilization is beyond the scope of this study. I will refer briefly to the following analysis by Macpherson of the value revolution inherent in the industrialization process.

Macpherson has devoted many of his illuminating writings to documenting the dramatic value changes which form the core of the industrial worldview. He points out that

> taking the world as a whole land through history, the right of unlimited individual appropriation has been the exception rather than the rule... What was new in this value judgment was the assumption of the rationality of unlimited desire [for material goods]. There had always been scarcity: men had always had to struggle with Nature to get a living. What was new was the assumption that the scarcity against which man was pitted was scarcity in relation to unlimited desire, which was itself rational and natural. Moral and political philosophers had from the earliest times recognized in mankind a strain of unlimited desire, but most of them had deplored it as avarice and had believed that it could, and urged that it should, be fought down. What was new from the seventeenth century onwards, was the prevalence of the assumption that unlimited desire was rational and morally acceptable.[9]

The ages-old opposition to materialism within Western thought extended without a break from the ancient Hebrews to the beginning of modernity and industrialism.[10] One progrowth opponent of the limits-to-growth position expresses the long and unified repugnance to materialism within preindustrial religious thought—Western and non-Western—when he complains: "the neo-Malthusians would have us be more generous and unselfish and less greedy and materialistic. No decent man would disagree, but are Forrester, Meadows, and Mishan more persuasive than Confucious, Buddha, Isaiah, or Jesus Christ?"[11]

Since our origins, all Western (and some non-Western), political philosophical, moral, and religious traditions have been strenuously opposed to the identification of human identity and values with the acquisition of material possessions. The view that, "I am what I have"[12] did not appear until the industrial revolution and the establishment of materialist social values. These values successfully challenged preindustrial normative traditions, virtually eliminating antimaterialism and replacing it with its contradictory evaluation of material goods to human nature and social life within the secular, value noncognitivist, industrial "dominant social paradigm."[13] The industrial materialist perspective was not only imperialistic for economic reasons (to attempt to satisfy its insatiable unlimited desire for material goods), but culturally as well, in the sense that such an industrial worldview and its values were extended not only to those living within such a society but to all other preindustrial cultures judged as "primitive" or "backward."

Before we conclude this brief point about the historical uniqueness of the industrial society and its values, especially its materialism, I would like to address those progrowth defenders who are skeptical of the possibility of ever achieving a transindustrial social order with fundamentally different values (such as nonmaterialism). To such skeptics, radical social change of this magnitude seems utopian and deleterious in its misleading and diversionary effects. Anyone pessimistic about the possibility of realizing such civilizational transformation need only to contemplate the extreme extent of social change in the revolutions from preindustrial, to industrial, to postindustrial culture. To be sure, a dramatic change in how postindustrial humanity lives will not be easy, and certainly not possible until systematic analysis beyond biophysical limits-to-growth discussions is conducted. Hopefully, a transindustrial revolution will bring us back to some of the traditional or "higher" values (as Dumont calls them), ending our modern industrial flight from them!

The Political Importance of Industrial Materialism

Since materialism is at the foundation of modern society as a whole, including its state's legitimacy, this social value could be said to be among the most important supports for this social order. Therefore, any attack upon materialism would threaten the stability of the entire industrial civilization resting upon it. This is precisely what the limits-to-growth critique involves; hence, the wide-ranging and vituperative reaction by defenders of the existing policy of ceaseless economic growth and the industrial values underlying it, primary of which is materialism. As we have discussed, the radical nature of the limits-to-growth criticism is merely implicit in the biophysical approach and mostly a yet to be fulfilled potential in the few normative limits-to-growth writings.[14] If the important social function of such a normative political discussion of the limits to economic growth addressing the nature and acceptability of industrial values is to be accomplished, then the dependence of modern industrial culture upon materialism as one of its base values must be recognized.

The industrial value of materialism is politically significant in yet another respect: in the Hobbesian view of human nature it presumes. Although the political philosophy of Hobbes was just barely intimated in our earlier discussion of liberalism, it must be noted that Hobbes's competitive, ever-restless, never-satiated conception of man is crucial in its contribution to the materialist depoliticization that is one of the defining characteristics of postindustrial society. With the prevalence of this Hobbesian industrial view of man, citizens of postindustrial cultures upholding its values are constantly seeking happiness or pleasure by pursuing the acquisition of material goods in a never-ending process—so long as they are alive—both for these goods' inherent or intrinsic value and the competitive nonmaterial, social esteem value that they signify.

To support this claim that Hobbes's view regarding the nature of humanity and its felicity is vital to understanding industrial civilization, I would like to cite some recent manifestations of this Hobbesian view (each made without reference to their seventeenth century intellectual ancestor). First, a progrowth economist, in the course of discussing the relationship between human needs, satisfactions, and happiness, asserts the following Hobbes-like claims: "it may well be that people are happier when they experience an increase in certain needs, even if these cannot be entirely satisfied." He also refers to a statement by Bertrand Russell: "to be without some of the things you want is an indispensable part of happiness"; and quotes French sociologist Henri Lefebvre: "*Plus l'être humain a des besoins, plus il existe*"; ["The more the human being has needs, the more he exists"]; and concludes with the possibility that: "what distinguishes man from animals if precisely the multiplicity and diversity of his needs so that... the more needs man has the 'better' he is a man."[15]

American economist Lester Thurow sounds quite Hobbesian when he writes against the limits-to-growth proposal of zero economic growth (symbolized by "ZEG"):

> If ZEG is taken seriously, it does not make sense. 'Small is beautiful' sounds beautiful, but it does not exist because it does not jibe with human nature. *Man is an acquisitive animal whose wants cannot be satiated.* This is not a matter of advertising and conditioning, but a basic fact of existence.[16]

Fellow economist Richard A. Easterlin in a very important and influential article entitled, "Does Economic Growth Improve the Human Lot?" concludes his empirical findings with a quote by sociologist George C. Homans: "Things like this have persuaded some people who would prefer to believe otherwise that any effort to satisfy mankind is bound to be self-defeating. Any satisfied desire creates an unsatisfied one."[17]

The Hobbesian idea that human self-satisfaction is impossible because of man's nature is even subscribed to by Ronald Inglehart, a political scientist devoted to bringing to the attention of students of contemporary post-industrial politics the existence and social significance of what he terms "postmaterialists," or, those citizens of affluent, advanced industrial societies who have turned to nonmaterial values. He observes: "high [human] satisfaction levels appear to be inherently fragile." He concludes with an almost direct Hobbesian influence:

> No government can make its people permanently happy [because such happiness is not humanly possible, according to this view of man]... But ultimately this may be a fortunate state of affairs. A society in which dissatisfaction were absent would be a society frozen in *rigor mortis* [like the dead man, according to Hobbes, whose desires are at an end].[18]

I have cited several contemporary reflections of Hobbes's view of human nature in an attempt to indicate the profound influence this "materialist" view has today in industrial cultures, particularly among economists and their reductionist worldview. Therefore, it should come as no surprise to learn from two students of welfare economics that a "popular elementary definition of economics [is]...that economics is the study of the allocation of limited means of satisfying unlimited human wants...."[19]

To remove material scarcity and achieve satisfaction leaving no unfulfilled desires would also remove this "rationale" for economic activity. With no legitimizing rationale, presumably both economic activity and its systematic study would also lose this reason for being. This produces the obvious conclusion that not only is materialist industrial society dependent upon such a view but so is the modern discipline of economics.

In my view, the core of Hobbes's conception of man is critical to our contemporary industrial society: the denial of any permanent human satisfaction necessitating endless seeking of the satisfaction of human desires. Temporary satisfaction of one desire merely leads, according to the Hobbesian view, to another desire; implied competition between actors and the resulting insecurity about their current status requires more efforts at more consumption endlessly until death. I have quoted contemporary sources to show the great similarity between their views of the growth-based world and Hobbes's on the basic level of the nature of humanity. These points accomplish two important goals: (1) once again to show the prime significance of political philosophical issues like the standard "nature of man," and, (2) to suggest that if this Hobbesian view of man can be refuted, then one very important means of support for the ideology of unlimited economic growth will be removed; and, with it gone, hopefully, a part of this position's rational persuasiveness and popular appeal will be undermined as well.

We confront yet again the centuries-old conflict between the Hobbesian and Rousseauian views of human nature and happiness. Is man morally superior or happier than nonhumans by having more needs, never being totally satisfied and constantly seeking new objects of desire until death? or, is the reverse true? Certainly such an issue, with its long tradition within Western thought and apparent unresolvability over the centuries intimidates any modern theorist and seems to be a candidate for avoidance.

Nonetheless, some observations upon this hoary problem are essential to our subject and must be addressed. (1) The questions of the nature of man and its derivative issue of the nature of human happiness are unavoidable in assessing social orders. Such questions are one of the primary elements within the field of political philosophy. (2) One position on this issue of the nature of man and human happiness is dominant within industrial society: the Hobbesian view. (3) The limits-to-growth critiques of industrial society are basically challenges to the Hobbesian conception of human nature: natural limits to the biophysical possibility of structuring a social order with such a conception of humanity; and, normative limits to the desirability of achieving, if possible, such a social order. These critiques assert implicitly—when they should argue explicitly—the alternative Rousseauian position where he clearly expresses his contrary views to Hobbes with regard to the noncompetitive nature of goods and the commendatory nature of their fewness rather than their multiplicity, as well as the presumption to avoid seeking social recognition—but more on Rousseau shortly. (4) Even if Hobbes is correct about man ceaselessly needing unfulfilled desires to be happy and that satiation of human desires is tantamount to death, the question may be posed whether these necessary desires must be material and competitive ones. Some limits-to-growth critics have raised the possibility of growth continuing in materially affluent, advanced industrial societies but not just as material economic growth (what one of them calls: "moral growth").[20]

With the idea of alternative, nonmaterial, noneconomic growth raised as an alternative, our imaginations may discover other social values to replace industrial materialist ones. Perhaps the first favorable presentation within political economy of the no-growth, stationary state, provided by political philosopher John Stuart Mill, may give us some inspiration. He admits that he is:

> not charmed with the [Hobbesian] ideal of life held out by those who think that the normal state of human beings is that of struggling to get on; that the trampling, crushing, elbowing, and treading on each other's heels, which form the existing form of social life, are the most desirable lot of human kind, or anything but the disagreeable symptoms of one of the phases of industrial progress.[21]

Mill then offers "the northern and middle states of America" as examples of civilizations in such a state of "progress" wherein "the life of the whole of one sex is devoted to dollar-hunting, and of the other to breeding dollar-hunters."[22] In contrast to this state and Hobbes's, consider Mill's ideal social order: "the best state for human nature is that in which, while no one is poor, no one desires to be richer, nor has any reason to fear being thrust back, by the efforts of others to push themselves forward."[23] We should note the key noncompetitive aspect of Mill's prescribed social order as well as the absence of the classical liberal's ubiquitous anxiety over relative downward mobility or, the "fear [of] being thrust back" while others "push themselves forward."

Perhaps in a transindustrial, noneconomistic, nongrowth-fixated social order, such nonmaterial, nonindustrial, noncompetitive values as family felicity, leisure, and friendships can grow.[24] To follow Schumacher's suggestion, Buddhist, nonmaterialist values might be considered.[25] Finally, the idea of "voluntary simplicity" or "simple life"[26] should be the catchall term to embody the nonmaterial values that might grow in a transindustrial social order characterized by material equilibrium. We return to the issue of the "composition of growth" or which aspects of the human experience should grow if—and it is a big "if" indeed—the growth of some human desires is absolutely essential to human happiness as Hobbes and the pro-growth defenders argue. It should be clear by now that this central social problem of which values ought to be selected, reinforced, and pursued by a culture with its practices and institutions organized to realize them is the basic normative issue of political philosophy.

One aim of this part and the volume as a whole is to show that the venerable political philosophical questions are still significant: the nature of humanity, human happiness, and goodness, and the adequacy of the materialist answer to these questions. (Regarding these deep theoretical issues, the materialist similarities between existing socialist and capitalist political economies and societies might be surprising.) I have attempted in this chapter to demonstrate the political significance of materialism to advanced industrial society. Now that the basic political importance of materialism has been explained, it is time to delve more thoroughly into its nature.

The Nonmaterial Normative Components of Industrial Materialism

Let us begin with the pursuit of the "deep structure" of what I mean by "unlimited competitive materialism" and the consequences of the phenomena referred to by this concept in advanced industrial society. It is essential to my overall argument that the important and historically unique industrial value of materialism be understood clearly and comprehensively beyond its ordinary superficial meaning: "emphasizing the human desire for material objects."

I introduce this discussion by citing two limits-to-growth critics of the industrial value of unlimited economic growth who view this value and the social policy based upon it as a social pathology of the industrial social order and yet, paradoxically, contend that such societies are not materialistic in the ordinary sense. One of them, Slater, states his objections to the characterization of materialism being attributed to American society as follows:

> There is much confusion about this issue in contemporary thought. The United States, for example, is described as a "materialistic" culture, apparently because it is deluged with material artifacts. Yet there has probably never been a people with less emotion invested in specific material possessions. Americans as a rule are Platonists when it comes to possessions—it is the *idea* or *form* of a house, car, chair or bowl to which they are attached rather than the specific object... [postindustrial] Mass production is based upon, and in turn encourages, a conceptual attitude toward objects. It is more difficult to particularize and love a house, shirt or car that is virtually identical with many others and will be abandoned for a replacement before long.[27]

Fromm makes a similar observation concerning the lack of emotional attachment to material articles, although for a different reason. Fromm poses "the puzzling question why contemporary [industrial] human beings love to buy and to consume and yet are so little attached to what they buy." His reply involves what he terms "the marketing character phenomenon" [what I shall call later "industrial materialism"]: "The marketing characters' lack of attachment also makes them indifferent to things. What matters is perhaps the prestige or the comfort that things give, but things *per se* have no substance."[28]

Now, one might think that these are odd passages to quote in a discussion stressing the significance of the materialism of industrial civilization, denying, as both thinkers do, attachment to material objects on the part of postindustrial (American) citizens and thereby apparently asserting the nonexistence of materialism within the industrial social order. Thus, let me quickly add that I have provided Slater's and Fromm's remarks as a way of introducing my own analysis of industrial materialism which emphasizes the complexity of the relation between the industrial consumer and material commodities, consistent with claims such as Slater's and Fromm's about Americans having little emotional investment in specific material things and the claim that for industrial consumers "things *per se* have no substance."

To start with, it is quite unfortunate that the term "materialism" has been preempted by the metaphysical philosophical theory claiming the ultimate constituents of the universe, including the human mind, to be of material nature or matter.[29] Within this philosophical context the opposing theory of reality to materialism is idealism or the view which holds that minds and their products (ideas) are the ultimate components of existence. One student of this issue writing in an introductory volume on metaphysics characterizes this philosophical debate between materialism and idealism as "probably the most conspicuous and the most deeply significant division" in the history of philosophy.[30]

From Slater's juxtaposition of the alleged materialism of American society with a reference to Plato's idealism and, furthermore, his contrasting material objects with their ideas or forms, it seems evident that Slater is using "materialism" in its technical philosophical meaning. I wish to make it clear that this is *not* the meaning that I intend in this discussion of industrial materialism nor do I believe it is what most perceptive analysts of industrial civilization have in mind when they claim this trait to be *the* main feature of such a society. Slater is drawing upon the metaphysical distinction between material objects as physical, tangible entities such as houses, cars, chairs, or bowls, and the nonphysical, nonmaterial ideas of them. However, this philosophical dualism, is, I believe, both inappropriate and misleading when inquiring into the social and political consequences of materialism as an industrial social value no matter how sound it may be as a metaphysical theory.

I wish to argue that if we are to fully comprehend the nature and social impact of the crucial normative doctrine of materialism within the industrial worldview we must disassociate it from the hoary philosophical theory of reality with the same linguistic label and think of it in a different—but not totally unrelated—light. Contrary to Slater, I prescribe that for purposes of analyzing and assessing postindustrial society we should conflate what he separates: material objects distinguished from our ideas of and about them (and purchasing material commodities from purchasing services as well). Our "conceptual attitude toward objects" (to quote Slater) should be considered, I contend, as part of what is meant by the materialism of industrial society. Moreover, I suggest that, from this analytical perspective of the postindustrial social order, what economists define as "services" should be included within this social order's materialist nature.

Supposedly, what a teacher or medical doctor (to use two examples of typically classified service occupations) provide is not a material, tangible object but nonphysical, nonmaterial knowledge. Such services, however, are nonetheless part of the materialist value structure of industrialism:

providers of such services (like teachers and medical doctors) desire monetary payment for their services in order to purchase material commodities—in fact, it is this payment which makes such provision of services economic "commodities" rather than charity. The use of material objects *cum* commodities in the delivery of the services (for example, books, medical equipment, drugs, etc.) is necessary—the monetary costs borne by the recipients for the services provided to them must be paid by them, usually with previous earnings as a result of exchanges involving material goods. Providers of services seek through their occupation and its monetary remuneration the opportunities to achieve the material expression or indication of their realizing industrial nonmaterial (I hesitate to say "spiritual") values and/or accomplishing some nonmaterial aims directly.[31]

One example of the former might be a medical doctor purchasing an expensive automobile in order to indicate success and to achieve social recognition and esteem (as shown in the Cadillac commercial quoted in the epigraph, "You are what you drive!"); an example of the latter might be these same nonmaterial values of social recognition and esteem being conferred upon members of service occupations *per se* because of their inherent socially valued traits, independent of the amount of their monetary remuneration, such as, medical doctor, judge, clergyperson and college professor. The last two are rarities within industrial society wherein highly valued occupations are usually accompanied by correspondingly high monetary remuneration for its members. Indeed, with these two occupations we may have the rare instances of the very lack of monetary rewards resulting in social admiration. Hence, they are considered as "callings" outside the normal market economy (with unique job security through tenure) and exclude the usual, unlimited materialist desires. This point about the relation between material commodities and nonmaterial values within postindustrial society requires further elaboration and shall be the focus of much that follows.

With regard to this relation between postindustrial commodities and values, Fromm's statement about the nonsubstantiality of "things" (or material commodities) within industrial society is most penetrating and profound in its consequences. It is not so much the physical or tangible composition of such things within the industrial culture that is socially significant; instead it is what these material objects *represent nonmaterially* to industrial man. To use Slater's formulation, the industrial *conceptual attitude* toward or the industrial *idea* of a house, car, chair and bowl is what is important more than the specific intrinsic, physical characteristics of these material objects. I submit that in order to comprehend the postindustrial social order, and its physical and normative vulnerabilities, one must recognize and fully appreciate what these material objects serving as commodities (because of their exchange value) mean; what social purposes they meet; what values they embody within this type of society; and whether such industrial social meaning is materially-based or not, or is both material *and* nonmaterial in nature.

Fromm's simple suggestion of "prestige" and "comfort" as the possible social meanings of industrial material goods must be pursued much more deeply. My claim here is that once industrial social analysts abandon the inapposite use of the metaphysical theory of materialism constructed in reply to the philosophical problem of the nature of ultimate reality *per se*, they can then treat Slater's and Fromm's assertions about advanced industrial society as consistent with, or part of, the concept of industrial materialism—not contrary to it as they appear to maintain.

The crucial nonmaterial aspect of the social value of unlimited competitive materialism within industrial civilization, necessary for illuminating the normative foundation and thus the possible points of attack by the proponents of the normative limits to growth, consists of two main, nonmaterial value attachments to material objects treated as industrial commodities: unlimited human desires and competitive success (including social recognition thereof).[32] As a Canadian team of limits-to-growth advocates explains: "The first belief of mass-consumption [industrial] society [is that] happiness is achieved through the accumulation of things." They add:

> Happiness depends on the accumulation of material goods in ever-increasing numbers. The degree of our happiness is supposed to be exactly proportional to the number and monetary value of things we possess. . . .[33]

One of the aims of the next chapter is to elucidate the unlimited and competitive nature of postindustrial values by drawing upon the rich tradition of modern political philosophy.

8

Materialism and Modern Political Philosophy

...the felicity of this life consists not in the repose of a mind satisfied. For there is no such *finis ultimus*, utmost aim, nor *summum bonum*, greatest good, as is spoken of in the books of the old moral philosophers. Nor can a man any more live whose desires are at an end than he whose senses and imaginations are at a stand. Felicity is a continual progress of the desire from one object to another, the attaining of the former being still but the way to the latter...I put for a general inclination of all mankind a perpetual and restless desire of power after power that ceases only in death. And the cause of this is not always that a man hopes for a more intensive delight than he has already attained to, or that he cannot be content with a moderate power, but because he cannot assume the power and means to live well which he has present without the acquisition of more.

—Thomas Hobbes[1]

...selfishness, which is always comparing self with others, is never satisfied and never can be; for this feeling, which prefers ourselves to others, requires that they should prefer us to themselves, which is impossible... So it is the fewness of his needs, the narrow limits within which he can compare himself with others, that makes a man really good; what makes him really bad is a multiplicity of needs and dependence on the opinion of others.

—Jean Jacques Rousseau[2]

To consume is one form of having and perhaps the most important one for today's affluent industrial societies. Consuming does relieve anxiety but it also requires one to consume ever more, because previous consumption soon loses its satisfactory character—like an addiction.

—Erich Fromm[3]

Hobbesian versus Rousseauian Conceptions of Man and Their Contemporary Relevance

Going back to the thought of Thomas Hobbes, who may be considered the founder (or cofounder with Machiavelli) of modern political philosophy, and certainly, as I hope to show, was the founding thinker of industrialism and its value of materialism, there emerges an important element within the intellectual history of this industrial value related to physical things.[4] This is the element within modern thought that probably has contributed to its confusion with the philosophical doctrine of the same name. We see this in Hobbes's revolutionary change from the ancient-scholastic tradition which prescribed that "the duty of the sovereign is...no longer 'to make the citizens good and doers of noble things.'" but to "furnish the citizens abundantly with all good things...which are conducive to delectation."[5]

Hobbes's philosophical materialism also contributed to this confusion between the philosophical theory of materialism and the industrial value I refer to by the term "materialism." His definition of "life" in *Leviathan* as "but a motion of limbs" is philosophical materialism in the extreme.[6] George Sabine calls this basic metaphysical belief of Hobbes, "scientific materialism" because Hobbes, according to Sabine, "grasped the principle [of Newton's theory of planetary motion] and made it the center of his system. At bottom, he held, every event is a motion and all sorts of natural processes must be explained by analyzing complex appearances into the underlying motions of which they consist."[7]

Hobbes's political philosophy, however, is not only noteworthy as a possible source of the misleading identification between the industrial value and the philosophical theory of materialism—since he held both—but much more importantly as the expression of the modern complex value of unlimited competitive materialism and its varied components. Some of these components are (1) individualism embodying the competitive nature of key social values such as social recognition, honor and vanity; (2) owing to constant threats to one's achieved material goods and social esteem, the requirement of the ceaseless striving for still more material acquisitions and power in order to protect one's previous acquisitions; and finally, (3) having this acquisition process end not with satisfaction or satiation but with death. The flavor of these ideas of Hobbes was suggested by the passage quoted in the epigraph to this chapter.

If this discussion were a history of the idea of industrial materialism it would require lengthy analyses of not only Hobbes's works—to my mind these contain industrial materialism's first and perhaps most influential formation—but, in addition, the political philosophies of Locke, Rousseau, Smith, Bernard Mandeville, David Hume, Jeremy Bentham, and J. S. Mill (to mention the major political thinkers within whose political thought this value played an important role), prior and supplementary to that great student of industrial materialism, Karl Marx. Such a huge task would encompass the political philosophical treatment of the origin and development of modern thought itself; as such, it is way beyond the scope of this part's aims or even the volume's taken as a whole.[8] Given our purposes, this prodigious interpretative project can happily be avoided. Nonetheless, I would like to touch upon the thought of some of these political thinkers merely as a way of fleshing out our understanding of the central industrial concept of materialism and its attendant values within modern industrial society. This brief excursion into the history of political philosophy will also help us appreciate the driving normative forces underlying economic growth ideology as well as the lethal threat to it constituted by the limits to growth and the social critique based upon them.

I refer to the thought and writings of the generally considered great political philosophers of Western history not to use them as authorities or as representatives of Western industrial culture but as the most insightful reflections into the nature of industrial and postindustrial society available to us. These writers' claims ought not to be accepted because of their scholarly reputation but because of the power of their imaginations and penetrating understanding of the human condition and its particular state within industrial civilization. Like anyone else's claims theirs must stand or fall upon the evidence provided.

Rousseau was perhaps the most penetrating early critic of modernity and its materialism. He recognized but dissented from Hobbes's main point about the significance for the modern industrial social order of competitive goods, especially social recognition or esteem, and the insatiable desire for them producing the necessarily ceaseless quest for such goods. Rousseau appreciated and attacked the pervasiveness of these values in his important concept of "selfishness" or egoism (*amour propre*), and that desire's unsatisfiability producing morally bad men (see, among other possible texts, the Rousseau passage quoted in the epigraph). He realized, like Hobbes, that the modern drive for competitive social recognition, honor, and selfishness could not be achieved by all.

Rousseau accepted as descriptively true, but prescribed against Hobbes's view of the zero-sum nature of modern goods especially their endless "multiplication" and their "dependence on the opinion of others."[9] Unlike Hobbes, Rousseau astutely perceived the unacceptable normative costs of founding a social order—like our modern industrial one—on such insatiable, competitive, and exclusive, and thereby unequal, values. This constitutes one of Rousseau's great contributions to modern thought.

In his account of the origin of modern inequality in *The Second Discourse*, Rousseau criticizes Hobbes for ignoring human compassion and provides an important footnote wherein he distinguishes between natural, noncompetitive self-respect (*amour de soi*) and social, competitive egoism (*amour propre*). Rousseau declares that these two emotions must not be confused.

Self respect [*amour de soi*, he writes] is a natural feeling which leads every animal to look to its own preservation, and which, guided in man by reason and modified by compassion, creates humanity and virtue. Egoism [*amour propre*] is a purely relative and factitious feeling, which arises in the state of society, leads each individual to make more of himself than of any other, causes all the mutual damage men inflict one on another, and is the real source of the [Hobbesian] "sense of honour."[10]

In the course of Rousseau's combined explanation and normative presentation of how modern social man became different—and morally worse—than his logical construct of isolated natural man, he emphasizes the fundamental importance and pernicious social consequences of the Hobbesian, vain (in *both* senses of that term: excessive self-concern and being futile) drive for social recognition by his fellow citizens/competitors. Rousseau captures the competitive nature of modernity and its unfortunate legacy in his *Discourse on the Origin of Inequality.*[11] Therein lies the basis for Rousseau's disagreement with Hobbes's assessment of man's nature and modern condition. Rousseau chides his predecessors in political philosophy, especially, of course, Hobbes, when he asserts:

The philosophers, who have inquired into the foundations of society, have all felt the necessity of going back to a state of nature; but not one of them has got there... Every one of them, in short, constantly dwelling on wants, avidity, oppression, desires, and pride, has transferred to the state of nature ideas which were acquired in society; so that, in speaking of the savage, they described the social man.[12]

This basic disagreement between Hobbes and Rousseau on the nature of man is widely noted by textual commentators and remains a profound point not only in the history of modern political philosophy but also for the light it sheds on the nature of social life in current advanced industrial societies. The nature of man has always been a primary, political philosophical theme since the beginnings of such inquiry with Plato. This essentially metaphysical and normative issue regarding the fundamental traits of human beings and the normative consequences that they imply, that is, which traits ought to be pursued to fulfillment and which ought to be rejected ("natural" versus "unnatural" traits, "true" versus "false" traits, of "authentic" versus "artificial" traits), and which ought to take priority when in conflict, show the fundamental importance of this issue not only for political philosophy but for the comprehension of the normative presuppositions of all civilizations.

The normative, political significance of the concept of humanity also manifests the improvement that this mode of normative discourse can make in understanding the contemporary plight of postindustrial citizens. Hopefully, it can thereby be suggestive of remedial or ameliorative action as well. From this perspective every culture, civilization, or social order (I have been using these broad social categories synonymously) is ultimately the institutional expression and embodiment of its values, for example, those contained in its conception of human nature. I believe this is so no matter how deeply embedded and hidden from critical self-examination these culture-defining values may be or how many obstacles are created by elites who have an interest in thwarting social analysis and the resultant social knowledge for fear of the disruptive consequences they both might inspire.

An insight by Camus is illuminating here: "Beginning to think is beginning to be undermined. Society has but little connection with such beginnings."[13] I would add the amendment: "especially normative thinking or thinking about a society's values"—particularly thinking about the socialized, taken for granted values which help constitute the society's dominant social paradigm. Two students of politics take note of Camus's point about the disinterest a society has—which is nonreified language means the disinterest its elites have—in stimulating a thorough, systematic, self-critical examination of one's own society. They relate it to the beginning of political consciousness:

Society [the elite] discourages original thought and covers up human origins of social facts in order to maintain itself in all its imperfection. Political consciousness begins only when we become aware of society's cover-up and oppose its conditioning [under the guise of "education" and noted for this social function since Plato] to the extent that it represses our human needs.[14]

The limits-to-growth controversy goes to the core values of industrial civilization and exposes the latter's reductionism of and pernicious effects upon the human condition through its specific values, such as materialism, leading to "the [industrial] repression of our human needs." Therefore, both the limits-to-growth critics and the advocates of limitless economic growth must, in my view, become more politically conscious. The participants on both sides of the controversy must explicitly and systematically address such political philosophical questions as the nature of man. These questions are at the roots of their respective positions however unfamiliar and intimidating they may find normative inquiry.

Rousseau's concept of human nature enabled him to perceive the normative dark side of the modern, Hobbesian, materialist society with its unlimited striving for competitive social esteem through material acquisition which he identified and attacked. Rousseau's critique of modernity included his recognition of the undesirable consequences of the industrial social order and its underlying values not the least of which was unlimited competitive materialism. Materialism produced, according to Rousseau (who may have been the first industrial social critic to observe this), modern alienation. Near the conclusion of his *Discourse on the Origin of Inequality*, Rousseau provides an eloquent assessment of modernity in a manner that can serve, I submit, as the watchword of the limits-to-growth critics' condemnation of industrial civilization:

> Civilized man, on the other hand, is always moving, sweating, toiling, and racking his brains to find still more laborious occupations: he goes on in drudgery to this last moment...He pays his court to men to power, whom he hates, and to the wealthy, whom he despises; he stops at nothing to have the honour of serving them....*social* [alienated] *man lives constantly outside himself, and only knows how to live in the opinion of others, so that he seems to receive the consciousness of his own existence merely from the judgment of others concerning him.*[15]

Rousseau concludes this searing indictment of a civilization characterized by what I prefer to call "industrial" or "unlimited competitive materialism" by noting that in such a social order we are "always asking others what we are, and never daring to ask ourselves.... [and] we have nothing to show for ourselves but a frivolous and deceitful appearance, honour without virtue, reason without wisdom, and pleasure without happiness."[16] These devastating words of Rousseau should not be accepted because of the stature of Rousseau within the tradition of Western political theory, but considered seriously as to their possible rational persuasiveness based on the evidence a contemporary can provide for their support. In political philosophy, as in all rational enterprises, evidentiary strength must determine preferability.

When we turn to the thought of Adam Smith a crucial move in the development of the industrial value of materialism is observed. He takes the Hobbesian-Rousseauian point about the modern drive for competitive social recognition, social honor, or what Rousseau termed *amour propre*—about which Hobbes seemed positive and Rousseau negative—and ties it directly to economic gain.[17] Smith, the moral philosopher, writes that

> it is chiefly from [the] regard to the sentiments of mankind that we pursue riches and avoid poverty. For to what is the end of avarice and

preeminence?...From whence...arises the emulation which runs through all the different ranks of men and what are the advantages which we propose by that great purpose of human life which we call *bettering our condition*? To be observed, to be attended to, to be taken notice of with sympathy, complacency, and appreciation, are all the advantages which we can propose to derive from it. It is the vanity, not the ease or the pleasure, which interests us.[18]

And, what, we may ask, are the nature and consequences of this "great purpose of human life" that Smith calls, "bettering our condition," which really amounts to nothing more than our seeking the approbation of mankind or public esteem? Smith, the economist, answers this question with the propensity in human nature to "truck, barter, and exchange one thing for another."[19] He adds:

...the principle which prompts to save, is the desire of bettering our condition, a desire which thought generally calm and dispassionate comes with us from the womb, and never leaves us till we go into the grave [compare this to Hobbes on the idea that it is only with death that the competitive urges cease]. In the whole interval which separates these two moments, there is scarce perhaps a single instant in which any man is so perfectly and completely satisfied with his situation, as to be without any wish of alteration or improvement of any kind [again compare to Hobbes's idea of the insatiability of man's desires until death occurs]. An augmentation of fortune is the means by which the greater part of men propose and wish to better their condition.[20]

From the perspective of this discussion of industrial materialism and its relation to unlimited growth, Smith's contribution cannot be overestimated. Two economic theorists make important comments upon Smith's path-breaking ideas both for the development of modern economics—which is renowned—and materialist-based and growth-based industrial society—which is rarely noted. One illustrates a point discussed earlier about the revolutionary materialist consequences of industrial society and its historical uniqueness when he remarks:

In distinction from previous societies where the pursuit of wealth and hard work were considered as inferior activities and as a curse, left to slaves, women, and inferior social groups, industrial society made the acquisition of wealth morally acceptable and considered it as a moral obligation. [Smithian] Economic thought justified this attitude by assuming that acquisitiveness and the propensity to truck, barter, and exchange in order to increase one's wealth is a basic human propensity. Here, a unique historical phenomenon, the acquisitive attitude, was interpreted as a universal human inclination.[21]

We should note the similarity between this criticism of Smith and Rousseau's critique of Hobbes: both critics charge their opponents with a misreading of human nature as a result of a faulty generalization from one particular historical period of society to man's basic nature—producing a possible reductionist error as well: confusing one trait of man with man's nature *in toto*. The major theme of my argument is echoed in Hirschman's work concerning the economic reductionism of modern industrial society when he comments upon the passage quoted above from Smith's *A Theory of Moral Sentiments*:

> ...Smith then takes the final reductionist step of turning [all of the human passions] into one; the drive for economic advantage is no longer autonomous but becomes a mere vehicle for the desire for consideration. By the same token, however, the noneconomic drives, powerful as they are, are all made to feed into the economic ones and do nothing but reinforce them, being thus deprived of their erstwhile independent existence.[22]

Here we have the most important aspect of industrial materialist thought that I have tried to elucidate thus far: "the final reductionist step" of making material economic gain the only "vehicle" for achieving the unlimited, competitive industrial values of social recognition, honor, social esteem, and so on, whereby the other noneconomically based human values merely "reinforce" the economic ones.

I hope that this brief historical survey of past political philosophers has clarified the nature of materialism as I understand that concept and have used it throughout this discussion and its relations to economic reductionism. It is of the utmost importance that industrial materialism not be oversimplified as merely a preoccupation with physical things when it encompasses a complex set of relations between tangible socially-defined goods or commodities and nonmaterial social values like social esteem and honor. The latter industrial social values or, as one student of political economic thought puts it, these "goods of the [industrial] imagination" require further examination.[23]

In an article explicating the political philosophies of Mandeville and Smith on the theme of "envy and commercial society,"[24] this student writes that in eighteenth century European society "while wealth brought with it the satisfaction of material goods, it seemed at least as important that it also brought recognition from others." Then he adds, significantly, I think, for understanding industrial materialism: "The benefit of basing economic activity in the desire for goods of the imagination was that such desires were unlimited. As Nicholas Barbon stated, 'The wants of the mind are infinite.' "[25]

We have seen, beginning with our discussion of relative wealth and positional or competitive goods in the previous part and of Hobbes in this chapter, what these industrial "goods of the imagination" or "wants of the mind" center upon: social esteem, social recognition, honor, pecuniary emulation, pride, vanity, envy—all competitively defined; in sum, Rousseau's *amour propre*. Hobbes, Rousseau, Barbon, and others have perceived that unlike biophysically based and thus limited desires of humans for material goods, such competitive imaginative goods are unlimited and insecure. Furthermore, because these latter traits of imaginative goods are both competitively and unlimitedly defined, desires for them are also insatiable. One limits-to-growth critic vividly expresses the limited nature of the human condition and how the unlimited nature of competitive goods contrasts with it: "No matter how rich he becomes a man has still but one pair of eyes, one pair of ears, one stomach, one sexual organ, a single brain and a single nervous system."[26]

The wisdom of the ages going back to the origins of Western civilization has recognized this profound deficiency in the unlimited—and thus unsatisfiable—quality of competitive goods of the mind or psychological goods. Before Rousseau, Epicurus stated: "If you live according to nature you will never be poor; if you live according to opinion, you will never be rich." Seneca, Epicurus's commentator, added: "Nature's wants are slight; the demands of opinion are boundless."[27]

To the ancient Greeks, as represented by Aristotle, *pleonexia*, "the insatiable desire to have more," is "a moral and political fault" which is deeply rooted in man's constitution, and which both a social order and its institutions must combat. While discussing Aristotle's extensive treatment of economic matters in the first book of his *Politics*, one commentator claims: "The ruling class must be educated away from *pleonexia*...which is part of all men's natural constitutions...."[28] Shulsky goes on to argue that because this insatiable desire is so deeply ingrained within man's nature, according to his interpretation of Aristotle, mere moral argument against it was viewed as insufficient. Aristotle therefore relied upon economic argument—his theory of natural and limited acquisition—which was intended to have greater appeal to his aristocratic audience.[29] Clearly this type of economic argument is of a different nature than its modern counterpart!

Aristotle's [morally-based, normative political] economics, unlike, for instance, the science of [modern, reductionist] economics as defined by Adam Smith, is as concerned with limiting man's desire for wealth as it is with showing him the means of fulfilling it.[30]

A critic takes issue with this interpretation of Aristotle on *pleonexia* being natural, and claims instead that Aristotle viewed this trait as the result of "unnatural" development and the social significance of money.[31] We can sidestep such esoteric textual battles over Aristotle's "real" intent since whether or not one views man's *pleonexia* as "deeply rooted in man's nature" is less important than the recognition that such an insatiable desire for more goods exists, is morally bad, and must be socially resisted and constrained.

If we accept the position that such insatiable desires are indeed natural (as Shulsky's Aristotle, Hobbes, and many other modern thinkers would claim, then, following Aristotle and contrary to Hobbes's view, such desires require limitation by social institutions and, at the very least, should be redirected from material objects either because of moral scruples or because unlimited consumption will eventually run up against biophysical limits— or both. Redirected *to* what? it may be asked. I answer: To noncompetitive, nonmaterial goals which include such qualities as Mill's ideal cited earlier, wherein humanity no longer desires to be richer than one's fellow citizens and is no longer fearful of losing what she or he already has attained because competitive success is not a social value (which thereby does away with competitive failure as well).

Hobbes's own analysis of the nature of social freedom, I believe, may be used against his own conception of man in society. His view was that freedom in society required some political limitation because unlimited freedom in such a context turned out to be no freedom at all, producing, in his famous words, a life that is "solitary, poor, nasty, brutish, and short," and marked by "continual fear."[32] Analogously, human desires may also require limitation (in balance with the limited physical means to satisfy them) in order to produce the desired sensation of human satisfaction. Unlimited desires might create the same, miserable, Hobbesian combination of unhappiness and anxiety as unlimited freedom.

I suggest that we view industrial materialism as a misguided and harmful effort to remove and/or deny the limits to human fulfillment— whether their source lies in man's nature or biophysical environment or both! We have already noted the erroneous denial of human limits involved in the industrialization process and this denial's relation to another erroneous modern denial of limits upon the human condition: death. Mumford explains:

The desire for life without limits was part of the general lifting of limits which the first great assemblage of power by means of the megamachine brought about. Human weaknesses, above all the weaknesses of mortality, were both contested and defied... from the standpoint of human life, indeed of all organic existence, this assertion of absolute power was a confession of psychological immaturity— a radical failure to understand the natural processes [and resulting limits] of birth and growth, of maturation and death.[33]

Modern man's futile efforts to "refuse to be what he is" (to use Camus's formulation), a limited being existing within a limited environment are, I believe, reflected in the policy of unlimited economic growth. Like the shock and terror that overtakes a dying person who has denied the limit of her or his mortality, advanced industrial society is experiencing the beginning of such a reaction in its current crisis brought about by our recognition of the collapse of our fantasies of limitlessness. This "mourning period for our fantasies" as Slater suggests can, I think, provide the start of a new and more fulfilling social order by casting off our social illusions, like unlimited and continuous economic growth, and getting back to—limited—reality.

Are men really as Hobbes suggested? What about the possibility of humans holding noncompetitive values that can be shared by all with no diminution in the satisfaction produced when they are fulfilled? Would such values turn the current postindustrial zero-sum game or Hobbesian universal war of human relations into a positive-sum game where cooperation and noncompetition is the name of the social game? Is humanity really better off generating more needs and insatiable desires or by reducing them, as Rousseau suggests? Must man live in the opinion of others and thus always be alienated and poor? These questions raise the issue of the nature of mankind and the values presupposed by a social order constructed on their answers. I have implied my own view of the superiority of the Rousseauian conception over the Hobbesian industrial one. This judgment informs my recommendation of an alternative transindustrial social order.

On the Psychopathology of Addiction and
Its Relevance to Materialism

Only when the liberal, modern, industrial view of man—which seems fully derivative from Hobbes's works and emphasized by the commentaries of Macpherson[34]—is rejected as perverse and pathological can its deleterious effects upon industrial society be recognized. So the limits-to-growth critics would argue, although very few of them actually go beyond purportedly scientific descriptions of the environment.

The infinite-desirer conception of man, and the social values and practices it generates, all provide the limits-to-growth literature with many opportunities for instructive analogies. Industrial materialism can be considered as a social stimulant wherein pathological confusion exists between ends and means because the means become ends in themselves. Society can be likened to a miser, or a narcissist, or to an addict who needs bigger and bigger doses to produce the same effect, creating a dangerous spiral heading for disaster. These psychiatric examples are used by critics of postindustrial, growth-based culture as analogies to the frustration and inevitable downfall of a society so characterized. Some illustrations of these limits-to-growth pathologies (in addition to Fromm's statement used in the epigraph to this chapter), are:

The practice of medicine may require the prescription of an addictive stimulant for the sake of good health. The amount of the stimulant is finite and limited by the end. When, however, one takes a stimulant for its own sake, the desire for it becomes infinite since it is no longer limited by a final goal but is an end in itself. The same is true of the output of the economic process which, rather than being used for the sake of achieving the final goal of life, tends to become the final goal itself. Since output is then not limited by any final goal, the desire for it becomes infinite. We get hooked on economic growth. To paraphrase Descartes, such a lifestyle would be based on the philosophical foundation: I make and I buy, therefore I am.[35]

Slater insightfully argues in a book aptly entitled, *Wealth Addiction*, about what he sees as the social pathology of addiction to wealth in advanced industrial societies (the Hobbesian competitive elements to this type of addiction, as Slater conceives it, should be noted):

Money is certainly an addiction, and one to which few of us are altogether immune...I doubt that we Americans can come to terms with our own money neuroses without understanding the more florid pathology of the very rich, for it is our envy and admiration of the rich that supports their habit and keeps us hooked ourselves...all wealth addicts are pushers by definition, because *wealth is the only form of addiction in which the addict gets high off other people's withdrawal symptoms*...addicts are tolerated...not because people are stupid but because they treasure the system that fosters wealth addiction. No such system could long exist if at least a bare majority of the population were not Closet Addicts—people who entertain the fantasy that they themselves will one day strike it rich. It is this secret dream that brings the Closet Addict into unwitting collusion with the Heavy Addict, a collusion from which the Closet Addict gains nothing and the Heavy Addict everything.[36]

This perceptive analysis provides an explanation of one of the most important phenomena of the American political system: why there is so much resistance to redistribution among the lower and middle classes when they would stand the most to gain from such a policy. Their "closet addiction" to wealth and their secret—but harmful—dream of "striking it rich" one day clearly work to the benefit of the already rich. Thus, it should be no surprise that this "American dream" is the strongest American myth; it has much real political force behind it! This is one fantasy whose recognition as illusory as well as its deleterious effects upon the nonrich majority, would make its mourning period both brief and emancipatory.

Following these examples of critics of industrialism emphasizing the undesirable and harmful effects of its values by using the analogy of the psychopathology of addiction, I would like to point out one aspect of addictive behavior which often turns out to be the basis of addiction: the avoidance of a negative experience.

Scitovsky points out that experimental evidence indicates that "one reason for the persistence of habits is that once they are established, they become painful to stop."[37] He goes on to analyze drug addiction and other types of more acceptable addictions (like "falling in love") by emphasizing the secondary opposing reaction to stimuli which grows more intense with each stimulus, more so than the primary reaction, for example, of the negative reaction of separated lovers.[38] "When this aftereffect becomes so unpleasant and so long-lasting that repeating the stimulus seems the best (though only temporary) way of eliminating it, addiction is established."[39]

Scitovsky applies this explanation to addictive behavior regarding status. Being addicted to status is indicated by the quintessential trait of all addictions according to the addiction theory subscribed to by Scitovsky: fear of loss. He writes concerning higher-status people in a Smithian vein regarding the greater pain of downward mobility or losing what we already have:

It ceases to give satisfaction after a while because it is taken for granted, but its loss can give much pain. People's striving to maintain their status seems better explained by their desire to avoid the pain of withdrawal symptoms than by their desire for any positive gratification.[40]

Fear of loss on the rich's part overwhelms any positive traits for society that they may otherwise perceive in an egalitarian-oriented redistributive policy.

If the limits-to-growth critics are correct in their charge of the addictive qualities of advanced industrial citizens' commitment to material goods and their symbolic value by applying the type of addictive theory offered by Scitovsky, we may be able to explain the pervasive anxiety noted by analysts, from Hobbes onward, of liberal industrial society characterized by unlimited competitive materialist values. Once one successfully attains competitive social esteem and honor through material acquisitions or indicators, the greatest fear is of loss in the sense of downward mobility or having these honors "snatched away." The famous advice of baseball's Satchel Paige—never to look back—cannot be heeded in a materialist postindustrial society where one's success is relatively or competitively defined. As Hobbes—and Marx—noted, increases in material goods (in profits) were necessary to protect what already was acquired by the individual or corporation against their competitors; a point vividly made clear in our own age of hostile corporate mergers.

Industrial citizens can never rest, never relax: they are always anxious about competitive declines and the possible loss of social values. As Hobbes noted, the drive for distinction is endless until death—and, of course, even there distinction is sought with expensive, "luxurious" funerals! Politically, the addictive characters of the industrial elite and their deepest desire to avoid the withdrawal symptoms of the loss of status (or downward mobility) makes them keenly resistant to social change. Habits must be broken and values changed before this powerful group will voluntarily or peacefully give up their competitive advantages to which they are addicted. What is the likelihood of this occurring?

Sadly, the industrial materialist addict, like all victims of addictive behavior, is doomed by the very nature of her or his addiction: as Hobbes noted unlimited, ceaseless, competitive strivings are such that when one object is attained he or she must pursue another endlessly until death. This Hobbesian conception of man at the foundation of industrial materialist values, therefore, leads to an undesirable conclusion. Frustration, dissatisfaction, fearfulness—all are impossible to avoid no matter how hard people try!

Who, consistent with one's sanity, would want to live in such a social order once these mistaken and pernicious ideas and values were recognized? When materially affluent citizens of advanced industrial society begin to experience the painful "withdrawal"—industrial crisis—from their materialist addictions owing to scarcity caused by the biophysical limits to growth in their environment, they will begin to attain political consciousness; that is, consciousness of the flawed and undesirable foundations of their society. Hopefully, this crisis, this despair, this mourning period for their industrial fantasies, will inspire them to turn to new values and conceptions to help them out of their pain, anguish, and ceaseless futile strivings—or, to use Camus's reference, their Sisyphian trials—which may be what the, thus far, small but increasing vanguard of antigrowth "postmaterialists," already indicate.

The complex nature of industrial materialism (unlike the purely philosophical theory) involves nonmaterial, competitive values which transform the material goods into means. If the desires for material goods by the materially affluent citizens of advanced industrial society merely serve as "vehicles" or indicators of the unlimited, competitive, insatiable, and nonmaterial "goods of the mind," then the desires for material goods themselves will become unlimited, competitive, and insatiable as well. Again, Hobbes is prescient when he observes the income elasticity of competitive nonmaterial goods: "All men naturally strive for honour and preferment; but chiefly they, who are least troubled with caring for necessary things" 'and "who otherwise live at ease, without fear of want."[41]

The commentator upon Hobbes who cites these remarks uses them in his attempt to refute Macpherson's (and other's) materialist ("possessive individualist") interpretation of Hobbes by showing that Hobbes's theory of social competition for honor and recognition was limited to very few English citizens—an aristocratic minority—in seventeenth century England.[42] While preferring to avoid historical and textual battles over the social structure of Hobbes's own society or the "real" meaning of his texts, we can say that the Hobbesian requirement of being "without fear of [biophysical] want" has spread to the most people in human history with the advent of advanced industrial society owing to its immense material productivity.

Thus, while this view may be correct about Hobbes's English society restricting the competition for social values to the relatively few affluent citizens, such a claim is not plausible in materially-rich, advanced industrial society. It is precisely because so many of its citizens' biophysical needs are materially and securely saturated that the competition for nonmaterial social esteem, honor, and recognition is so vicious, unending, fearful, and ultimately frustrating.

One of the most telling points against the promise of the alleged advantages of unlimited economic growth is made evident when the panoramic history of Western thought is considered from Epicurus to Hirsch regarding the nature of socially defined goods. As was discussed in part 2 merely increasing material goods in materially affluent, postindustrial society will not only not increase human satisfaction—now defined in postindustrial society as competitive success at attaining relative or positional goods—but, in fact, will *worsen* such competition and diminish the possibility of any one individual succeeding, or finding any satisfaction at all—temporary as the latter might be until the next struggle. Veblen explains why

material economic growth will never satisfy Hobbesian, industrial materialist values:

> In the nature of the case, the desire for wealth can scarcely be satiated
> in any individual instance, and evidently a satiation of the average or
> general desire for wealth is out of the question. However widely, or
> equally, or "fairly," it may be distributed, no general increase of the
> community's wealth can make any approach to satiating this need, the
> ground of which is the desire of everyone to excel everyone else in the
> accumulation of goods. If, as is sometimes assumed, the incentive to
> accumulation were the want of subsistence or of physical comfort,
> then the aggregate economic wants of a community might conceivably
> be satisfied at some point in the advance of industrial efficiency; but
> since the struggle is substantially a race for reputability on the basis of
> an invidious comparison, no approach to a definitive attainment is
> possible.[43]

This impossibility within industrial society to attain industrial values leads
to constant dissatisfaction and insecurity about whatever accomplishments
have been made: early liberal anxiety intensified and writ large!

One point I would like to emphasize is that material "goods [within
industrial society and especially within materially affluent, advanced industrial society]... acquired a surrogate value as currency in the competition
for honour and power which became all-consuming"[44] and thereby make
clear the crucial nonmaterial element within the industrial value cluster
termed "materialism."

We would be remiss if this cursory perusal of major modern political
philosophers' views of materialism within industrial society omitted the
work of Karl Marx, especially his concept of the "fetishism of commodities" and the nature of the goods in general within industrial capitalism
expounded within a section of his monumental work, *Capital*.[45]

Marx begins the section on commodity fetishism with an astute observation of particular importance in any effort to understand the nature of
industrial society: "A commodity appears, at first sight, a very trivial thing,
and easily understood. Its analysis shows that it is, in reality, a very queer
thing, abounding in metaphysical subtleties and theological niceties."[46] One
could view Marx's efforts in *Capital* (indeed, in all of his economic works)
as aiming toward clarification of the "metaphysical subtleties and theological niceties" of commodities within industrial capitalist society as part of
the broader question of the overall nature of commodities within such a
society, the subject of this portion of his work.[47] One metaphysical subtlety
stressed in this discussion of industrial commodities and their accompanying

materialist value system is the relation between material objects as commodities when possessing exchange value and the nonmaterial value attributed to them that do not inhere in their physical composition or are socially imposed. One major accomplishment of modernity—the industrial organization of society and materialism broadly understood in the manner discussed here—is the transformation of the social view and role of physical objects treated as commodities and their symbolic surrogate value.

The exclusive physical orientation of materialism was probably immortalized in the philosophical materialist theory of Marx against the idealism of Hegel emphasizing the capitalist perversion of human desires toward material objects treated as economic commodities within industrial capitalism.[48] Marx wrote that within the capitalist social order, "Individuals exist for one another only insofar as their commodities exist."[49] He introduces the concept of the capitalist fetishism of commodities in order to explain the distortions, illusions, and mystifications of industrial capitalism, and in this regard this discussion parallels the illusions and mystifications associated with unlimited growth ideology within advanced industrial society. He states:

> The existence of things *qua* commodities [within capitalism] and the value relation between the products of labor which stamps them as commodities, have absolutely no connexion with their physical properties and with the natural relations arising therefrom. There is a definite social relation between man, that assumes in their eyes, the fantastic form of a relation between things.[50]

An interpreter of this concept of Marx explains mystification of capitalism in the following manner:

> Marx means that individuals, in this [capitalist] mode, make contact with one another only through the exchange of their commodities. For this reason, exchange value appears to be a relation between commodities—this commodity is worth so much of that commodity— but in fact it is a relation between people, between labor-times of workers.[51]

Another commentator on Marx captures the main materialist point of Marx's concept of the fetishism of commodities and its deleterious effects when he writes:

> Relations among people in capitalist production assume the form of relations among commodities. The resulting commodity fetishism

reinforces consumerism, for it emphasizes the importance of material goods—rather than social relations—as the primary source of individual welfare.[52]

Marx compares the "fantastic form of a relation between things"—the creations of the capitalist mode of production or "fetish"—to the fantastic creations of religious people to whom "the production of the human brain appear as independent beings endowed with life.[53]

Without getting involved in the infamous controversy over whether Marx was an extreme or qualified philosophical materialist and economic determinist,[54] I would rather note his fetish idea derived from an analogy between a distorted and false human meaning of (economic) reality and physical things *cum* commodities within capitalism, and his belief of the distortions of religious ideas brought about by religious faith and thinking. Marx criticizes the dehumanizing consequences of this fetishism within capitalism but from the point of view of our concerns with industrial materialism and the nature of commodities within industrial society; his point is worth noting beyond the confusion of physical reality created by such fetishes.

As we have seen, the nonmaterial attachments to the acquired physical objects treated as commodities or social goods with exchange value impose social meanings upon industrial values, such as: social recognition, social esteem, competitive success, and so on. All of these components of what I have termed "materialism" in industrial culture—whether capitalistically organized or not—could be deemed fetishes in Marx's sense: human creations that distort or mystify reality, and in this sense Marx's account of this concept is pertinent to our discussion. The error of reductionism seems to come to the fore once again in the nature of the contemporary plight of industrial man; man's nature and social life have been reduced to the desire for material goods both for what they are (their intrinsic, physical characteristics) *and* what they represent in a society characterized by unlimited competitive materialism.

The psychologist Abraham Maslow has said: "Man does not live by bread alone—*if* he has enough bread."[55] Certainly postindustrial man should not live by seeking pure luxurious or positional goods merely to indicate defeat of the other competitors in this very serious social game, while hundreds of millions of other human beings search in vain for adequate food and other requirements for survival. Such growth-addicted social policy is not only unproductive of human happiness and a threat to our natural environment, it is unjust. The key to understanding the specific nature of the materialistic reductionism of unlimited economic growth as a social objective is recognizing the crucial distinction between material (or economic) welfare and *human* welfare. Postindustrial, growth-based society, its values and worldview, all misidentify these two different sources of human satisfaction. By not giving human welfare its due as a component of human happiness, we produce a society which virtually reduces all of human needs to Maslow's lowest physiological and safety needs and ignore the higher normative, self-actualization needs or erroneously define these latter needs in terms of material goods alone; or, in other words, commit the error of reductionist materialism.

Beginning with Hobbes, the core of the reductionism of industrial materialism has been the denial of the possibility—or even desirability—of material saturation thereby supporting the unlimited nature of material wants and the economy ceaselessly attempting to satisfy such endless wants. From VCRs to car telephones to large projection televisions to videotape cameras to highly expensive, luxury cars, Madison Avenue (and increasingly, Japanese, consumer electronic corporations) creates a market for goods and produces a profit so that others may compete for and consume such luxurious items *ad infinitum, ad nauseum*, but with differential status results depending upon the all-important timing of the acquisition.

...most people seem to think that wants are inexhaustible. They do not expect the utility of income additions to become zero or even to decline [despite the hallowed place within modern economics of The Law of Diminishing Returns]. The idea that there may be some point at which not only the stomach, but the whole body, including head and heart, is fed, if not fed up, is usually denied...Dissatisfaction with one's material condition is regarded as the stimulus of life. Our hopes and ambitions are tied to material "progress." Our enterprising spirit requires it as an outlet. Efforts to achieve economic growth have created their values and vested interests. Saturation appears as a threat of greater dimensions than a mere problem of economic policy.[56]

Central to the materialist's denial of the saturation and the resulting endless nature of material wants, is the fundamental claim that the continuous net increase in material goods will produce a continuous net increase in one's welfare or happiness.[57] Although this claim is false, it is the heart of the reductionism of industrial materialism. *The entire Hobbes-Rousseau-Veblen-Hirsch tradition of analyzing the relativity or competitive nature of industrial goods necessitates a grim conclusion regarding the futility of industrial values where the only respite from pursuing unfulfilled wants is death!*

This point is confirmed in Easterlin's well-known empirical research on the nature of human happiness. He writes emphatically for the limits-to-growth position:

The increase in output itself makes for an escalation in human aspirations, and thus negates the expected positive impact on welfare...
If the view suggested here has merit, economic growth does not raise
a society to some ultimate state of plenty. Rather, the growth process
itself engenders ever-growing wants that lead it ever onward.[58]

Here we have a policy of unlimited and continuous economic growth
with a normative basis of industrial materialism producing a citizen with
infinite desires created by the very process that is supposed to satisfy them
but cannot. Therefore, instead of being a *means* to human satisfaction,
unlimited and continuous economic growth seems to be the reverse: a
producer of dissatisfaction, frustration, and anxiety. Various limits-to-growth
critics of industrial civilization have offered different reasons for this sad
conclusion: a lack of time to consume (Linder); the impossibility of everyone attaining competitive goods (Hirsch); the confusion over wants and how
to satisfy them (Leiss); and, the limited natural resources as well as the
limited levels of tolerance for industrial pollutants (the biophysically-based
environmental critics). What I have tried to do in this volume, particularly,
in this part, is to focus upon yet another reason for the demise of industrial
civilization: its value structure, and especially its unlimited, competitive
materialist values.

Whether one emphasizes Hobbes, Rousseau, Smith, or Marx or any
other great, modern political philosopher within the Western tradition, or
relies upon the post-Marxian social thinkers from Veblen to Hirsch, most
penetrating analysts of modern life and thought address the nature of
commodities, the physical characteristics of material objects, and the nonmaterial social values attributed to them within modern industrial society. It
is their keenness of insight into the nature of industrial and postindustrial
society and not their luminary status within this tradition that should compel
one to consider their views. This is what makes them deserving of the title:
great political or social theorists. I say this to inform the reader of how I
perceive the proper use of the ideas of these theorists of industrial society as
contained herein.

Industrial Values and Commodities

I would like to begin this portion of our discussion on industrial values and commodities by referring to yet another treatment rejecting what is
termed the "materialist approach to consumption" in favor of an account
based on an "anthropology of consumption," provided by an anthropologist
and an economist.[59] These authors make a key point about the nature of
industrial goods which is central to understanding industrial materialism and

its social consequences. They prescribe that the consumption of commodities as a "live information system" whereby "[material] goods assembled together in ownership make physical, visible statements about the hierarchy of values to which their chooser subscribes."[60]

Of critical importance for my argument about this claim is the implicit, broader normative, nonmaterial component to the consumption of material goods within industrial society and industrial values: material goods' representative or symbolic function making "visible statements about the hierarchy of values of their choosers." (This essential point about the normative function of industrial commodities as well as their competitive aspects—and the ultimately insignificant intrinsic value of the goods themselves—are all clearly revealed in the current American T-shirt slogan: "The one with the most toys when he dies, wins"!) I say, "broader normative, nonmaterial component," meaning broader than if one restricted the meaning of industrial materialism to the philosophical sense only. Many authors use this definition as the basis for rejecting what they consider to be "the materialist approach to [industrial] consumption." Once this narrow and misleading philosophical meaning of materialism is given up, the broader, dual nature of industrial materialism as a social value and the nature of consumption within industrial society will become clearer, encompassing its combination of physical and nonphysical normative constituents.

Thus, in the confusing metaphysical terminology (which I recommend be abandoned in this sociopolitical context), industrial materialism—contradictorily—consists of *both* materialist and idealist elements! This is why such a philosophical perspective is inappropriate for understanding the foundations of industrial society and should be dropped. Material goods or commodities, like Slater's house, car, chair, or bowl, all convey, express, symbolize, have attached to them, act as a vehicle for, and make statements about, the nonmaterial values of the culture they are consumed within, like Hobbesian, competitive social recognition within industrial culture.

Leiss is perceptive on this point in his discussion of human needs. He presents the necessary materialist element of human needs and adds that

every facet of human needing has a symbolic correlate in the sense that the material exchanges of life are mediated (i.e., interpreted through the cultural of reflective transformations of impulses) by means of elaborate social interaction patterns. Neither the material nor the symbolic aspects can be reduced or collapsed into the other; nor ...can the two be separated...*I believe that the human system of needs in every culture is an indissoluble unity of material and symbolic correlates.*[61]

He subsequently mentions the theory of consumption of the American economist Kelvin Lancaster, in which industrial commodities are conceived as complex entities consisting of both physical and empirical traits. These are seen by Lancaster as objective; the products of one relation between their physical makeup and their observable characteristics, and a second relation between these latter characteristics and their human consumers "involving [their] individual preferences"—what I consider these commodities' normative element.[62]

According to Lancaster, "a producer is ultimately selling characteristic collections rather than goods."[63] Leiss offers the following "bundle of characteristics" with regard to food and other consumables for illustrative purposes: nutritive content, convenience of preparation, packaging of portions, appearance and texture, and so forth."[64] Following Lancaster's characteristics theory of consumption, the task before the analyst of industrial society consists of discerning the bundle of industrial characteristics reflected in this society's pattern of consumption and assessing both their realization and acceptability. Indeed, unlimited competitive materialism is an essential bundle of characteristics for industrial society manifested in its commodities and modes of consumption. Again, the nature of industrial materialism turns out to be more complex than initially thought. If Lancaster is correct, it is these value-based, value-reflecting characteristics rather than their embodiments within material goods or "vehicles" that are most important.

The upshot of Lancaster's theory of industrial consumption, according to Leiss, is that industrial commodities "are not straightforward 'objects' but are rather . . . temporary collections of objective and [culturally] imputed characteristics—that is, highly complex material-symbolic entities."[65]

This point is very important for assessing any culture especially an industrial culture with its rampant materialism. Industrial culture, particularly in its advanced form and through its several immensely powerful media of mass communication, can send its normative imputations to consumers of the physical commodities—like the Cadillac advertisement—more effectively than any other previous social order. (On the great effectiveness and social significance of advertising within advanced industrial society, see the previously cited Ewen and Key volumes.) The message of this advertisement merely makes explicit what any advanced industrial citizen learns early: that an automobile in this culture is far more than the mere bundle of its physical characteristics. This material commodity, like all others in this society, is a complex whole consisting of physical and normative characteristics imputed by the culture containing many nonphysically based social values; in the case of an automobile, "You are what you drive!" Even the least culturally sophisticated industrial citizen knows the typical social values reflected in a Cadillac (or its expensive, "luxurious," distinction-conferring equivalents like a Mercedes-Benz or BMW, etc.).

What is innovative in Lancaster's view is his insight that in industrial society consumers are more interested in the bundles of such characteristics as social distinction or esteem imputed to many types of goods (for example, luxurious goods like Cadillacs, diamond rings, boats) rather than the specific goods themselves. The discerning interest among industrial consumers regarding these various characteristics reflects their value hierarchies.[66]

Here, another explanation for Slater's and Fromm's observations noted earlier about industrial citizens not caring about specific material goods is provided. If Lancaster's view is correct, what matters more to materially affluent residents of advanced industrial societies are the culturally imputed values reflected in the commodities' "characteristics collections"—which are really social values represented by these material goods—rather than the specific physical goods conveying these collections (values). To the Hobbesian, vanity-driven, social esteem-seeking consumer, when possessions or goods no longer supply the competitive materialist bundle of characteristics or values, the social value of that specific commodity is diminished; some examples of this phenomenon are a small, black and white television set; a once expensive and status-conferring resort, now affordable to middle classes; or a B.A. college degree. Such goods no longer convey the social distinction they once did, and therefore, have lost their competitive materialist value.

I do not agree with Leiss's value noncognitivist conclusion that the key relation between the consumer's values and the characteristics *cum* commodity is "a subjective, psychological matter."[67] Experienced individually, yet generalizable within a culture, the characteristics consumers apply to material goods reflect the essential social values which constitute the normative foundations of that social order as a whole. If the industrial civilization's values are competitive and based on an endless striving for satisfaction that cannot be achieved because of the unlimited nature of industrial desires (industrial felicity being defined by Hobbes as "a continual progress [struggle?] of the desire from one object to another") and, furthermore, if these insatiable industrial values are neither desirable in themselves nor maintainable owing to the biophysical limits which conflict with their limitless scope, then the particular values of industrial civilization—and their social institutional reflections (which define a civilization or culture)—are both in danger of extinction *and* do not deserve acceptance.

How astute was Marx's remark in *Capital* about an industrial commodity being a "very queer thing, abounding in metaphysical subtleties and theological niceities." Material goods or their collections of characteristics (values) carry significant normative (political) import. They reflect the values of any culture and in the materialist industrial culture they reflect its most important values. This normative element of material goods' duality of social meaning increases in significance as the material affluence of industrial society increases; more and more people do not consume solely to satisfy limited biophysical needs or to obtain the intrinsic characteristics of the consumer goods within such a society because of its material wealth.

I have attempted to sketch out the core values of industrial civilization which I have termed "unlimited competitive materialism," by referring to some political philosophical analyses. This examination, beginning with Hobbes, of modern, political philosophers' analyses of modern society has revealed that the relationship between industrial, material commodities and industrial values, including the conception of human nature, lies at the foundation of industrial materialism. Furthermore, we have seen that this materialism is characterized by ceaseless competition and the unlimited nature of individual desires producing anxiety and preventing satisfaction. Modern political thought provides an understanding of the industrial worldview that emphasizes the normative expressive function of the huge increase in the number and variety of industrial material goods as well as the competitive and limitless nature of the accompanying values. At the very creation of industrial society Hobbes insightfully noted its point of vulnerability (along with other of its materialist traits) when he observed:

All [modern] society therefore is either for Gain, or for Glory; (i.e.) not so much for love of our Fellowes, as for the love of our Selves: but no society can be great, or lasting, which begins from Vain Glory; because that Glory is like Honour, if all men have it, no man hath it, for they consist in comparison and precellence [i.e. precedence or excellence].[68]

In *Leviathan*, Hobbes defines "vainglory" as glory "grounded in the flattery of others, vainly supposed by himself for delight."[69] Hobbes perceptively relates the competitive vainglory at the foundation of industrial society and its self-destructive consequences. The Hobbesian jungle and its "war of every man against every man" continues in new forms in the advanced industrial society and unless its normative foundation is changed will threaten its continued survival.

Industrial materialism as an industrial social value must be viewed as broader in scope and more significant in consequence than the mere desire for material, physical objects *cum* commodities. This essential industrial characteristic includes within it nonmaterial spiritual values which are selected, transmitted, and reinforced through industrial culture and its juvenile and adult socialization processes. Material commodities have a complex dual nature: physical in their material constitution and nonmaterial in their normative, symbolic function as expressive of unlimited competitive industrial values or ends. In this setting physical characteristics become not only indicators of industrial values but, in addition, the means to achieve them thereby permitting—even encouraging—the confusion of means with ends that prompted Tawney's characterization of industrialism by just such a confusion.

In this discussion I have connected what Slater divided: the car, chair, house or bowl contain their respective sets of ideas. The notion of industrial materialism explicated here includes what Slater's term, based on his misleading philosophical conception of "materialism," excludes: "the conceptual attitude toward objects." Once this is recognized one can see how American society is, indeed, materialistic to the extreme.

Actually, such a normative symbolic component for material goods was not unique to industrial society—if we accept Lancaster's account of consumption in which the material goods of all societies have some normative cultural element—surpassing their mere physical set of characteristics. What *was* new in industrial culture, in the words of the political philosopher Herbert Marcuse, was the greatly increased possibility of a "materialization of ideals"[70] created by the fantastic material productivity of this industrial society. Just as science holds the metaphysical tenet that all empirical phenomena have a cause, modern industrial society appears to hold that all human values—or the ones that are most significant—have a material expression or indication and the concomitant view that those values that are unable to be so materially expressed are downgraded in importance. This idea, in part, characterizes the materialism of industrial culture.

Part IV

Transindustrial Values

Replacing the Addiction to Unlimited Economic
Growth with Nonmaterialism, Noncompetition,
Participatory Democracy and Community

9

Social Transformation into a Transindustrial Community

The exhaustion of Modernism, the aridity of communist life, the tedium of the unrestrained self, and the meaninglessness of the monolithic political chants, all indicate that a long era is coming to a close. The theme of Modernism was the word beyond: beyond nature, beyond culture, beyond tragedy—that was where the self-infinitizing spirit was driving the radical self. We are now groping for a new vocabulary whose keyword seems to be limits: a limit to growth, a limit to spoliation of the environment, a limit to arms, a limit to torture, and a limit to *hubris*—can we extend the list? If we can, it is also one of the relevant portents of our time.

— Daniel Bell[1]

In the end, education is our only solution—education of ourselves toward a fuller understanding of both the evolutionary leap mankind struggles to effect and the requirements for a successful transformation to the transindustrial society. All we have learned of psychotherapy suggests that it is at the precise time when the individual most feels as though his whole life is crashing down around him that he is most likely to achieve an inner reorganization constituting a quantum leap in his growth toward human maturity. Our hope, our belief, is that it is precisely when society's future seems so beleaguered—when its problems seem almost staggering in complexity, when so many individuals seem alienated, and so many values seem to have deteriorated—that it is most likely to achieve a metamorphosis in society's growth toward maturity, toward more truly enhancing and fulfilling the human spirit than ever before.

—Willis W. Harman[2]

The Complex and Incomplete Nature of the Limits-to-Growth Critique of Industrialism

I strongly believe and have maintained throughout this discussion that the recent scientific literature elucidating the biophysical limits to economic growth and the limits themselves present an unprecedented and lethal challenge to advanced industrial society. Nonetheless, the mere assertion of the existence of these limits to the continuation of the growth-based industrial civilization—no matter how well substantiated empirically—is incomplete and thus inadequate to the task of achieving the required, planned transformation of our civilization. This type of planned social transformation is necessary, I think, if humanity is to avoid accidental, uncontrolled, and cataclysmic change caused by crossing the limits-to-growth thresholds. As I have attempted to show by uncovering some of the specific normative foundations of the industrial worldview, *some* industrial social change is inevitable because ours is a collapsing civilization committed to the impossible goal of ceaseless growth—the "megalomania of self-infinitization" of modern industrial man.[3] Therefore, the basic issue we confront is not whether postindustrial society will undergo change, but whether that unavoidable change will be controlled by humanity to further its aims or threaten the continued existence of all planetary life.

The biophysical limits-to-growth critique of industrial society should be accompanied by an examination and assessment of its normative bases or else the acceptance by the general public of any scientific claims regarding the presence of such limits to ceaseless economic growth will lead only to superficial reforms of the status quo. This approach will also ignore: the fundamental normative structure of postindustrial society; the consideration of this structure's social consequences; and, the recommendation of a desirable alternative set of values. We are all too familiar with timid, "business as usual" proposals such as charging polluters more in taxes or increasing the price of a scarce mineral. These sanctions perpetuate the very industrial values that got us into the crisis in the first place.

Such a circumscribed and conservative social policy will leave intact—and thereby reinforce—the deeper, growth-addictive values described earlier; for example, unlimited competitive materialism. As I have argued, a rationally persuasive and practically effective limits-to-growth assault on industrial civilization must include a systematic examination of its core values as well as empirical findings of its biophysical threats. This leads to industrial value analyses and to the normative limits to growth; analyses and limits that are largely ignored by scientific contributors to the biophysical limits-to-growth literature.

If the biophysical limits do, in fact, exist (as I am convinced they do, although a full scientific discussion of the many technical issues of empirical measurement, data collection, and threshold definition is both beyond the scope of this work and my competence), I contend that we must address the normative forces that drive postindustrial societies to approach and even cross these limits: postindustrial social values. These values threaten all life on our planet owing to the global impact of the technologically powerful, postindustrial social order. If the biophysical limits-to-growth literature provokes difficult and often avoided normative self-examination, then this may be its most important and emancipatory legacy.

Even if unlimited growth in postindustrial society is environmentally sustainable and will not—contrary to the biophysical limits-to-growth advocates—eventuate in ecological disaster, I would argue that this type of society is nonetheless fundamentally flawed in its values and the resulting quality of life for its members. Therefore, a value assessment of industrial civilization will suggest that our social order—although dominant for about two hundred years in the West—should be transformed and improved regardless of biophysical limits or the limits-to-growth controversy.

Let us suppose that the claims of the alleged biophysical limits to economic growth are not, in fact, valid, as the progrowth opponents to the empirically-oriented, limits-to-growth position such as Herman Kahn and Julian Simon contend (see discussion of these critics' views in part 1). The fundamental—hence logically prior—normative component to the limits-based attack upon industrial civilization still remains as powerful as ever. In this instance, the attack would shift from the assertion of the empirical *impossibility* of the survival of the growth-addicted postindustrial order to its normative *undesirability*.

It is essential to recognize the complex nature of the limits-to-growth challenge to industrialism encompassing *both* empirical and normative components. It should be noted in this regard that our discussion of the nature of the limits to growth has gotten progressively more complicated. We started in chapter 1 not distinguishing at all between the types of limits. In later chapters, an argument was presented to distinguish between normative and empirical limits. As we shall see, even finer analytical distinctions may be required to separate out empirical limits that are not biophysical (such as political limits). Also, I shall introduce the category of conceptual or logical limits that are neither empirical nor normative in nature, although they do have profound empirical and normative consequences (such as Hirsch's "social" limits which are partly conceptual, having to do with the nature of competition, and partly normative, involving postindustrial, positional social values).

Moreover, the analytical or conceptual separation of these different components, each with their respective scientific, logical, and normative criteria, must be kept in mind for the purposes of assessing claims made within each domain. Their logical independence must be noted as well so that one type of challenge to industrialism may be met successfully with little or no bearing upon the other. For example, industrial society based upon the fundamental value of unlimited economic and population growth may be possible indefinitely because the earth and its resources are limitless (the implausibility of this notion when stated explicitly illustrates the weakness of the unlimited economic growth ideology!), but such a society may, nevertheless, still be normatively unacceptable because of its contravention of essential human values. The alternative is that an impossible society may still be normatively preferable—like a Platonic ideal—and thereby become socially important as a goal for its citizens to approach asymptotically, providing direction and guidance for public policy as well as for individual conduct.

I see two implications of the limits-to-economic-growth position: (1) there are unavoidable and ineliminative biophysical limits to industrial society's fundamental value of unlimited economic growth. This value and the entire civilization built upon it must be replaced or transformed; that is, endless economic growth is not possible for very much longer without seriously damaging feedback effects in the environment. We have become increasingly aware of the dangers after the great publicity of several environmental threats during the summer of 1988. And, (2) even if, *per impossible*, a growth-based postindustrial society were achievable, considering the normatively-based portion of the limits-to-growth critique of the industrial worldview and social structure, it is still not desirable and thus should be transformed in any case.

Once we comprehend this complex and divisible character of the limits-to-growth argument, I believe we can better focus upon the ensuing debate over the merits of industrialism by applying the respective empirical, normative, or logical criteria of assessment to each side and their own arguments without confusion: both to the limits-to-growth advocates' assault upon industrial civilization and their implied prescriptions for social transformation, and to the replies by supporters of the postindustrial status quo who endorse its value system including unlimited economic growth.

If we treat the limits-to-growth theorists' argument as purely empirical—which is quite likely given that most of their writings concentrate on claimed biophysical limits—then the primary public policy questions facing contemporary citizens of advanced industrial society are technical ones: how to retain our current postindustrial values in a different but more feasible manner; for example, shifting to solar energy as we shifted in the past from coal to petroleum, or integrating more scientific expertise in public policymaking. On the other hand, if we accept the value-based objections to industrialism—both the empirical and normative aspects of the critique of the industrial worldview and society—then the issue before us would be the profound, traditional, political philosophical challenge of judging and selecting alternative values, and creating corresponding appropriate social institutions to realize different values: to create "the design of a new civilization."

One political scientist who is ecologically informed (a rare combination) reflects upon the complex nature of this crucial social design process as follows: "Social design refers to a creative social change process by which preferred and viable social futures can be envisioned, collectively debated, and eventually implemented through mutually agreed upon transition strategies."[4] He goes on to describe five tasks involved in this notion of social design that convey the multidimensional and multidisciplinary elements required in transforming industrial society: (1) analyzing the biophysical limits to future economic growth; (2) analyzing what makes continuous economic growth attractive and where resistance to change is likely to occur; (3) outlining a vision of an alternative, sustainable, non-growth-addictive society; (4) developing a transition strategy for reaching the prescribed social order; and, (5) implementing transition strategies.[5]

Thus, designing a new society is not only a combined empirical-normative process, but also combines thoughts and actions. This is a point often overlooked by political philosophers, self-confined as they are to abstract theorizing, and by activists committed to social action to achieve transformation. Pirages perceptively urges advocates of postindustrial social transformation to go beyond merely formulating and prescribing a new social order (however difficult these goals may be to achieve), and to concern themselves with the crucial task of implementing the proposed new social order:

> Utopias are useless in the absence of action rules for creating them. Such a transition strategy must be well-grounded in social theory as well as relevant to real world problems and decision... Social design for sustainable growth requires action as well as study and talk. Without willingness to get involved in social, economic, and political processes, alternate futures and transition theories are meaningless.[6]

Another political theorist makes a similar point in concluding his analysis of the limits-to-growth controversy. He characterizes the limits-to-growth theorists as:

> short on—like most utopian thinkers of the past—... any clear strategy of how to get from where we are today as a nation and a world to where we should be in their view. There is only a limited sense of how one mobilizes for change either in terms of identifying basically (and perhaps necessarily) disaffected groups, mobilizing them, or grasping and using the levers of power to change policy on the rules of the game... The great fundamental paradox therefore is that although

the new relationship of human society to technology and nature shakes the foundations of political philosophy as we have known at least in the West, it does little to replace these foundations.[7]

One major goal of this portion of the discussion is to assert and defend the claim of the failure of many of the limits-to-growth advocates to appreciate the several different aspects of their necessarily broad-ranging enterprise: the normative critique of industrialism, the proposal of an alternative and superior social structure, and the presentation of strategies of social transformation; all essential to a rationally convincing and practically significant formation of their argument.

The importance of the limits-to-growth critique of industrialism and the quintessential political, philosophical inquiry into designing an alternative transindustrial society is beginning to be recognized. I hope to stimulate interest in this daunting but necessary endeavor vital to the welfare of our planet and all its inhabitants: to transform advanced industrial society dependent upon unlimited economic growth into a society that is neither preindustrial or totally anti-industrial but *beyond* the industrial worldview and social structure—a transindustrial society. In this more desirable social order, I think that the following phenomena—among others—should be true: the limits to economic growth will be accepted and thus the unlimited growth ideology will be discarded; and, the social order will be repoliticized so that a full-fledged political life is institutionally supported in order to make its decisive contribution to human development and once again become "a way of living."[8]

The empirical biophysical orientation of the limits-to-growth supporters has resulted in neglect of postindustrial values and the omission of essential normative political issues. They have not contemplated, proposed, or rationally defended values and social institutions to replace the current dominant industrial values (such as unlimited economic growth), nor have they considered how any proposed alternative social order might be reached.

One might conclude that what I have attempted to do in this discussion is to pick up the dropped baton initially carried by the authors of the first Club of Rome report by reasserting the paramount significance of industrial values to the entire limits-to-growth debate. Perhaps my exhortations to normative political theorists, policymakers, and the general public as well as the sample analysis contained herein will be more successful than the Meadows team's implied prescriptions for a normative agenda which unfortunately concluded a volume exclusively devoted to computer projections of empirical descriptions of physical entities and processes.

To my mind, the central question of the limits-to-growth debate is: *whether feasible or not, should the advanced industrial worldview and social life, wherein both are based upon unlimited economic growth, be judged desirable and worthy of continuing as presently constituted and copied throughout all other societies?* If the answer to this profound question is in the negative, as I have argued, then much political action needs to be inspired, instructed and taken to appropriately change the postindustrial social order founded upon continuous and limitless economic growth and its accompanying ideology. However, before such political action to transform the existing postindustrial values and social structure can be effectuated, potential political activists require some definition—even if only partial—of a conception of an alternative social order. A new civilization must be designed which will improve upon what people now or in the near future confront and find to be unsatisfying and/or dangerous.

Transformational or revolutionary action will be difficult to mobilize—let alone implement—without a set of alternative social goals and practices implied by a different worldview and values informing such action. This is so, unless, of course, one wishes to be exclusively negative in one's critique by advocating the destruction of current social aims and arrangements and leaving it to others at a later, and presumably more propitious, time to create a new social order; for example, as with certain anarchists' positions such as the nineteenth century, Russian anarchist Mikhail Bakunin's "creative destruction."[9] The risk here is that the new yet to be determined society could be worse than the one changed. Furthermore, by omitting a vision of a supposedly superior, alternative society the achievement of social transformation is thwarted because the proposed theoretical structure or "city coming into being in speech," as Plato formulates it in *The Republic*,[10] can neither guide political action, so that people know what to strive for, nor provide the evaluative criteria with which to judge how successful their action has been in creating a new—and supposedly better—civilization.

The omission of evaluative criteria derived from a projected social ideal precludes the restriction of the revolutionary means chosen that are consistent with the envisioned ends. This last point refers to the possibility of contradiction arising between revolutionary means and social goals; something the twentieth century has witnessed frequently with respect to political violence as a means of social change.

Therefore, the predominance of the biophysical limits-to-growth literature exclusively devoted to empirical matters and overlooking what a different, more normatively desirable, society would be like is unfortunate and detrimental to transforming postindustrial society. What is needed is a presentation of an alternative social order, one not characterized by the deficient values of industrialism. Here the criticism, cited earlier, strikes a responsive chord: the limits-to-growth literature has indeed "shaken the foundations of [modern] political philosophy" yet "it has done little to replace these foundations" or even *examined* these fundamental political questions!

One can almost hear an objector to the biophysical limits-to-growth argument immediately rising in protest and saying: "All right, if the industrial social order is doomed by the limits you emphasize, what do you prescribe as an alternative, and, moreover, how shall we realize this new limits-cognizant society?" In my view, it is inadequate to spend 98 percent of a work pointing out inevitable ecological limits and their apocalyptic consequences without providing a transition to a fundamentally different society. It is not sufficient to claim that drastic and immediate social changes are necessary in order to avoid dire consequences, while devoting very brief space or thought to the form such changes will take and even less to their implementation.

What is the nature of the good society? This quintessential question of normative political theory begun by Plato and continuing to the present is raised again by the scientific, biophysical limits-to-growth claims regarding the eventual unsustainability and demise of postindustrial society. This empirical literature containing projections of the death of industrial civilization can demonstrate, in a society where systematic normative inquiry is generally ignored because of value noncognitivism, the importance of pursuing an inquiry into the nature, assessment, and replacement of industrial values; it thereby arouses the interest of the public for debate on vital matters of policy. In these respects, the biophysical limits-to-growth literature serves normative and transformational purposes.

Having noted that much of the limits-to-growth critique of industrial society is flawed because its proponents neglect normative issues and the prescription of alternatives to industrial values, I should mention another source of weakness in this literature. It is produced by those few limits-to-growth theorists who do not commit the mistake of ignoring industrial values entirely or merely providing a cursory discussion of them. There is a small subset of advocates who claim the existence of biophysical limits to growth who do address the key question of an alternative ideal to industrial society as a result of their understanding of the impossibility of both the current industrial institutions and the continuation of the values reflected in them. Sadly, these conceptions of an industrial order transformed into a normatively preferable and ecologically sustainable society are usually presented very briefly and constitute the final chapter of a volume filled with despairing doom and gloom news about the death of industrialism.[11] In spite of this, I think they should be examined because of the significance of such ideal "cities in speech."

After reading the limits-to-growth studies described above, I decided to term this error present in most of the biophysical approaches as the "absence-of-means-to-social-transformation" fallacy, or, more simply, the "absence-of-means" fallacy. What I have in mind by this fallacy is the failure on the part of the authors who recommend transformation of the industrial culture to consider how to implement the new and purportedly better society; what Pirages called a "transition strategy." They fail to raise the difficult but unavoidable political question: "How do we get there from here?" In *The Republic*, Plato, in the words of Glaucon, asked Socrates regarding the ideal society: "Is it possible for this regime to come into being and how is it ever possible?" Socrates replied that such a question is the "biggest and most difficult, the third wave" (the third wave coming to shore was traditionally thought by the ancient Greeks to be the biggest one).[12]

It is not sufficient merely to delineate a proposed superior or even ideal social order. As soon as its proponent succeeds in persuading us to agree with her or his prescription, someone (and not necessarily an unsympathetic critic), will rightfully raise Glaucon's question. After all, this is a question that has haunted normative political theorists since Plato's time with the pejorative label of "utopian" waiting to be applied as the *coup de grace*. One contemporary social theorist has characterized political theories as "utopian" when they have "no change strategies."[13] Regrettably, most of the biophysical limits-to-growth studies that do address the creation of a new society (a small portion of the total literature) seem to be utopian in Alvin Gouldner's sense.

Before I continue this point about the general omission within the limits-to-growth literature of implementation strategies for alternative social orders, as well as the previously noted ignorance of the critical role of the foundation values to industrial civilization, a recent and encouraging exception to this absence of politically sophisticated, limits-to-growth analyses should be mentioned. Lester Milbrath's *Envisioning a Sustainable Society* is noteworthy for its explicit recognition of the essential role of values to politics, the possibility of rational discourse about values, the latter's importance in the current postindustrial crisis, and, moreover, the need for limits-to-growth critics of postindustrial civilization to propose alternative values and a way of life as a replacement for the unsustainable industrial social order.[14]

To Milbrath's credit, his book is important in its attempt to fill the void that characterizes the limits-to-growth position regarding the nature of a society freed of growth-addiction and how it would be constructed. It provides a detailed presentation of nonindustrial, sustainable values and the postindustrial transformation process. Given the aims of my own argument, it should be no surprise that I find much of Milbrath's work valuable. My diagnosis of what fatally ails postindustrial civilization is quite compatible with Milbrath's efforts to define a value structure for a sustainable society and to present the manner in which this alternative normative structure may be realized. I hope that Milbrath's volume is the forerunner of a large genre of such political works.

Precisely because I consider Milbrath's vision of a sustainable society so admirable in its intentions, I regret that I must register my disappointment with its specific arguments. Space does not permit a thorough assessment of this work, so I shall restrict my critical remarks to these: (1) Milbrath prescribes "life in a viable ecosystem [as] the centerpiece [or, 'most fundamental value'] of a value structure for a sustainable society;"[15] (2) with all of Milbrath's discussion of how the new, sustainable society that he envisions is to be achieved, there is a paucity of any detailed considerations of how the resistance of the postindustrial elite will be overcome; (3) by citing previous revolutions in such places as China and Iran as support for the possibility of radical social change, Milbrath ignores the fact that all previous social transformations have occurred in preindustrial societies and that no social revolution has yet occurred in any postindustrial society like the United States;[16] and, finally, (4) by borrowing the analysis of revolutions and paradigm shifts in science provided by Thomas S. Kuhn, Milbrath begs the key issues of whether revolutions in academic disciplines are like revolutions in society, including whether the powerful social elite have more resources to withstand transformation than the academic powers that be who are supposedly devoted to knowledge and its enhancement.[17]

Let me expand upon the first point. By proposing the viability of the ecosystem as the most fundamental and important value in the new social order, Milbrath's vision becomes vulnerable to the charge of antienvironmentalists like Richard Neuhaus to the effect that mere biophysical survival within a viable ecosystem, is not sufficient. Neuhaus pointedly asks, "Who wants to breathe clean air in a racist society?" and then goes on to assert, "Survival may be a precondition for developing a moral purpose, but survival itself is not a moral purpose."[18]

To be sure, Milbrath's hierarchy of values includes justice, equality, freedom, and other important moral values;[19] however, having a linear value hierarchy wherein all other values are subordinated to a single ecological factor of ecosystem viability is problematic. It is undercut by all the difficulties associated with a monistic value structure (as opposed to a pluralist value structure whereby more than one value is primary and in different respects), and it falls prey to the naturalist fallacy (wherein the charge is made that from a fact alone value cannot be deduced).[20] Of course, these are very large and controversial issues requiring discussion that would take us far afield. My only objection here is that Milbrath entirely overlooks these possibly damaging criticisms to his enterprise.

I would also like to address elite resistance to transformation. There is a basic political fact of postindustrial social life that must not be overlooked: although the number of citizens in advanced industrial societies who perceive themselves to be, or actually are, the beneficiaries of its social goods may be declining, the social group supporting the postindustrial *status quo* is still formidable indeed. This is because the manipulated masses suffer from false consciousness, and the upper class—or postindustrial elite—possess immense political and economic power. The well-endowed elite, by virtue of their superior wealth, income, power, and status, are able to avoid many of the most damaging traits of postindustrial society, but importantly for our later discussion concerning the prospects for the transformation of postindustrial society, the elite cannot escape all of them!

Certainly, I believe Milbrath is correct when he states that rational argument alone will not bring about social transformation.[21] I also agree and have argued that unlike rational argumentation, current ecological crises within postindustrial society can act as a catalyst for social change. Facing environmental hazards may cause us to become disillusioned with our fantasies, and to realize that these fantasies are undesirable, impossible, and manipulative.

What if the powerful postindustrial elite do not change their views and values, holding on to their control of society and its bases for power: governmental institutions, economic wealth and the mass media? In a volume specifically devoted to how an envisioned and prescribed society is to be realized, the reader expects more discussion of this momentous obstacle to social transformation than Milbrath provides in his book's brief final section which is dependent upon a highly conjectural, *biological* theory of creative evolution.[22]

Milbrath, and others who address the transformation of society, confront the unavoidable issue of how such a new society is to be reached. This includes prescribing how to overcome the powerful opposition by the postindustrial elite to any fundamental change in society, including changes in social values that might produce a great negative impact upon their currently high social position and luxurious styles of material life. Here the insightful, sixteenth century, political theorist of practical politics, Niccolo Machiavelli, deserves mention regarding this point about the powerful obstacles to radical social change:

> It must be considered that there is nothing more difficult to carry out, nor more doubtful of success, nor more dangerous to handle, than to initiate a new order of things. For the reformer has enemies in all those who profit by the old order, and only lukewarm defenders in all

those who would profit by the new order, this lukewarmness arising partly from fear of their adversaries, who have the laws in their favor; and partly from the incredulity of mankind, who do not truly believe in anything new until they have had actual experience of it.[23]

For the aims of those prescribing industrial society's transformation, Machiavelli's last comment about the incredulity of mankind about anything new should be emphasized. Whether for Machiavelli's reasons or not, it certainly appears to be true that the proposals for new social values and institutions (i.e., "initiating a new order of things") are usually greeted with deep initial skepticism (and perhaps excessively demanding requirements as well), which must be overcome if the prescribed social transformation is to occur.

To make matters worse for the advocate of industrial social transformation, owing to the immense powers of communication and social influence available to the postindustrial elite, even the middle and lower classes can be—and have been—manipulated. persuaded, or socialized to support the industrial value structure and institutions in order to maintain what few advantages the middle class possess over the poor. The elites also perpetuate the growth-based hope that members of both groups—especially the poor—will acquire more social goods and status *later*: the "American Dream."[24]

Until now, these methods of sustaining the elite-serving, postindustrial social order have been quite effective, but they are to be challenged severely by the limits-to-growth argument and its inspiration of new social movements and change. Nevertheless, we must not underestimate the staying power of the postindustrial elite and their predominant worldview supported by an enormous variety and quantity of resources. One historical fact previously noted weighs heavily upon those prescribing or predicting the transformation of industrial society: the absence of such a successful revolutionary development throughout the reign of industrialism. Although the twentieth century has been a revolutionary age, all the revolutions have occurred in preindustrial societies: Russia, China, Cuba, and other wars of national liberation.

Theorists proposing postindustrial transformation as well as activists (such as members of the various Green parties, begun in West Germany in the early 1980s and now present in several countries in Europe and North America)[25] must address how the resistance of the small but hegemonic elite and the manipulated masses can be negated or transformed. We must also examine how the masses' support for the postindustrial social system can be undermined, causing them to become receptive towards a better and more satisfying social order.

The reader might (prematurely) conclude at this point that any limits-to-growth theorist who predicts the death of industrial civilization and prescribes the establishment of a transindustrial society is guilty of utopian naivete. On the contrary, advocates of limits-based, postindustrial social transformation would reply (as I think Milbrath would) that it is those members of the faithful who accept the gospel of industrialism and its dependence upon the continuation of both unlimited economic growth and the postindustrial status quo, who are utopian. Their naivete will become increasingly evident as the limits to growth get closer and the dangers to society increase; when the apocalyptic consequences of growth-addiction begin to materialize and the flawed normative foundations of postindustrialism are exposed. Time is running out, as some popular media have begun to suggest with regard to several environmental threats recently made prominent: global warming, stratospheric ozone depletion, acid rain, deforestation, ocean pollution, and so on.

Ecological reports are intended to convince us that there are limits to the amount of pollutants industrial societies can spew into the environment and can be absorbed safely before they threaten human and nonhuman life. Furthermore, they assert that there are absolute limits to the amounts of available precious natural resources required for industrial life and a rapidly expanding global human population with ever-increasing material demands. Such studies suggest that these limits constitute an insurmountable barrier and challenge to the continuance and globalization of an onrushing post-industrial social order founded upon the belief in unlimited economic growth that denies—*and must deny if it is to remain intact*—the existence of such limits. Underlying the limits-denying postindustrial institutions, I have argued, are progrowth values constituting the core of the problem of post-industrial civilizations' continuity and desirability.

The Meadows team, in *The Limits to Growth* volume, deserves credit for emphasizing the important role of values—a point that I have not seen made in any of the many reviews or commentaries upon this influential work—among their recommendations for the transformation of endangered growth-dependent postindustrial society to a sustainable one marked by material equilibrium. However, they raised this significant normative point on page 186 of their 188-page book, while the remainder of their volume ignored values or wished social problems away amidst computer projections of the eventual collapse of the industrial social order. The authors of this founding document of the limits-to-growth position have left a legacy of omitting normative factors in subsequent biophysical, limits-to-growth writings.[26]

Another deficiency of the limits-to-growth literature (including those works which specifically claim that industrial civilization is seriously threatened by self-destruction) occurs in making normative judgments that such a society ought not survive because of value faults, in addition to the unfavorable scientific prognosis. The weakness here involves the failure of the authors of such volumes to provide much detail—beyond the usual vague sketch or one or two specific reforms—about the nature of a supposedly superior alternative to the industrial social structure; one that is more desirable because it will fulfill more of mankind's normative (or nonmaterial) needs and values consistent with environmental limits. In some instances, specific radical proposals to improve current industrial life are mentioned and discussed briefly, but the required discussion of implementation is absent.

Some examples of these theoretically isolated and too-narrow prescriptions for social change are: the establishment of both maximum and minimum limits on income and wealth;[27] marketable licenses to have children;[28] school age children (above the age of 12 years) working one day per week during the school year outside of school;[29] the implied elimination of the private automobile (called, "surely, one of the greatest, if not the greatest, disasters that ever befell the human race");[30] a proposal to replace the nuclear family with the extended family within "large commune-type living units" and rearing children in communal environments;[31] and, finally, a prescription for a "relative pay reduction for society" applied to currently defined top jobs.[32]

Radical proposals such as these are usually intended as only one element of a transformed new society, yet the envisioned social order is described incompletely or not at all. I think it is important to point out a dilemma that limits-based advocates of industrial society's transformation face if they contemplate the new civilization to be a participatory democratic one as well—which they usually imply, given their criticism of the strongly hierarchical or unequal nature of postindustrial society. Theorists who support participatory democracy would hold the position that the self-governing people themselves should decide their collective destiny, including the critical elements of social life, such as social structure and values. Therefore, any prior judgments made and presumably implemented by the democratic revolutionary who prescribes the transformation of industrial culture are by definition contradictory to his or her claimed commitment to democracy. "The final shape of the democratic order is importantly contingent, not only because it is generally impossible to predict exactly what will happen in the future, but because open-endedness is built into the democratic order itself."[33]

On the other hand, if no picture of the future democratic society-to-be is drawn, even in the form of a rough sketch, citizens of advanced industrial civilization—or of any deficient society deserving of transformation—would remain unclear as to the nature of the proposed social order and would thereby weaken their possible commitment to it. What replacements for existing social institutions and what underlying alternative values are to be exchanged for the current social values in order to achieve the prescribed social change? Most modern citizens will choose what they have known (as Machiavelli conjectured), however undesirable it may be (barring, of course, the extremes of destitution or environmentally-caused self-destruction), over not knowing what they are going to get by way of a new social order. This "bird in the hand" reaction constitutes, I think, a powerful conservative force thwarting attempts at basic social change.

This is especially true for the postindustrial middle class where the miseries of postindustrial life and its preoccupation with competitive success are mitigated somewhat by material possessions and the self-knowledge of superiority to the lower classes. Therefore, negative critique alone is not sufficient to accomplish the transformation of postindustrial society. Any prescribed social structure and its foundation values must be well-delineated by advocates of social change to serve as inspiration, guide, and a source of mobilization. Only then can a movement for postindustrial transformation be successful—especially if such social change is to be realized peacefully and democratically!

What is the proper response to this dilemma of the democratic social revolutionary? It lies, I believe, somewhere between no description of the alternative society and an excessively detailed one which eliminates the prerogatives of policymaking citizens in the future. A suitable balance needs to be found if social theorists are to meet both their theoretical obligations as well as the practically important goals of providing an outline of the nature of life in a new social order. This crucial and extremely difficult aim of social theory can only be begun here, but I urge students of contemporary society and scientific experts on the biophysical limits to postindustrial society to join me in going beyond the challenging task of assessing the desirability and determining the feasibility of postindustrial society. We must proceed further to prescriptive discussions of its successor: a genuinely transindustrial society (Milbrath's 1989 contribution is a good start in this direction).

Our current advanced industrial society should be transformed in the radical sense, encompassing its normative foundations, not merely in the narrow temporal sense of the postindustrial. The latter is nothing more than a linear extrapolation of past industrial trends and values with the old industrial values remaining intact; the former requires a fundamental transformation, including its value structure.

An initial conceptual framework of how a complete inquiry may proceed is provided in a valuable essay by Michael E. Kraft who addresses the unavoidable political nature of the environmental crisis, the limits to economic growth position, and the issues involved in moving to a sustainable society.[34] Kraft provides four components of a full-fledged political analysis of the possibility and desirability of the industrial social order that summarize much of what I have in mind. Especially noteworthy are the complex empirical and normative analyses required and the need for a discussion of the transitional issues raised by industrial social transformation. He writes that the "agenda of political concerns" of such a transformation should consist of: (1) normative considerations (value clarification, evaluation of political conditions, and prescriptions for reform); (2) scientific analysis (description and explanation of ecological problems and political actions); (3) futuristic projections or predictions (specification of likely consequences and possible alternative futures); and (4) strategic analysis (how change might be brought about).[35]

Kraft, too, is skeptical about the value of the limits-to-growth literature as presently constituted. He is critical of the scientific analyses alone or accompanied by vague utopian proposals for reform.

Most of the authors cited above [limits-to-growth contributors such as: Caldwell, Ophuls, Pirages, and Ehrlich, specifically listed by name by Kraft on page 185] conclude their discussions with a set of recommendations which they predict (or simply hope) will alter the unfavorable climate of present politics...The central problem is that these partial and limited descriptive analyses of current politics and probable "deficiencies" do not provide the necessary information and guidance. To improve upon this work we need more expansive and more fully developed explorations, including critical examination of the full ramifications of these political characteristics. Put most broadly, what we need is more and better explanatory, evaluative, prescriptive, and strategic analysis to begin providing some meaningful and useful answers to the questions of what changes are really necessary and how they might be implemented.[36]

Further scientific analyses of the biophysical limits to growth must go forward to address the progrowth scientists and growth-addicted policymakers who insist that no such limits exist, especially since the deterioration of the environment seems even more imminent with new evidence of biophysical threats such as ocean pollution, stratospheric ozone depletion, ambient ozone increase, deforestation, global warming, and world overpopulation. More concentrated effort is also needed in evaluative and prescriptive analysis. We must investigate how advanced industrial societies are to move from the current structure to a new one—especially given the resistance by prosperous postindustrial elite members and manipulated hope-filled masses. I intend to provide some initial replies to the important issues raised by Kraft, particularly about a strategy for social change.

I prescribe that an alternative, nongrowth-addicted, sustainable society be considered transindustrial and that this product of the transformation of industrial society should utilize the material affluence produced by the postindustrial social order. It must go on to transcend industrial society in order to remedy its several defects: dependence on ceaseless, limitless economic growth, materialism, harmful competition, and depoliticization. This is to be accomplished by creating a nongrowth, nonmaterialist, non-competitive, repoliticized, participatory democratic community wherein public life is "educative" in this sense: the "intellectual, emotional and moral capacities [of people] have reached their full potential and they are joined, freely and actively in a genuine community"[37]

The Anxieties of a Civilization in Transition and Optimism for the Transformation of Postindustrial Society

In chapter 1 we discussed the widespread pessimism characterizing contemporary thought in advanced industrial societies. From the "utterly terminal pessimism" of Kurt Vonnegut, Jr., to Woody Allen's no-win choice of "utter hopelessness or total extinction," to the limits-to-growth advocate E. J. Mishan's view of industrial civilization heading for the abyss, the doom and gloom label for the limits-to-growth position appears thoroughly appropriate. Indeed, the threats of apocalyptic outcomes made by the limits-to-growth critics of industrialism are an essential element of their argument.

The threat of a dangerous result if sufficient change in the social forces producing the particular postindustrial social order is not achieved is central to the dystopian logic for social change, as was exemplified in George Orwell's novel *Nineteen Eighty-four*. The doom and gloom character of the limits-to-growth position is an indispensable element and not the idio-syncratic orientation of some specific thinkers with peculiar or pathological, psychological perspectives on the contemporary condition of humanity.

Yet, radical social change is disturbing on both the individual and social levels, even when the replacement factors—be they new values, social practices, institutions or worldviews—are clearly delineated and accepted. When these needed social substitutes are incompletely known or formulated along with considerable popular and elite resistance, however, the already extensive costs of social change are exacerbated. As we in the late twentieth century witness the frightful ecological, social, and normative portents of the beginning of the end of industrial civilization, we are still groping for the answers to many difficult questions about what life after industrialism will be like and how we will reach it. Thus, we can appreciate and identify with the nineteenth century reactions of two Englishmen: political theorist John Stuart Mill, and poet and critic Matthew Arnold, who wrote about their English society as it underwent rapid social change to become the first and most industrially developed in the world. Both thinkers described the pain of living in a period of cultural transition: from a lost preindustrial age where religious faith dominated, to a yet to be established, secular, fully industrial age (the liberal Mill felt less melancholy pessimism and grief than Arnold, who longed for the lost religious era).[38]

In his essay, "The Spirit of the Age," Mill writes: "The first of the leading peculiarities of the present age is that it is an age of transition. Mankind have outgrown old institutions and old doctrines, and have not yet acquired new ones."[39] In the famous second chapter of *On Liberty*, devoted to the topic "of the liberty of thought and discussion," Mill provides an insightful characterization of mid-nineteenth century, industrializing English society as follows: "In the present age—which has been described as 'destitute of faith, but terrified at skepticism'—in which people feel sure, not so much that their opinions are true as that they should not know what to do without them,"[40] Mill experienced in his day, and we experience in our own, the anguish of being caught in the midst of cultural transformation. In it, the old world and its worldview, social values, and goals, our whole identities—both social and individual—are dead or dying; while the new one promising all that we require as individuals and social beings has yet to be created. Humanity is left adrift lacking the effective—agreed upon by social consensus—cultural paradigm necessary to give meaning and worth to our perceived world and to ourselves.[41]

To those who object to my analogy here between Mill's nineteenth century British society's transitional stage and our own advanced industrial society, I pose the following query: are we not still "destitute of faith but terrified at skepticism"? Especially now, when general value noncognitivism reigns, we in the contemporary age are socially destitute of normative knowledge, not only of religion, but of politics, morals, and art. Nonetheless, we remain terrified at skeptical relativism—involving even the last bastion of confident objective knowledge: natural science (as indicated by the vehemence of the debate over scientific realism within the philosophy of science).[42] It does not seem an exaggeration to say that matters have gotten worse in this regard in the one hundred years since Mill lived.

Lionel Trilling's description of Arnold's poetry is quite pertinent to the issue of social transformation raised here.

Arnold's poetry [he writes] in its most characteristic mood is elegiac—
it mourns a loss, celebrates the lost thing, and tries to come to terms

with deprivation. What is the thing that is grieved for?...It is the loss of a certain culture—that is to say, of a certain body of assumptions, looking at the world and of responding to it, a certain quality of temperament which seems no longer available.[43]

Arnold powerfully captured the anxiety of a person living between two worlds, between social paradigms, and between comforting stable value systems in a social limbo when he lamented:

Wandering between two worlds, one dead,
The other powerless to be born,
With nowhere yet to rest my head.
Like these, on earth I wait forlorn.[44]

How similar are the limits-to-growth critics of industrialism, its values and way of life! They recognize and appreciate their society's impending demise, but have yet to conceive a new social order—let alone its full realization. The mournful mood evoked by Arnold's passage above compares with Vonnegut's "utterly terminal pessimism" or Mishan's unmitigated despair; contemporary thinkers are indeed "wandering between two worlds, one dead"—the industrial one—while its replacement, a transindustrial society, seems "powerless to be born," truly "L'époque de Malaise"!

During the 1970s and 1980s, new ecological concerns made the public aware that the life goals and values derived from the postindustrial worldview might be doomed by environmental limits. This, in addition to the doom and gloom of the limits-to-growth writings seemed to warrant grim characterizations. It can be seen how such pessimism about the environment could lead to social paralysis, or to fatalistic escapism. Either might thwart action to transform postindustrial culture, thereby delaying the start of the process of creating a new and better social order. Even if the worst scenario of the cataclysmic effects of a continuation of current growth-based policies are ultimately avoided, pessimism might prevail.

Therefore, it is essential to emphasize that the end or death of industrial civilization will not necessarily bring the apocalyptic termination of life on earth! It *will* mean the end of the world, but only one world; it could mean merely the end of a particular (and defective) social order! For people who have absorbed its worldview uncritically and completely, and furthermore, who have adjusted successfully to the resulting social structure and values, the impending loss of a civilization does appear to be terrifying. They will experience the death of the only desirable—and for the industrial elite, self-serving—world they know as a totally destructive, and therefore traumatic, phenomenon rather than what it actually is: the passing of a specific, elite-benefitting world that indeed can and should be transformed.

When the flaws of a social order are understood, and its fantastic elements and promises (like industrialism's unlimited economic growth) are recognized and appreciated for what they are—impossible dreams preserving the ruling group's control and benefits—they should be cast aside. The loss of social fantasies causes immediate despair but the mourning period for their death should be temporary and surmountable. As both Slater and Harman emphasize, such despair is both appropriate and necessary to the achievement of social and individual transformation.

I believe that both Slater and Marcuse are right in their claims that the recognition of the limits upon social fantasies (although such recognition creates despair) and the awareness of one's servitude together constitute a necessary step to liberation. However, such cognitive insights are not the only steps required; political action and change are necessary for social transformation to occur. First, we must avoid the paralyzing despondency and hopelessness which could lead to genuine apocalyptic self-destruction caused by inaction and inertia which support the *status quo*. Second, in order to create a new and superior civilization while avoiding some of the anxiety as expressed by Arnold, we must proceed beyond mere recognition to the creation of a superior replacement for the dying civilization. Third, we must be prepared to take social action to implement these social visions. Of course, for this goal to be achieved the broad question of the strategies for social change must be addressed.

Even sophisticated political theorists such as Philip Green fall prey to expressions of discouragement about transforming postindustrial society. Reflecting upon the state of social theory in America, he writes:

> *all* serious, critical, intellectual endeavor among us is academic, for critical intellect here is detached (I cannot think of any exceptions) from any mass movement that might want to make use of it; to put its theories into effect. My purpose is precisely to be of ultimate, practical use. I have to admit, though, that day when that wish might be granted is undoubtedly a long time off.[45]

He ends his discussion of a genuine participatory democratic theory and society with the words:

> this book and these proposals exist, for now at least, within the realm of ideas alone, and not of action. That is, as it has to be, unfortunately. The philosophers can only interpret the world in our various ways, someone else will have to change it.[46]

I note this voice of pessimism (man others could be cited here) about the feasibility of advanced industrial society being transformed in deference to the possibility that it is accurate, however despairing such a conclusion might be. The evidence for discouragement regarding this revolutionary project is considerable. However, I would like to emphasize that there are several important sources for encouragement regarding the possibility of the radical social change of postindustrial society.

Let me begin with some responses to Green's characterizations of social theory in America. It is true that social theorists seem to be largely confined to the American academies, which is to say isolated from the general public and restricted to conveying their thoughts in esoteric journals with only themselves as the audience. Moreover, if their ignoring of the limits-to-growth controversy is any indication, they have also overlooked the key problem impinging upon our contemporary way of life.

Yet, Green's statements are misleading when one considers the intellectuals critically involved in various organizations comprising the worldwide environmental, disarmament, and antigrowth movements, wherein their contributions do inevitably lead to thoughts and action to transform the world, not just American society. As we shall see, there is evidence that perhaps the people themselves are leading the theorists in expressing the miseries of industrial civilization; when the theorists do get around to providing a radical alternative worldview there will be many people ready and able to take appropriate action for change. The day when this might occur may not be as far off as Green claims.

While the main Platonic problem of uniting philosophical knowledge with political authority has not been solved in twenty-five hundred years of Western political thought, I think that political philosophers must not abandon the social transformation efforts to others, especially those action-oriented revolutionaries who appear to be specially constituted for such a task. It could be argued that a revolutionary group informed solely by its own lights and not enlightened by a social theory would contribute to the obvious excesses of revolutionary behavior. We must understand that because the process of social transformation is so complex involving several types of discourse and action, the analysis and recommendations of the political philosopher are a vital part of the entire effort.

Action may indeed be taken by others, but where, why, and for what purposes we must act are all indispensable elements of proper political action. As I intend to make clear, the social conditions within advanced industrial society may be more ripe for the transformation of this social order and its growth-addicted ideology than the pessimists believe. What may be the most damaging weakness for the revolutionary position is the lack of a defensible, realistic, alternative political philosophy to provide the newly emerging social movements with inspiration, guidance, and resources for mobilization and organization. We need more sociopolitical analysts "hacking away at the roots" of industrial evils and proposing ways of eliminating them.

As several limits-to-growth theorists have noted, the death of one culture should mean—if we do not terminate all human life first—the challenge of creating a more desirable and sustainable one: the task of "designing a new civilization." One political student of contemporary society presents a central point in the position upholding the possibility of transforming postindustrial life: contemporary revolutionary praxis must address the issue of taking advantage of the disintegrative aspects of postindustrial society (he says, "capitalist order"), while at the same time "preventing the unavoidable upheaval from turning into an inevitable catastrophe."[47]

This social theorist chooses one aspect of the Orwellian revolutionary dilemma: the problem of changing social consciousness which requires a change in the existing social institutions; yet the latter can occur only when the former occurs. "Until they [the masses] become conscious they will never rebel, and until after they have rebelled, they cannot become conscious."[48] This option of changing social consciousness or the dominant social paradigm formulates one of the most important conclusions to be derived from the limits-to-growth case for fundamentally changing postindustrial society: "the revolutionary project should take a cultural form, focussing most of its attention on the liberation of some consciousness rather than on the seizure of state power." In brief, this recommended revolutionary perspective emphasizes the process of "conscientization," a term made popular by the social theorist and activist, Paolo Freire.[49]

Nevertheless, change of consciousness alone is not sufficient to bring about a successful social transformation; such consciousness change must lead to effective political action. As Orwell understood, the former is necessary to the latter. However, as Slater and Marcuse both emphasize, before any change in either consciousness or social life can occur, there must be recognition of a problem, of negative outcomes (such as servitude), of a dilemma necessitating a choice, or, I would add, of the fantastic and manipulatory nature of our postindustrial social goods.

Successful social remedies to postindustrial ailments require recognition of conditions demanding treatment. To continue the medical analogy, a social analogue to pain is needed to sensitize us to the presence of some disorder. No matter how shocking and disorienting the initial recognition may be, we must not succumb to the temptation (as some individuals do regarding threats to their own health) of burying our heads in the sand and practicing denial. We may view the actual limits to growth, the scholarly literature providing evidence and demanding social change, and the social movements for postindustrial transformation—the latter two emerging in the 1970s—as performing the political equivalent of warning signs of a medical malady: in need of early and extensive treatment.

The writings on limits and the antinuclear, environmental, and voluntary simplicity movements expose the urgent need to make ultimate value choices, and the realization that all of us cannot have all that we desire. This crucial lesson is as old as Western civilization and thought itself. As has been discussed, the Greeks of antiquity always emphasized limits and opposed, as did the ancient Hebrews, limitless luxury.[50] However, in the euphoria associated with the endless material affluence promised by the tremendous productivity of the industrial machine, this millenia-old insight was (temporarily) rejected and erroneously believed to be obsolete.

Let us recall Camus's remark that humans are members of the only species that refuse to be what they are. The industrial era, lasting only about 250 years in the West, may be viewed as an entire society's refusal to be what its members and environment are: limited!

One limits-to-growth advocate waxes biblical when he tries to capture the violence committed by industrial growth values to the wisdom of the ages which stressed limits. After noting Jesus' reply to Satan that man does not live by bread alone, Daly writes:

Man, craving for the infinite, has been corrupted by the temptation to satisfy an insatiable hunger in the material realm...The proper object of economic activity is to have *enough* bread, not infinite bread, not a world turned into bread, not even vast storehouses full of bread. The infinite hunger of man, his moral and spiritual hunger, is not to be satisfied, is indeed exacerbated, by the current demonic madness of producing more and more things for more and more people. Afflicted with an infinite itch, modern man is scratching in the wrong place, and his frenetic clawing is drawing blood from the life-sustaining circulatory systems of his spaceship, the biosphere.[51]

As this passage suggests, a major precept of the limits-to-growth position is that for all of its inconceivable power the industrial megamachine has not accomplished the impossible: overcoming the existential limits of the human condition which provided the bases for the limits-emphasizing tradition as old as Western civilization. "Modernity has accomplished many far-reaching transformations, but it has not fundamentally changed the finitude, fragility, and mortality of the human condition."[52]

Those who assert the existence of the limits to economic growth attack one of the most important components of the industrial worldview and charge it with a fatal flaw. This understanding could be considered as one of the catalytic or precipitating developments (or one of the several required) for socially transforming the industrial civilization discussed by students of revolutionary theory and movements. One such student defines a revolutionary or "precipitating event" as:

> a catalyst that galvanized already existing elements and helped forged them into a social movement. The role of a catalyst...is to provide the focal connection that in turn brings different ingredients together and transforms what was previously diffuse and passive into something focused and active. The catalytic event is not itself sufficient to generate collective behavior, but it is the indispensable filter that helps give form and direction to the otherwise unrelated components of change.[53]

Another student of revolution defines a "precipitant" of revolution analogously to a precipitant in a chemical reaction: "it promotes a drastic and immediate reaction amongst preexisting ingredients."[54] It is important to note the necessity for "preexisting ingredients" and the "galvanizing effect" of revolutionary catalysts. To the limits-to-growth critics of industrialism, the biophysical and normative ingredients demanding industrial social transformation are present, and they anticipate that the increasing limits-to-growth consciousness will galvanize the preexisting social elements into an effective social movement for revolutionary change.

An encouraging aspect of this view of the limits to growth and their recognition as constituting revolutionary precipitants is that they are usually unpredictable. Two advocates of the transformation of American society end their work in an attempt to reply to the apparent futility of their aim by noting the unpredictability of revolutionary resistance to the existing order:

> Who predicted the Lordstown strike? Who predicted the strange refusal of Rosa Parks to move to the back of the bus? Who predicted the upsurge of both black and white Americans who joined in that refusal?...Who predicted massive domestic opposition to the war in Vietnam? Who predicted that millions of women would suddenly demand the obvious, that they be treated with the respect accorded equal human beings?[55]

We should not be discouraged about the prospects for transforming postindustrial society because we cannot conceive of the scenario of postindustrial transformation in specific and detailed form. Who knows or can predict where the next possible revolutionary precipitant event will occur? We have already had the oil price shocks of the 1970s; the Santa Barbara, the *Exxon Valdez* Alaskan and other oil spills; the Three Mile Island and Chernobyl nuclear accidents; the Love Canal toxic waste disaster; the Bhopal chemical accident; the garbage disposal crisis; ocean and beach pollution; the "greenhouse effect" producing global warming; stratospheric ozone depletion; and so forth.

These events have served to awaken the limits consciousness and social action for change as evidenced by increased popular support for worldwide environmental organizations and Green and Green-type anti-industrial movements. In addition, the experience of the futility and unsatis-factory nature of the Hobbesian, materialistic, competitive values has caused millions of people to renounce such values and adopt countercultural (that is, anti-industrial) values such as voluntary simplicity. Let us hope that the transformation of advanced industrial society will occur prior to the final "big bang" event that will "precipitate" an end to our species' and planet's survival!

Ecological indicators of social disorders are also possible catalysts for change in combination with frustrations and anxieties that are less publicly visible and more difficult to communicate. The elite are insecure about maintaining their vaunted positions and the industrial masses seek elite stations in vain. This must be recognized before it is too late, argue the advocates of the limits-to-growth critique of postindustrial civilization.

Ecological limits are now reported daily (as seen during the summer of 1988 drought in the United States, and the extensive coverage of the 1989 Alaskan oil spill). Dangers to the environment are witnessed personally by observant citizens: polluted recreational waters and beaches; the increasing number of contaminated fish or the absence of fish altogether owing to pollution; problems associated with the removal of nuclear and human waste materials; discovery of toxic dump sites near their homes; insufficient energy to cool homes during peak summer months; the threat of radon in their homes, and so on. Other limits are inwardly experienced in their daily fruitless attempts to realize the postindustrial "dream" of a secure, luxur-ious, competitively superior and everlasting life; witness the New York State Lottery's current advertising slogan: "All you need is a dollar and a dream!" With the odds of winning at eight million to one, winning is indeed a dream! All this increases stress and produces many forms of human misery in the postindustrial citizen, family, and society. These signs are likely to be recognized and responded to by increasing numbers of postindustrial citizens, constituting the revolutionary conditions to be precipitated by a catalytic event.

As Slater has argued, personal (and, I would add, social) change requires a disillusionment with the current values and beliefs. There are indications of such disillusionment that should encourage advocates of transformational change within industrial societies: the persistent and various environmental groups throughout the industrial nation-states even through poor economic times when progrowth critics expected a return to the priority of materialism and economic values;[56] the rise of new social movements throughout the postindustrial world, like the Greens, proclaiming alternative nonmaterialist values; and the workplace democracy movement increasing the autonomy of workers as well as humanizing the nature of industrial work. All of these challenge the dominance of existing postindustrial values and social conditions. They also reveal that the educational, conscientizing, disillusioning process pertaining to postindustrial life and values has already begun. The excesses of limitless industrialism—ecological, normative, and, if you will, spiritual—implying the existence of limits beyond which "excess" is defined, are beginning to be understood by the postindustrial public at large!

Part of the meaning of the death of industrial civilization will be the recognition of the failure of its antipolitical ethos and attempt at the reduction and implicit ideological suppression of politics. The fear of explicit politics experienced by antipolitical, progrowth defenders of industrialism follows from the latter's fundamental antipolitical, antinormative nature. Once the basic values, tenets, and concepts of industrial growth ideology are changed, Western Civilization's original high esteem for politics and its study, begun by Plato and Aristotle, may return in a repoliticized, transindustrial social order. The acceptance of the limits-to-growth position and the demise of the industrial value system and social practices will result in a transvaluation of explicit politics, "explicit" because politics was never actually eliminated or successfully suppressed by the industrial social order but merely in the consciousness of the manipulated industrial masses), restoring politics to its rightful place in transindustrial society as a comprehensive discourse of the highest importance.

The Possible Dynamics of Industrial Social Transformation to a Transindustrial Community

As the epigraph for this book, I quoted Oscar Wilde's paradoxical statement about the tragedy of getting what one wants. In the advanced industrial world where human wants are limitless in number, boundless in variety, and ceaseless in creation, "getting what one wants" appears to be the social definition of individual happiness (or, writ large, a prosperous society); certainly the opposite of a tragedy, let alone the "worst" tragedy. Given this understanding of industrial society, Wilde's words seem perverse—a consequence probably not unintended by Wilde, a nonconformist who satirized the industrial mores of his time.[57] The profundity of Wilde's point can, I think, be an excellent beginning to our discussion devoted to the transformation of postindustrial society.

The first human tragedy according to Wilde exists "in this world" (it should be noted that this phrase is ambiguous: it could refer to the human condition on the whole, or specifically to Wilde's late nineteenth century, British society which was the first and most advanced industrial one during this period),[58] and refers to an obvious fact of life experienced by all humans at some time and one which most people endured concerning very basic, material wants prior to the industrial revolution and its widespread affluence: "not getting what one wants." The tragedy occurs when a person who does not get what she or he wants becomes disappointed and frustrated. Alexis de Tocqueville, that acute student of American life in the nineteenth century, expresses this same point:

> In America I have seen the freest and best educated of men in circumstances the happiest to be found in the world; yet it seemed serious almost sad even in their pleasures [for the reason that they] never stop thinking of the good things they have not got.[59]

Little more need be said of this ubiquitous human trait. It is the second of Wilde's tragedies that calls out for explanation: how can *getting* what one wants constitute a tragedy, let alone "much the worst" tragedy? To address this question is one general aim of my book.

An unlikely source for illumination regarding Wilde's remarks is the former American secretary of state and international political scientist, Henry Kissinger. His analysis on national television in 1970 about Americans during the agonizing period of the Vietnam War provides an uncanny resemblance to and clarification of Wilde's thoughts. Kissinger said:

> To Americans usually tragedy is wanting something very badly and not getting it. Many people have had to learn in their private lives, and nations have had to learn in their historical experience, that perhaps the worst form of tragedy is wanting something badly, getting it, and finding it empty. And to get this sense of historical humility and of limitation, which is the experience through which we are now going as a people, is extremely painful.[60]

Whether Kissinger knew of Wilde's statement is not important. What is significant is the phenomenon of getting what we want and finding it empty, which, I think, is what Wilde was driving at with his characterization of it as the worst tragedy (and also what Hirschman emphasized in his discussion of the significance of human disappointment). It seems easier not to get our wants satisfied at all and to keep our values and goals intact.

A more typical source (a philosopher) identifies three causes of fundamental value change. He terms one, "value erosion" or "realization erosion," which seems to be of help in understanding Wilde's point:

> The status of a value can be eroded away when, in the wake of its substantial realization in a society, the value "loses its savor" and comes to be downgraded by disenchantment and disillusionment. Some examples would be: *"efficiency"* in the era of automation, *"progress"* in our age of anxiety, *"economic security"* in a welfare state, and *"national independence"* for an "emerging" nation in socio-economic chaos.[61]

These ideas concerning one of the prime movers for people to change their values—achieving them and then discovering that they have "lost their savor''—help us to see the explosive impact upon the existing social order of the value erosion process. Realizing one's values and becoming disenchanted with them because of their emptiness—or in Wilde's formulation, getting what one wants and experiencing "real" tragedy—leads one to examine them critically and to be receptive to change for the better. When such values or wants lie at the foundation of society, the possibility of the transformation of the dominant social paradigm and resulting social structure is suggested by this concept of value erosion or Wildean tragedy.

Although discussing the nature of humanity is a time-honored tradition within the history of political philosophy, one of its mainstays throughout the ages since Plato, I shall bypass such a discussion here except to make the following few comments. If, as I contend, the Hobbesian, ceaselessly dissatisfied concept of man is normatively undesirable and false, then reliance by the industrial worldview and social structure upon it as a basic support undermines industrialism severely. Talk about doom and gloom! The basic limits-to-growth position is no match for the foundations of industrial civilization in grim assumptions! This should be one of the points made by limits-to-growth advocates and informs my discussion as well.

Instead of Hobbes's gloomy conception being treated as part of genuine human nature it should be considered an element of the mistaken industrial ideology. If the Hobbesian notion of insatiable humanity is correct, it leads to the unhappy conclusion that people are unable to reach satisfaction of their wants except for ephemeral experiences. We are like professional sports teams who have only moments to enjoy a world championship before they are asked about the next season: in the locker room while still celebrating the final victory of the current season! A writer analyzing the "thrill of [competitive] victory"—let alone the "agony of defeat"—notes its dark side and then concludes his point about the trials and tribulations of winning—the "worst tragedy" of getting what one wants—in his critique of the excessive and harmful nature of postindustrial competition, by quoting a commentator on The Dallas Cowboys football team winning The Super Bowl. These sentiments surprisingly echo Wilde's:

> Despite their excitement, however, winning fails to satisfy us in any significant way and thus cannot begin to compensate for the pain in losing... *Winning offers no genuine comfort because there is no competitive activity for which victory is permanent*... Subjectively, the status of being envied and targeted by others may be superficially gratifying, but it is also deeply unsettling. Objectively, the reality is that it is only a matter of time until one becomes a loser again. [quoting a commentator on the Dallas Cowboys] The problem is this: even after you've just won the Super Bowl—*especially* after you've just won the Super Bowl—*there's always next year*. If "Winning isn't everything, it's the only thing," then "the only thing" is nothing—emptiness, the nightmare of life without ultimate meaning.[62]

Despite the grim possibility that Hobbes's view of mankind is correct, I still maintain that the industrial assumption of humanity as a limitless desirer is erroneous in its materialist exclusivity. Perhaps, as Hobbes and other advocates of this position hold, humans will always experience discontent and endless searching for satisfaction of their limitless wants, ceasing only with death. But, why must such endless searching be directed toward limitless wants of a material nature alone, dependent upon material possessions?

What I wish to suggest is (even if the infinite-wants view of human nature is accurate), after our material wants are satisfied, why not move on to truly nonmaterial ones, such as normative-based desires? These include the political values of freedom, equality, democracy, self-realization, and fulfilling work, or what Daly calls (perhaps too narrowly) "moral growth," to distinguish it from material growth.

Let us consider the possibility of life's "higher" desires being nonmaterial, as in psychologist Abraham Maslow's hierarchy. Maslow proposes a scale of human values culminating in self-actualization consisting of equally important components, as expressed by one interpretation of his theory: "love, truth, service, justice, perfection, aesthetics, [and] meaningfulness."[63] We may, in this instance, still envision an Hobbesian person endlessly flitting from one want to another as they become satisfied or until failure or death but, at the very least, the wants or satisfied desires would be significantly different from the standard, postindustrial, materialist-based ones, especially in their social consequences. They would be predominantly nonmaterial, normatively enhancing, socially improving, and noncompetitive as well as ecologically sustainable. These values would have a profound political, economic, and social impact on the current postindustrial societies. One political student of the American business system recognized this when he stated that the American (or any postindustrial) economy's "success depends upon the deliberate squandering of resources" and then goes on to ask a fascinating question reflecting these nonmaterial desires and their effects upon our society: "Walking through the woods on a snowy evening may be just as pleasant as riding a snowmobile, but is it as marketable?"[64]

The problem of the nature of human wants and expectations is essential to social life. Human disappointment—produced by discrepancies between reality and our expectations—depends upon our values. This simple point is profoundly important to both our individual and social lives, as well as to stimulating the thought and action which will lead to social transformation.[65]

I am sensitive to the charge that my discussion thus far bears only remotely upon its stated subject of the dynamics of postindustrial transformation to a new social order. However, I am convinced of the great significance to my theme of the nature of human tragedy and its relation to human expectations and values. This idea is often missed by analysts of contemporary postindustrial society, falsely leading them to reach pessimistic conclusions about the chances for radically changing the current hegemonic postindustrial order. I believe that human tragedy (as contemplated by Wilde and Kissinger), human disappointment (as interpreted by Hirschman), the erosion of human values because of their realization (as analyzed by Rescher), and the decreasing marginal utility (according to the discipline of modern economics) all reflect a potentially fatal flaw within materially rich, competitive, advanced industrial society. This flaw is implied by the limits-to-growth position and could be exploited for the purpose of transforming society for the better.

Industrial civilization is being killed by its own success. Although more citizens of such a culture have acquired more material goods than in any past social order, these citizens increasingly find such goods unsatisfying, producing the experiences of tragedy and disappointment; the negative consequence of erosion of values or value change is also occurring. These developments, important in our late stage of industrial civilization, hold much potential for its transformation.

The richer we are in material objects either individually or socially (and the United States is the wealthiest society in the aggregate, materially speaking, in history), the greater our feelings of disappointment and tragic apprehension. Why is this so? The following factors are important in answering this question: (1) competitive limits for the increasingly larger role of social position or competitive goods in materially affluent, advanced industrial society mean that relative wealth is *logically* not available to the members of the society as a whole;[66] (2) time limits; (3) consumer satisfaction limited by the mass production process economically required to distribute material goods throughout the entire economy when what is really desired is actually the competitive status or social esteem indicated by such goods (see part 3): and, finally, (4) ecological limits regarding: the production and safe removal of toxic and nontoxic wastes (illustrated recently by the difficult social problems of the safe disposal of nuclear waste, or by the vagabond New York garbage barge in 1988 unable to get approval to dump its supposedly nontoxic waste after a trip of thousands of miles and months at sea); ocean pollution of bathing and fishing areas; atmospheric pollution; and the supply of food, arable land, minerals, energy sources, and so forth.

Despite these negative results of the industrial drive for self-infinitization, we must not ignore the materially poor, nonindustrial societies whose members experience the pain of the unfulfillment of their necessary wants or needs (see Jerome Segal's gloomy analysis for such countries unless drastic action is taken immediately). Indeed, it has been emphasized throughout this discussion that for such societies, economic growth to end basic deprivation, if not catch up to materially rich, advanced industrial societies, is necessary and desirable (implying relative or even absolute material losses for the wealthy societies).

The difference in degree of human misery—both individual and social—experienced by citizens of advanced industrial and nonindustrial societies can be contrasted but is very difficult to weigh comparatively for lack of commensurability; for example, spiritual versus physical hunger, loss of community versus lack of physical shelter, alienating labor versus ill health, and so forth. However, we should not forget Aristotle's basic point that mere living is a prerequisite to living the good life. The lives of the residents of materially poor countries are presently endangered as will be the whole human species if the industrial value of limitless economic growth continues unchecked by the existential limits of the human condition.

Hirschman's perceptive analysis of the social significance of disappointment for value changes (what Rescher termed "value erosion"), and the effects of Wildean tragedy which may be viewed broadly as a type or subdivision of disappointment with what our satisfied wants produce, can inform the achievement of industrial social transformation and illuminate the direction toward which such transformation should aim. Furthermore, these phenomena go beyond rational argument which is severely limited as a catalyst for social change, as Milbrath notes. These are trenchant experiences that can be recognized and acted upon by the least sophisticated advanced industrial citizen.

Perhaps what is truly satisfying and ultimately the most valuable about nonmaterial, noncompetitive goods or wants are their apparent indefinite or even infinite limits and public nature. In contrast, the typical, advanced industrial goods are usually materialist-based and highly competitive even if, at their most basic level, they seem nonmaterial (Hobbes's vainglory; Rousseau's *amour propre*; our "being number one"). Nonmaterial, noncompetitive goods are not vulnerable to the weaknesses brought about by the decreasing marginal utility and zero-sum traits characteristic of their limited and competitive counterparts; for example, does our love for someone decrease in satisfaction as it grows? Does our appreciation for a beautiful poem become lessened by others' similar appreciation of it? (See Milbrath for his envisioned new order's values: "cooperation, love, compassion, justice, self-restraint, nonviolence, and trust.")[67] Do not such questions appear misplaced about such desired goods?

A basic characteristic of lower wants is that their satisfaction is subject to scarcity and to diminishing returns. If one person gets more of a material good, the other must necessarily get less. Nonmaterial values such as knowledge, faith, self-realization and others are neither subject to diminishing returns nor diminish in quantity when shared with others. Potentially they are infinitely expandable and are not subject to scarcity in the sense that material goods are.[68]

Would not a society that had the capacity to provide for all of its members' biophysical needs (as the few advanced industrial societies can) be a superior one normatively if it then turned its attention to realizing nonmaterial, noncompetitive values rather than pursuing competitive goods, especially social status, through endless material acquisition?

In part 3, I presented a critique of the infinite wants of the mind and unlimited desires of the imagination. Beginning with the ancient Greeks' emphasis upon moderation and their concept of *hubris*, continuing with the Stoics and Epicureans to Rousseau and the contemporary economic theorists Daly, Hirsch and Hirschman, Western thought has condemned "infinite wants of the mind." However, I think it is crucial to add that the particular goods of the mind attacked in this twenty-five hundred year old tradition, as well as those which are quintessentially industrial (like *amour propre*), are inherently competitive. Therefore, given the nature of a competitive Hobbesian society where even the temporary winner cannot rest secure, Hobbes's striving competition or our own striving to be number one with its resulting anxiety about downward mobility for those few fortunate people who make it to the top—where winning is the *only* thing—is an endless pursuit. It is because of the insecurity caused by constant threats in this "war of all against all," from everyone seeking each other's titles or indications of competitive success (e.g., Super Bowl champion, highest class rank or salesperson with the most sales in dollars, etc.), that the Hobbesian industrial man *must* endlessly desire power in order to protect what one already possesses. It is the competitiveness itself, not necessarily the normative nature of the wants, that is deleterious.

Horne, a student of Mandeville's thought, captures this moral/political tradition of rejecting the competitive goods of the mind when he writes:

> it is in the nature of honor that few can possess it, that the competition for it becomes intense, that its possessors become haughty and arrogant, and that those without it become resentful and envious. Moreover, if goods of the imagination—recognition or vanity—provide a constant and powerful motivation to economic activity because they are without limit, it is only because they are without lasting satisfaction.[69]

I suggest that the reason why such nonmaterial goods (referred to by Epicurus, Rousseau, Hobbes, Horne and those in our own society, tied as they are to the acquisition of material goods through postindustrial conspicuous consumption) are ultimately unsatisfying is their competitive nature; therefore, contrary to Horne's assertion about such goods being "without limit," they are actually quite limited in their capability to provide human satisfaction by their very nature as sources of competition. This supports Hirsch's main point about the ultimately dissatisfying character of positional or competitive goods: all seek them and by definition only a few can have them—for example, winning the Super Bowl. Such goods are indeed "without lasting satisfaction," as Horne says, or socially harmful not because they are without limit but rather because of their stringent limits of temporary comparative worth.

If the nonmaterial goods could be noncompetitive as well, the longstanding criticism against the unlimited goods of the mind or nonmaterial goods might be obviated. We must discard the pernicious, Hobbesian, and ceaselessly competitive view of human nature and society which still prevails among other industrial social values and its structure. I believe that we should conceive of individual and social humanity in a noncompetitive manner and replace our malignant conceptions and values with public, nonzero-sum, nonmaterial social goods or cooperative goods. In this way, people would have an interest in satisfying the desires of others because by doing so they satisfy their own desires.

Alfie Kohn, in his criticisms of competition as a social value makes two very important points pertinent to our discussion: (1) competition creates scarcity; and, (2) competition preserves the existing social structure and values. His perceptive remarks are worth noting:

> A competitive economic system offers itself as the best way to deal with scarcity...while quietly *promoting* scarcity...Manufactured scarcity, of course, is not limited to economic matters. Every contest that is staged (the most facts memorized, the fastest runner, the most beautiful) involves the creation of a desired and scarce status where none existed before.[70]

On the conservative nature of competition, this critic of industrial competition writes of the attempt by competitive winners to convince losers that each got what they deserved:

> Despite the outrageous arrogance of this view, winners are sometimes successful in persuading losers of its validity. This has two consequences: (1) the losers' contempt for the winners is mixed with self-contempt, and (2) the losers will set about not to change the system (a move that would in any case be dismissed as "sour grapes") but only to become a winner next time. *Thus there is no one to press for structural change.*[71]

The consequences of Kohn's point—so politically profound—have been observed by many analysts of contemporary industrial society, but especially poignantly by students of Marx. They call attention to the members of the lower class of such societies who rather than taking action to transform their unequal social orders are instead pre-occupied with becoming "winners" themselves, however unlikely this prospect may be. The devil in the piece is not the nonmaterial nature of "goods of the mind" but their limited nature imposed by competitive, exclusive, and erroneous limits-denying traits. The truly unlimited goods are the nonmaterial and noncompetitive or public ones.

Here Marx and Engels's ideal of noncompetitive human association wherein the "free development of each is the condition of the free development of all" is important. To create such a society where the human development of each member is inextricably connected to every other—man's political or social nature first asserted by Aristotle is implied—I think requires the creation of a genuine community as opposed to the competitive, Hobbesian, postindustrial, "lonely crowd," whose members' only shared trait is the endless desire to defeat each other; a society where the slogan:

"Whoever has the most things when he dies, wins," accurately reflects this conception of postindustrial society as a materialist-based contest and nothing else.

While the concept of "community" has been a theme within political philosophy since its origins with much political thought and writing on its nature and value,[72] let me state in the briefest terms possible (since a full discussion of this concept is beyond the scope of this chapter) what I wish to convey by the use of the term: a social order with non-Hobbesian, non-industrial values. This explains its presence in the title of this part as one of the essential components of an alternative society to the postindustrial one; one to which I prescribe postindustrial civilization be transformed. Adding "democracy" to this briefest description of the transindustrial society I recommend also contributes, once elaborated upon, to a society wherein equality, freedom, the self-development of each person through an active public life and self-fulfilling labor, are valued.[73]

Another important virtue of nonmaterial, noncompetitive goods of the mind or Maslovian higher needs is that owing to their intangible or mental nature they can be eliminated or changed by the very mind that created them in the first place—by value changes—unlike material-based, physical goods which remain intact despite value changes and transformed world-views; while man does not live by bread alone, man cannot live without bread!

I would like to reinforce Hirschman's point about the great political significance of human disappointment especially with regard to stimulating thought and action about social transformation by referring to a recent theory of the causes for revolution known as the "relative deprivation theory," specifically, a subdivision of it: the "J-curve" hypothesis. While space does not permit a full exposition of this theory of political change, I present it briefly to further support the claim made here concerning the causal relation between experiencing a discrepancy between our expectations and perceived reality (or disappointment) and transformational politics.

A political scientist in his discussion of relative deprivation informs his readers that:

the concept of RD [relative deprivation] was first used systematically in the 1940s by the authors of *The American Soldier* to denote the feelings of an individual who lacks some status or conditions that he thinks he should have, his standards of what he should have generally been determined by reference to what some other person or group has.[74]

Although the concept of relative deprivation was introduced in the 1960s by James C. Davies's contemporary, political scientific *locus classicus* to explain revolution,[75] the idea of people's value expectations not being fulfilled by current social conditions constitutes a cause of revolution that probably dates back to the Greeks. In his *Politics*, Aristotle proposed the explanation that the masses sought revolution to achieve their desire for more equality and democracy and the oligarchs did the same in order to achieve their conflicting desire for more inequality.[76] Both groups, according to Aristotle's analysis, appeared to experience a sense of discrepancy between what they wanted (or what they considered to be just rewards) and what they got.

Of course, this idea that dissatisfaction regarding one's relative social success spurs political action is a staple of modern political thought. In the seventeenth century Hobbes—perceptive as he was about modernity—foresaw the profound importance of competitive, socially defined goods for which the modern industrial citizen would ceaselessly strive, while never attaining lasting satisfaction. One hundred years before Hirsch's analysis of the inevitable and unavoidable social limits to growth engendered by the competitive or relative definition of goods within advanced industrial society, Marx and Engels clearly recognized the significance of socially-defined goods in industrial capitalist society. They wrote: "Our desires and pleasures spring from society; we measure them, therefore, by society and not by the objects which serve for their satisfaction. Because they are of a social nature, they are of a relative nature."[77]

In that same work, *Wage Labor and Capital*, Marx and Engels express the main point about how industrial humanity's desire for relative or competitive goods necessarily produces dissatisfaction and frustration which could become the driving forces for transforming such a society. They refer to a man who lives in a small house which

as long as the surrounding houses are equally small... satisfies all social demands for a dwelling. [But] let a palace arise beside the little house, and it shrinks from a little house to a hut. The little house shows now that its owner has only slight or no demands to make; and however high it may shoot up in the course of civilization, if the neighboring palace grows to an equal or even greater extent, the occupant of the relative small house will feel more and more uncomfortable, dissatisfied and cramped within its four walls.[78]

It certainly seems as if these commentators upon modernity have accurately described one of the essential characteristics of industrial life and worldview: its extreme competitiveness leading to disappointment and dissatisfaction for most of its members. We merely have to thoughtfully observe the barrage of daily advertising in advanced industrial society to recognize how much of our social values are basically competitive: "keeping up with the Joneses," "being number one," and the corresponding dread of failure or decline.[79] We have already quoted Slater's idea of an addiction to wealth—and competitive success—in the previous part; this addiction has the unique quality of having the addict get high on the withdrawal symptoms of others similarly addicted. Mishan reflects the extremity of the degree of competition in advanced industrial society with his illustration of this society's perversely competitive value system wherein a worker would prefer a lesser loss than other workers over a lesser gain than that received by others.

In addition to mentioning Rousseau's and Veblen's respectively acute analyses of the critical role of competition in modern society Bell's simple statement should probably be the final word on this competitive aspect of industrial civilization: "If consumption represents the psychological competition for status, then one can say that bourgeois [industrial] society is the institutionalization of envy."[80]

Despite this powerful body of evidence regarding the competitive and social nature of goods in the industrial social order, the issue of the causal relation between human disappointment brought about by relative deprivation (competitive losses), revolutionary action, and social transformation needs more explicit discussion and defense.

The derivative J-curve hypothesis of the general psychological, relative deprivation theory emphasizes one of the three possible forms of relative deprivation that can have revolutionary consequences according to its advocates: (1) when value expectations are roughly constant and the social reality declines; (2) when the value expectations rise and the social reality remains roughly constant; and, (3) when value expectations rise and social reality declines. Davis called this social situation the J-curve because the sharp drop off of social conditions relative to expectations appears to form a sideways "J" (roughly: ⟋⟎) indicating a sharp and sudden reversal in social desires and expectations being met; that is, after some success in meeting social wants circumstances take a sharp turn for the worse.[81]

What should be noted about the J-curve hypothesis of revolutionary action is that as derivative of relative deprivation theory in general, the discrepancy between the satisfaction expected and the actual satisfaction achieved forms the basis of human effort to transform society.

The rapidly widening gap between expectations and gratifications portends revolution. The most common case for this widening gap of individual dissatisfactions is economic or social dislocation that makes the affected individual generally tense, generally frustrated.[82]

In short, disappointed, dissatisfied, frustrated people will take action to radically change their social conditions in an effort to become more satisfied.

What is important for our discussion about relative deprivation theory and the J-curve hypothesis? First, we considered the uncontentious but significant fact that advanced industrial society was the first society on a collective level to be so materially productive and therefore well-endowed as to be capable of satisfying the basic biophysical needs of all of its citizens (or at least, in the event of inadequate distribution, those of many of its citizens), so that its members could shift from wondering where their next meal would come from (or how their other basic needs would be met) to concentrating their attention and efforts on achieving competitive social status (or other forms of competitive success, or "vainglory" in Hobbes's language); hence, the importance of relative wealth or scarcity in advanced industrial society.

As Galbraith observed and we discussed earlier, a hungry man (or a person deprived of the basic biophysical needs for survival) does not look to see what food his neighbor receives when he eats for the first time in quite a while. Human survival needs are absolute and not relative (or competitive or positional) in nature (for example, tolerable temperature extremes, quantities of water, calories, vitamins, minerals, etc.). This is important for social and political consequences: your satisfying these absolute basic human needs does not detract from my doing so. No zero-sum competition exists; the goals providing the satisfaction of such needs are truly public (as long as sufficient supply for all is available) and thus could spur social cooperation for their satisfaction.

Herein lies the power of Hirsch's argument about the social limits to growth—their logical or conceptual nature as well as the empirical limits caused by the phenomenon of overcrowding—but, I believe, he should have made reference to the long history of these ideas within political thought. Postindustrial society promises its citizens what it cannot deliver logically or empirically: everyone winning! The competitive nature of industrial social values and corresponding goods ensures that not only can comparatively few people succeed, but their temporary success is always threatened by the relative advancement of others—why Hobbes said that man must ceaselessly seek more power and why Satchel Paige advised never to look back—for they may be gaining on you!

Thus, human disappointment seems to be produced by what relative deprivation theorists highlight as the *necessary* discrepancies between the (impossible) expected, competitive values and the actual values realized within postindustrial society. A sense of relative deprivation creates feelings of disappointment, dissatisfaction, and frustration, and these feelings could be the bases for social transformation. If Hirschman and the relative deprivation theorists, especially advocates of the J-curve hypothesis, are correct, when value expectations rise and industrial social reality declines (and is therefore unable to satisfy these expectations) the psychological and social conditions are ripe for social transformation.

Admittedly, being "ripe" for social transformation is a vague term referring to a very complex phenomenon. As critics of relative deprivation theory assert, more precision in defining the thresholds is necessary.[83] A prominent student of social change raises an important point against relative deprivation theory and the J-curve thesis when he pointedly asserts: "people's rising expectations are being disappointed all the time without revolution...."[84] This simple remark seeks to correct what is perceived to be an error within relative deprivation theory and parallels the earlier analysis of revolution emphasizing the need to consider both social consciousness and social structure. He continues:

> that whether widespread discontent actually couples with a revolutionary situation depends on structural circumstances that have little or no connection with the generality of discontent. Those "structural circumstances" include the military vulnerability of the state, the internal organization of its opposition, and the character of coalitions among classes.[85]

Without going into the details of the very large debate among contemporary social scientists over the precise causes of revolution, one may still accept this point by viewing psychologically based, relative deprivation as insufficient for social transformation; other factors, which are termed, "structural circumstances," are also needed (as we have discussed earlier). This observation about discontent being ubiquitous without resulting in revolution is illuminating and is reinforced in advanced industrial society by the absence of revolution despite the miseries of lower and middle class life (and furthermore, by the conservative orientation of the members of these classes sometimes even greater than even the upper class). This particular fact has caused contemporary Marxists (like Habermas and Gorz) to reconsider where the revolutionary class will emerge. The question remains: can the biophysical limits to growth provide some of the structural requirements for postindustrial transformation in addition to the psychological or consciousness component of radical social change?

One important conclusion of the relative deprivation theory is that poverty *per se* does not cause revolution—if it did, revolution and revolutionary activities would be a constant set of phenomena on the world scene or, at least, far more frequent than they are. From this revolutionary perspective, rather than the issue being why there is so much political violence in the world, the pressing social issue should be why there is so *little* political violence relative to the enormous extent and severity of destitution in the world. Actually, it is the failure of materially affluent societies to fulfill the rising expectations of materially richer people—not the abject poor—which leads to dissatisfaction and revolutionary efforts. This suggests that one should expect transformational sentiments and action to come from a dissatisfied middle and even upper class rather than from the more objectively and materially deprived lower or underclass. Whether such a transformational middle or upper class does emerge remains to be seen, but the early signs of industrial middle-class members supporting new social movements for change like the Greens and their alternative anti-industrial values such as postmaterialism or voluntary simplicity would seem to confirm this theoretical anticipation.[86]

A key question to be raised concerning this point is: can the ecological, biophysical limits to growth provide some of the structural requirements for industrial transformation carrying us beyond the psychological dynamics of disappointment? Indeed, ecological limits will exacerbate the already existing warfare between groups within advanced industrial society because of the competitive nature of postindustrial social goods and values. People seeking to avoid air pollution, toxic waste sites, overcrowding, nuclear power plants, polluted beaches and water bodies, acid rain, and all the disamenities now being recognized as generated by the advanced industrial social order will heighten the already high level of competition characterizing such a society. Middle-class members who thought they were on their way to elite exclusivity and competitive success will, sooner or later, realize that they are lagging behind the elite in their ability to avoid industrial miseries; what Hirsch calls "defensive" expenditures to protect one's place will rise rapidly, as objective and relative conditions worsen or threaten to do so.[87]

It will not merely be the disappointment of unfulfilled expectations for advanced industrial populations that is most politically meaningful; eventually the upper and middle classes will scramble to protect what competitive benefits and advantages they already possess from attack by either the lower classes' advancement or ecologically-caused degradation. In this regard, Adam Smith's claim, so important to liberalism, that the pain from the loss of what one already possesses is worse than the gain of having an expectation fulfilled, is crucial. "Man's suffering was more intense," Smith wrote, "when we fall from a better to a worse situation than we ever enjoy when we rise from a worse to a better."[88]

Liberal, industrial, competitive values are flawed because they are not open or available to most. Even those who temporarily attain them by winning remain ceaselessly insecure! Furthermore, they are predicated upon an undesirable (Hobbesian) conception of humanity as well as upon the achievement of values made empirically impossible by objective limits to material growth in a world of over five billion people characterized by finite resources and tolerance ranges for various waste products. Not only will the citizens of advanced industrial societies experience the anxiety of realizing the emptiness or erosion of their attained values, but they will find that the biophysical, lower, Maslovian needs—previously bracketed as met or taken for granted so that the higher ones might be addressed—will reemerge with a vengeance, thrusting such citizens into despair as they realize that their fantasies are dead.

This may be sufficient to provide the needed fuel for questioning the legitimacy or worthiness of continuing the current postindustrial social order. Here we should recall Tawney's point about how mankind does not reflect upon their social order until compelled to do so by some "practical emergency." This could be so, less because of human nature than a society's elite's interest and capability—especially in technologically advanced industrial society—to thwart critical social thinking; Camus's remark about thinking being subversive strikes a responsive chord here. I think that the limits-to-growth-inspired, postindustrial crisis presents just such a "practical emergency" to stimulate industrial citizens to be subversive by social thinking, by "reflect[ing] upon questions of economic and social organization," as Tawney expressed it.

Moreover, moving to the realm of action, many analysts of revolution have noted that most people do not initiate social action for transformation unless moved to do so by impinging social developments. In the current social situation such developments could include experiencing a combination of Wildean tragedy, human disappointment and the shaking of the smug middle and upper classes' confidence about their biophysical survival needs being met. Such experiences may be sufficient to break through the conservative Orwellian circle of industrial societal continuity wherein consciousness and social structure reinforce each other as well as the powerful advanced industrial means of socialization and social control possessed by postindustrial elites. The elite passengers on the supposedly unsinkable *Titanic* may have been slower than others to realize that the ship was—incredibly—taking on water, but they did eventually recognize the reality and grabbed for life vests and rafts. I think collectively we are somewhere near—and getting closer all the time—to this latter appreciation of our situation but clearly we are not quite there at this time. This is especially true for those rich, postindustrial citizens whose powers to deny despair (experienced as the mourning period for fantasies) and to avoid postindustrial disamenities are greater than their nonrich, fellow citizens!

Let us recapitulate. Limits-to-growth theorists have argued—though not in sufficient clarity or evidential detail—that growth-addicted, advanced industrial society is not sustainable. One nonphysical reason that we can now understand is that increasing numbers of the citizens of such societies experience deep feelings of disappointment or relative deprivation when their expectations are always rising—competitively—and are not, *cannot*, be satisfied; both because of physical and conceptual limits, the latter referring to the exclusive nature of competitive industrial goods and values. This produces more and more postindustrial persons open to the transformational message and willing to take appropriate political action; members of the powerful elite are included so that this psychological/normative change can have social structural implications. While it is true that disappointment, discontent and insecurity by themselves are not sufficient to transform postindustrial society, they can provide the essential background conditions, once mobilized and organized, to help form an effective social movement for societal transformation. Importantly, these conditions can assist in the formation of the instrument for social change by shaping its goals (as with the new anti-industrial social movements, the most prominent of which is tied to the environment and stopping its further deterioration).

Moreover, as a result of disappointment, Wildean tragedy, and value erosion, the postindustrial elite (the current members of the beneficiary class within the dominant, postindustrial social paradigm and structure) might come to a realization unique in history. The elite, postindustrial consciousness may be shocked into change by increasingly conspicuous limits to growth as well as by the profoundly challenging nature of the limits-to-growth literature: the futility, insecurity, and disaster looming in our foreseeable future (unlike the predicted long-range disaster of our sun burning up in several billion years), and a future filled with the preoccupation of seeking to maintain their relative advantages and ceaselessly fend off all of the others seeking to replace them. The enjoyment of the elite's present success seems short-lived, unstable, and increasingly inadequate relative to both the concern and effort expended in attaining such "success" in the first place, and the rising costs of maintaining their celebrated position on top.

If both the temporary postindustrial elite (or the successful competitors in the contests that constitute most of the postindustrial social order) as well as the lower- and middle-class members can be made to realize that the value structure of this civilization is erroneous in several respects making it unworthy and impossible (even if preferred), then the social transformation of such a society will not be the highly unlikely prospect claimed by the social-change pessimists and defenders of the status quo.

Critics of this view might reply that to grant this condition is to beg the question because such a fundamental normative change supports social transformation since such a value change *is* part of social transformation. Orwell's point becomes relevant again: How can consciousness (or value change) be an effective agent of change without changing the social structure and vice versa?

In rebuttal, the limits-to-growth advocate can answer that the biophysical limits to growth, such as toxic waste discovered in one's community or even under one's home; nuclear accidents; shortages of potable water, crude oil, clean air, edible fish, arable land, or vital minerals; environmentally caused disease such as cancer—to name just a few local, rather than global, manifestations within advanced industrial society—are frightening enough to act collectively as a catalyst, or as Tawney's "practical emergency," for the transformation of postindustrial society. They force the recognition of the very high—possibly deadly—cost of the achievement of attempting to realize industrial values by continuing "business as usual."

Such a realization may result in dissatisfaction and the ongoing sense of relative deprivation for most postindustrial citizens—including those who are successful in the short run. Our final despair for industrial civilization is the mourning period for the industrial fantasy of unlimited economic growth spurred by the consciousness of the ultimate and unavoidable limits of the earth, the human condition, and the nature of human (competitive, materialist) satisfaction. And, as has been emphasized, this final despair is imperative if genuine individual and social transformation is to occur.

The public's reaction to the increasingly visible limits to growth will make the possibility of postindustrial social transformation more likely. In a society like ours, wherein the people who yearn for the achievement of postindustrial values as well as those (few) who have already achieved them are both doomed to dissatisfaction, is transformation truly impossible? I think not, and have attempted to show in this section that the stimuli necessary for transformation are already present and increasing in social significance. In addition, while not detailing a specific revolutionary program or strategy containing the structural changes needed for a successful transformation, I think that with such limits-to-growth catalysts there are sufficient grounds for encouragement warranting further inquiry and efforts in this direction (in the manner of Milbrath's most recent effort). The question of the specific form and goals of such a transformation of postindustrial society should be one of the main topics for contemporary social theorists, policymakers and the general public. I hope that this discussion has pro-

voked enough interest and has provided sufficient rational evidence to convince members of these groups of both the justifiability and urgency of such
a project.

To sum up the main thrust of this chapter, I believe that the current
industrial crisis centering on the limits to growth can be instrumental in
getting citizens of advanced industrial societies to recognize the erroneous
nature of the dominant postindustrial social paradigm, its way of life, and
values. As a consequence, this crisis will stimulate these citizens to be
conscious of their society's deficiencies inspiring the destruction of the
limitless growth illusion as well as the illusory materialist reductionism of
humanity, society, and politics. What I have in mind here is that the entire
growth-addictive conceptual apparatus that supports postindustrial society,
the industrial ideology containing the Hobbesian conception of humanity,
liberalism, materialism, and competitiveness—all must be destroyed as well.
Such a cleansing process will pave the way to begin the necessary transformation of postindustrial society to a transindustrial one; one not bur-
dened by these weaknesses that are potentially fatal to our planet and all of
its inhabitants.

By this discussion I intend to becalm those who, like Woody Allen,
believe that our future consists only of choices between different means to
disaster. It is essential to stress that we are merely losing a fantasy, a dream
of industrialism that in actuality was and is a nightmare to most of the
world's population in its ecological, social, political, and individual consequences. Its victims are many and varied; there are impoverished billions
who suffer because of global injustice as a result of industrial ideology and
individual "losers" of advanced industrial societies who do not "make it."
There are living creatures of the animal world sacrificed for industrial
"progress" and a "successful" elite racked with anxiety about losing their
competitive, superior status and experiencing downward mobility: the "has
beens." Hard-working "stiffs" toil at alienating jobs motivated by the false
hope of a more materially rich future for themselves and their children, not
realizing the irreversible costs to themselves. Blameless but blamed victims
of the competitive, Hobbesian, industrial "jungle" are sent the inaccurate
message that they were given their chance and failed. People are made to
suffer because of the immeasurable demands of competitive, materialist
industrialism, while "disenfranchised" persons, or members of the underclass, are not even permitted the opportunity to fail because of various types
of societal discrimination resulting in enormous self-doubt and loss of
self-esteem.

For all of these persons—an overwhelming majority of the earth's
population—the mourning period for the industrial, limitless growth fantasy
should be a short and easy one once the realities and deficiencies of indus-

trial civilization are recognized. Furthermore, when the immediate, unhappy consequences of their initial awareness of the perverse and illusory nature of ceaseless economic growth as the primary social goal are over, the victims of industrialism can turn to the urgent and real problems confronting us all: those associated with the creation of a superior, sustainable civilization to replace the illusion-based, unequal and undemocratic, postindustrial one. After all, the industrial social order and framework are no more than about two hundred and fifty years old; it is *not* one that has been with us since the beginning of time nor is it the consummation of humanity's nature as industrial ideologues are inclined to imply. In fact, as we have seen, this industrial paradigm, its values, and social institutions have contravened the long history of Western thought, human nature and its environment by the denial of limits!

10

Conclusion:
Towards a New Transindustrial Society

> Ironically, the pain of a collapsing culture is also an opportunity:
> to change is hard, but not to change is impossible.
>
> —George Lakey[1]

The Nature of Transindustrialism

It is impossible for me to provide a detailed prescription of the social order to follow the unacceptable and dangerous postindustrial one. We are at an early stage of both the worldwide crisis and the transitional period between our old, declining civilization and a new one. Such a prescription would be merely another construction of one person's vision. Furthermore, such a personal account of the transindustrial society would defeat what I conceive to be one of the new society's major characteristics: a genuine participatory democracy wherein it shall be the right and responsibility of its own citizens to determine their particular institutional structure and specific public policies. Nonetheless, I believe that some very general indications about this new worldview, its values and social life, in contrast to industrialism and its social arrangements, should be made. It is important to provide some content to what the limits-to-growth theorists and I have argued is a necessary alternative to postindustrial values and society.

First, and perhaps foremost, the reader must not think of transindustrial civilization as completely anti-industrial. I have tried to convey this important point by adopting the label "transindustrial" in order to make clear the transcendent nature of the new social order's values and structure. In this manner, I hope to avoid the impression that this "post-postindustrial" society is being recommended as a means to return to some rustic preindustrial "Golden Age," when life was "simple" (and, it turns out, poor!). Transindustrial civilization, as I conceive of it, shall not be an agriculturally-based culture nor a primitive way of life preoccupied with meeting the daily challenge of material subsistence. *I do not prescribe nor consider it feasible to totally discard all of the components of advanced industrial society.*

In my view, we have the potential for the first time to meet *all* of humanity's basic survival needs—those needs of all of the more than five billion members of our species—as a consequence of the immense material productivity of a scientifically advanced and highly technologically innovative culture. This goal should be essential to the values and structure of transindustrial society. The average transindustrial citizen will require—and be able to achieve—liberation from everyday biophysical concerns that currently preoccupy one-quarter of the earth's population and obtain the concomitant leisure time to develop and fulfill itself. Moreover, there should be time for education and participation in the demanding yet satisfying public life and collective decisionmaking which should characterize the democratic transindustrial community.

This idea of retaining some of contemporary industrial civilization's distinctive features within the transindustrial social order—while, of course, eliminating others—may be comprehended better, I think, by considering the famous formulation of the dialectical process defined by the nineteenth century German philosopher Georg Wilhelm Friedrich Hegel. As dense and obscure as Hegel's thought and writings are reputed to be—even to the extreme of unintelligibility—it may seem odd that I suggest utilizing an Hegelian concept for clarification of the nature of the transindustrial society. Nevertheless, despite this reputation of opacity—well-deserved in other portions of Hegel's philosophy—I do believe that the idea of the Hegelian dialectic, specifically Hegel's use of the German verb *aufheben* (to sublimate), can indeed illuminate an important but difficult to grasp element of transindustrial civilization.

In the course of his interpretative biography of Hegel, Walter Kaufmann attempts to clarify Hegel's terminology, including the salient verb *aufheben* by relating both its category meaning and Hegel's interpretation.

Aufheben (sublimate) means literally "pick up" [writes Kaufmann] ...it is quite common in ordinary speech: it is what you do when something has fallen to the floor. But this original sensuous meaning has given rise to two derivative meanings which are no less common: "cancel," and "preserve" or "keep." Something may be picked up in order that it will no longer be there; on the other hand, I may also pick it up to keep it. When Hegel uses the term in its double (or triple) meaning...he may be said to visualize how something is picked up in order that it may no longer be *there* just the way it was, although, of course, it is not cancelled altogether but lifted up to be kept on a different level.[2]

Hegel addresses the richness of this complex German concept in a note to his *Logic* on the term "*aufheben*." Hegel writes:

Aufheben and *das aufgehobene* (*das ideele*) is one of the most important concepts of philosophy, a basic determination which recurs practically everywhere...what is sublimated...is *mediated*; it is that which is not, but as a *result*, having issued from what had being; it is therefore *still characterized by the determination from which it comes*.

Aufheben has in the [German] language a double meaning in that it signifies conserving, *preserving*, and at the same time also making cease, *making an end*. Even conserving includes the negative aspect that something is taken out of its immediacy...to be preserved —Thus what is *aufgehoben* is at the same time conserved and has merely lost its immediacy but is not for that reason annihilated.[3]

Without entering into the many interpretative and substantive puzzles presented to the reader by Hegel's philosophy or the large secondary literature regarding Hegel's conception of the dialectical or sublimation process, these passages will suffice for our specific purpose of illuminating one aspect of the nature of transindustrial society and its relation to its immediate predecessor: advanced industrial society.

Using Hegel's analysis of *aufheben* or sublimation, I envision a sequence whereby advanced industrial civilization, its values and social structure are *both* "canceled" and "preserved" in the Hegelian sense of this central concept to his philosophy. This entails "not being cancelled altogether but lifted up to be kept on a different level" (to quote Kaufmann's interpretation), or preserved within a different form, sublimated, "but not for that reason annihilated" (to quote Hegel); or, "picked up in order that it will no longer be there just the way it was"; it is transformed.

To my mind, transindustrial society will "still [be] characterized [in part] by the determinateness from which it comes"—advanced industrial society—even though the latter is *aufgehoben* or sublimated. In this conception of the transformation of industrial society relying upon Hegel's analysis of the sublimation process, the postindustrial social order is both ended *and* preserved, transformed through sublimation; in this case, as a result of the revolutionary and politicizing process associated with the recognition of the limits to economic growth and the appreciation of their social consequences for industrialism.

An illustration from the world of mathematics is useful here in an attempt to clarify this point further. Consider the mathematical variable symbolized by the letter a and its relation to the product of the multiplication process: (a) $\times$ (a) or a^2; a is "included" within the product a^2 or preserved but is has clearly ended its initial identity—although "not cancelled altogether." Similarly, I conceive of transindustrial society essentially ending or canceling objectionable aspects of the industrial values—some of which have been discussed in this volume: limitless economic growth, materialism, and competitiveness—its worldview and derivative social institutions, while at the same time preserving the spirit of scientific inquiry, knowledge, technological applications, and some other values associated with postindustrial civilization. In brief, the sublimation of these industrial characteristics to "a different level" will occur achieving a normatively higher—more desirable—ecologically sustainable level within a new social order embodying more rationally preferable core values and social life.

It is crucial that the limits-to-growth critique of postindustrial civilization not be dismissed as some contemporary version of the nineteenth century Luddite attack against that quintessential component of early industrial society: its use of the machine to replace human labor. I do not commend transindustrial society or the transformation of postindustrial society so that we (in the postindustrialized world) may retreat to a bygone agrarian, preindustrial era. One critic of the new, anti-industrial social movements formulated his attack on such alleged antediluvian aims as follows: "the *petit bourgeois* (members of the new social movements]...seeks the new society in the past: in a mythical and mystical past, the reestablishment of which is intended to prevent the impending downgrading."[4] I disagree with this description of the new social movements and certainly deny that this characterization applies to my own concept of the transindustrial replacement of industrial society. My view definitely does not include "seek[ing] the new society in the past" for the following reasons.

First, there are aspects of preindustrial life sometimes romanticized by critics of industrial civilization—and regarding *such* romanticizations the words "mythical" and "mystical" may be justified—that are themselves unacceptable. The many undesirable elements of preindustrial life in England, lest glorification of this social order by sought as a remedy for the ills of contemporary industrial society, must be considered. In an historical discussion, an author wishes to convey to his readers in the late twentieth century the miseries of the "lost" world as compared to the industrial one with regard to family, working conditions, social relations among rigidly hierarchical classes, and individual and public health in preindustrial England. His findings are startling to any critic of advanced industrial society—flawed as the latter is—who might seek a replacement for it in preindustrial life:

> The world we have lost, as I have chosen to call it, was no paradise or golden age of equality, tolerance or loving kindness...the coming of industry cannot be shown to have brought economic oppression and exploitation along with it. It was there already.[5]

One datum to fill out this grim picture of preindustrial English life may be used as illustration of his supporting evidence (as if current post-industrial observers of life in poor, preindustrial, Third and Fourth World nations should require more evidence):

It will be obvious by now how crucial expectation of life turns out to be when comparing our own everyday experience with that of our [preindustrial] ancestors...Life expectancy at birth in seventeenth century England seems to have been in the low thirties[!]....[6]

Second, even if the description of life in preindustrial English society provided here were not so negative, and even if such a view of preindustrial life were contested and judged on the whole to be desirable despite the social problems delineated, reconstructing the preindustrial, agrarian social order is not a realistic possibility for a global population of over five billion people and increasing all the time. Merely providing the basic material necessities of life for such a huge aggregation of humanity will require all the scientific knowledge and technological means that advanced industrial researchers and technicians can muster.

It would be cruelly misguided to prescribe to the advanced industrial nations of the world—currently the materially richest (in the aggregate)—to decrease their production levels of goods and return to a simple (and materially impoverished), preindustrial way of life. Such a policy would be a death sentence for hundreds of millions (if not billions) of people dependent upon advanced industrial material productivity. Thus, in spite of my favorable references to the ancient Greek *polis* and some of its admirable value traits, especially the primacy accorded politics and public life, do not misconstrue my remarks to imply that we in the advanced industrial world could—or should, even if possible—go back to some antiquated preindustrial utopia.

The enormous challenge confronting the citizens of advanced industrial society is to accomplish the sublimation of their culture; to have their social order *das Aufgehoben* in the Hegelian sense of preserving some of its traits, like aggregate material productivity, while ending or canceling its deleterious normative foundations. This can be accomplished, it seems to me, by replacing such industrial values as unlimited economic growth and competitive, materialist-based social esteem with (not necessarily completely new) more acceptable values utilizing industrialism's productivity to greater human benefit by avoiding self-destruction and the social ills of industrial civilization.

The possibility exists, I believe, in a transindustrial social order to create much more leisure time for the stimulation, development, and realization of nonmaterial social values higher than the industrial ones, such as the aesthetic pleasures derived from "walks in the snowy forest." Nonmaterialist transindustrial society could also, for example, ease the presently immeasurable harm and alienation of preindustrial labor by switching to such a transindustrial value and social structure as a genuinely participatory democratic community which encompassed democratic organization in the workplace as well.

Humanity needs more, not less, technological creativity and advancement to eradicate the old and new scourges of mankind, like cancer and AIDS. We must also introduce the benefits of a materially satisfied life to those who have yet to have their basic needs met by the material fruitfulness of industrialization. Like the authors of the first Club of Rome report, I have recognized throughout this discussion the urgent requirement for economic growth in the destitute areas of the world where such growth is essential to the satisfaction of survival needs; it is a prerequisite to the spread of transindustrial society worldwide beyond the few currently advanced industrial societies. Simple justice, globally applied, requires it.

The alternative transindustrial values cannot be comprehensively delineated here but should, I think, be considered briefly. They will reflect the general thrust of my argument for the transformation of industrial values after the deficiencies of the dominant ones are recognized, our industrial fantasies are eradicated, and the social despair associated with our mourning for them—the industrial civilizational crisis—are over.

Inglehart attempts to support empirically the proposition that "the evidence indicates that PostMaterialism is a deep-rooted phenomenon. Despite the recession of recent years, it not only persisted but increased its penetration of older groups."[7]

In the same article he defines the following as postmaterialist goals, or what I would call "transindustrial values": "more say on job;" "less impersonal society;" "more say in government;" "society where ideas count;" "more beautiful cities;" and, "freedom of expression."[8] These survey questionnaire options do reflect the transindustrial values that I have focussed upon: workplace democracy, community, and a more fulfilling and free life for all. Examples of postmaterialist or transindustrial movements according to Inglehart are the women's movement, the consumer advocacy movement, the environmental movement, and the antinuclear movement.[9]

At this point, let us anticipate some of the later discussion about the possible significant role of the new social movements within advanced industrial societies in achieving the latter's transformation. Because I think their members' understanding and recognition of the urgency for alternative values and social structure to the dominant postindustrial ones is the most comprehensive, I would like to introduce the Greens' conception of transformational values as suggestive for transindustrial civilization.

The Green, anti-industrial paradigm, labelled "the politics of ecology" by one British Green party leader, provides a detailed source for transindustrial values in contrast to industrial ones. He realizes that what is involved in the difference between these values is no less than the differences between two complete worldviews or social paradigms. Consider the following contrasts between the values of industrialism and ecology or transindustrialism:

The politics of industrialism	The politics of ecology
An ethos of aggressive individualism	A co-operatively based, communitarian society
Materialism, pure and simple	A move towards spiritual non-material values
Anthropocentism	Biocentrism
Patriarchical values	Post-patriarchal, feminist values
Economic growth and GNP	Sustainability and quality of life
High income differentials	Low income differentials
Demand stimulation	Voluntary simplicity
Employment as a means to an end	Work as an end in itself
Hierarchical structure	Non-hierarchical structure
Dependence upon experts	Participative involvement
Representative democracy	Direct democracy
Sovereignty of nation-state	Internationalism and global solidarity
Environment managed as a resource	Resources regarded as strictly finite[10]

While a full discussion of each of these important normative conflicts between industrial and transindustrial values would be beyond the scope of this chapter, I hope that this list will help stimulate both normative political theorists and political scientists, and provoke the postindustrial public to pursue more deeply the many issues raised by such a transindustrial value scheme: building cooperative communities to achieving spirituality; shifting to a biocentric view wherein all life is considered valuable with no inherent superiority given to the human species; realizing sexual equality; accomplishing economic equality and providing self-fulfilling work to all; establishing a participatory democracy; and realizing global solidarity and justice. Finally, we must recognize the trait that inspired the whole trans-industrial vision and movement for social change: the limited nature of the earth's resources and the human condition, and create a new social order consistent with these limits.

In addition to the British Green party, the American Greens should be mentioned. The American confederation of local Green groups, known as The Committees of Correspondence—a name taken from the grass roots political organization during the American Revolution—offers the following "Ten Key Values," which constitute the criteria for membership.[11] It is important to note, especially for the industrial convergence thesis discussed earlier, that these values are considered by the American Greens as "not being addressed adequately by the political left or right." The Green movement's "plague on both your houses" approach throughout the world is symbolized by their slogan that Green politics is "a politics that is neither left or right, but in front."[12]

The Greens' "Ten Key Values" are: "ecological wisdom; grass roots democracy; personal and social responsibility; nonviolence; decentraliza-tion; community-based economics; postpatriarchal values; respect for diver-sity; global responsibility; and, future focus."[13] Each of these values is followed by a series of questions to further delineate what is intended and to indicate briefly the possible extensions and applications of these ideas. One example will suffice as an illustration of this document. Regarding "ecologi-cal wisdom," the American Greens ask:

How can we operate human societies with the understanding that we are part of nature, not on top of it? How can we live within the eco-logical and resource limits of the planet, applying our technological knowledge to the challenge of an energy-efficient economy? How can we build a better relationship between cities and countryside? How can we guarantee the rights of nonhuman species? How can we pro-mote sustainable agriculture and respect for self-regulating natural systems? How can we further biocentric wisdom in all spheres of life?[14]

Merely to continue listing the possible alternative values in a trans-industrial social order will not be productive and the ones already men-tioned in previous discussion are sufficiently suggestive for the reader to obtain an idea of some of these transindustrial values as an outline of a social order built upon them. It seems that the (usually implied) values of the limits-to-growth critics of industrialism and the values of these explicit advocates of alternative, transindustrial, social paradigms, and values over-lap considerably. This is just as one would expect based on the industrial values under attack by their critics and their normative opposites: unlimited economic growth and unlimited competitive materialism. We should observe that all anti-industrial theorists usually share a recognition of the false and undesirable nature of preindustrial promises: impossible, limitless, material accumulation and self-contradictory, competitive, success for all.

It is important to note in considering this inventory of transindustrial values that postmaterialists' values, or the Greens' basic values of "ecology, social responsibility, grass roots democracy and nonviolence,"[15] or what I have intended to convey by the title of this part contain the same central thrust: all aim to transform the current preindustrial worldview and institutions to create a new, more sustainable, and humanly fulfilling civilization. This transformation will ensure, following Schumacher's subtitle, that "people mattered;" or to refer to the British Greens' manifesto: "Politics for life;"[16] or my emphasis here: "politics as a way of life and self-development," in addition to a deep respect for nonhuman nature and the ecological interdependence of all life on earth. When I refer in the subtitle of this volume to "the repoliticization of advanced industrial society" it is this kind of politics that I have in mind.

I conclude this presentation of transindustrial values by quoting the European Greens' motto: "Europe will be Green or not at all"[17] and rephrasing it as: "Human civilization will be Green—or transindustrial—or not at all!"

One illustration may help to clarify the transcendental nature of the transindustrial society and its values. The limits-to-growth theorists' advocacy of alternative transindustrial values does appear to form a consensus. This normative agreement includes emphasis upon the creation of a genuine democracy whereby all adult citizens are to have the opportunity to participate fully in their society's public decisionmaking process. This participation is considered a vital component to the establishment of an ecologically sustainable and desirable transindustrial social order.

But this democratic aspect of the transindustrial value scheme as well as several others within it, including cooperative communities, economic equality, self-fulfilling work and international justice may seem vulnerable to the same charge that limits-to-growth advocates make of industrialism: illusory or impossible goals. For example, regarding participatory democracy, progrowth—usually elitist—defenders of the present postindustrial hegemony routinely denigrate the recommendation of participatory democracy for large advanced industrial societies as "unrealistic," or exemplifying the "fictitious communality" of the "mythical and mystical" past. I am sure that a similar charge of unrealizability would be made by these progrowth defenders of the status quo to other transindustrial values.

Here I disagree, and my reasons may illuminate some earlier points about the transcendental nature—in the Hegelian sense of sublimation—of the transindustrial worldview and social structure. This culture need *not* invoke some utopian, preindustrial character full of illusory and impossible, if not downright undesirable, values; rather, it can become a genuine, trans-industrial society utilizing the material accomplishments of its predecessor. For example, technological innovations already accomplished in advanced industrial societies and those projected for the foreseeable future provide the technical means for mass communications (even two-way) among a population as large as the United States. This effectively challenges the usual complaint that mass participatory democracy is practically impossible. There is an expanding literature on "teledemocracy" (or "video democracy"), explaining how through the use of cable television technology, once insurmountable obstacles to communication necessary for discussion and debate in the collective decisionmaking process may indeed be overcome.[18] The *existing* Warner-Amex CUBE System used in Columbus, Ohio, the two-way video communications network established in Reading, Pennsylvania, and videotext service[19] all demonstrate the means for large-scale political participation in a way not dreamt of by the opponents—or proponents, for that matter—of participatory democracy.

With current technology (computers, fax machines, etc.) and the technology yet to come, communications, town meetings, public discussion, and collective decisionmaking could all become feasible across thousands of miles and between millions of people. The capability and potential of world-wide communications was demonstrated by the 1985 "Live Aid" rock concert that was reportedly viewed by an estimated audience of two billion people across the entire globe. Why not utilize such technological improvements in communications to realize old democratic values thought to be unrealizable and thus purely utopian! If one of the central values of trans-industrial society—participatory democracy—is to be achieved in the current world of over five billion people, recognition of the contribution of science and technology will be imperative—but, of course, this alone will not be sufficient. Improvement in other areas such as good education and material needs of life being met would be needed as well. As I have tried to show throughout this part, transcending postindustrial society means rejecting some of its attributes while preserving others.

There should be no apology for the apparent lack of truly novel values among those mentioned as transindustrial social values. We cannot return to the social structure of past preindustrial societies on the global level, nor should we desire to. Nonetheless, the normative insights and experience of earlier societies can provide a rich source of values and suggestions for institutions in a transindustrial culture to come. One Green party leader hits this profound point squarely: "The more I find out about ecology, the more I realize that there is nothing new in what we are saying. Green politics today is the rediscovery of old wisdom made relevant in a very different age."[20]

Similarly, I modelled my prescription for the repoliticization of a transindustrial civilization after the Greek *polis*, implemented in a fundamentally different social setting, utilizing available advanced industrial technology. Throughout the history of social thought, nonmaterial values and human needs were applicable and possibly even present, but precious few individuals could rise above the preoccupations of materialist, biophysical survival to realize them. I reiterate that we should not define the challenge confronting humanity during the current crisis of industrial civilization as involving the creation of completely new values and institutions. Rather, I think we should recognize the wisdom of some of the old values and define the present task facing mankind to be one of accomplishing such goals as: "cooperatively based, communitarian society"; "direct democracy"; "a move towards more spiritual nonmaterial values"; and "voluntary simplicity."

Claus Offe, a contemporary social theorist, also perceives this point about the lack of novelty in the transindustrial social movements' values. However, he goes further than I would allow by claiming that:

> *All* these values and moral norms advocated by the proponents of the new political paradigm [my transindustrialism] are firmly rooted in *modern* political philosophies (as well as aesthetic theories) of the last two centuries, and they are inherited from the progressive movements of both the bourgeoisie and the ruling class.[21]

He concludes that because of their values shared with modernity, the new social movements' normative orientation is neither "postmodern" nor "premodern."

> The values advocated and defended by the new social movements [Offe asserts] are not "new" but part and parcel of the repertory of dominant modern culture, which obviously would make it difficult to think of [these] movements as flowing from either "premodern," or, for that matter, "postmodern" subcultures.[22]

I hope that the ways in which my view differs from Offe's analysis here are clear. In contradistinction to Offe, I believe that there are strong, antimodern values inherent within the limits-to-growth critique of postindustrialism and its associated new social movements like the Greens or the many worldwide environmentalist groups. These include the ones discussed in this volume: respect for nature and the limits presented by finite nature and humanity; an antigrowth-based, rejection of the modern denial of limits; anti-individualism; anticompetitiveness; and, antimaterialism. In short, I have argued that transindustrialism's anti-Hobbesian, antiliberal values are really antimodern at their core. Furthermore, the ancient veneration of political life and criticism of excessive materialism and individualism, so important to the transindustrial social order, are not consistent with modern social life or modern economic and political thought as we have seen.

While I, too, do not believe that the transindustrial society must have *all* new values—there are enough unrealized old ones that, if adopted and fulfilled, would dramatically improve the quality of life for transindustrial citizens—I cannot agree with Offe's characterization of the new social movements. I consider the overwhelming number of them to be social organizations for radical change of the present postindustrial paradigm and society toward a limits-accepting, transindustrial society. Even groups that appear not to be so characterized may actually imply such change, but because their members have failed to examine both their own normative foundations and industrialism's, they have overlooked their own political thrust.

It is important to realize that designing a new civilization need not involve starting from scratch with regard to values. Most likely, the creativity required by such a huge task will lie in the implementation of old values through a specific institutional structure and public policies within the contemporary advanced industrial social setting. I would argue, in opposition to Offe's view, that transindustrial social movements are not really modern nor are they completely antimodern. As Ely concludes, they present "neither antimodern or modern values" but "an alternative modernity outside the terms in which . . . modernization have been formed and conceived."[23]

Transindustrial groups, in my view, should be demanding a sublimated modernity wherein some elements of modern social structure (such as science and technology) and some modern values (such as respect for tolerance and individual autonomy) are retained; *in this latter sense, and in this sense only,* transindustrial society is modern or "preserved" in Hegelian language. However, these modern aspects will exist within a distinctively antimodern civilization wherein such fundamental modern values as unlimited economic growth are "cancelled." Perhaps this is what Ely means by an "alternative modernity"?

I want to emphasize that the transformation of industrial society into what I have termed a transindustrial one is both antimodern *and* modern; we transcend modernity in the Hegelian sense of sublimation—to cancel and preserve on a different level. To quote two old adages: let us not throw out the wheat with the chaff, or the baby with the bathwater!

The New Social Movements and Industrial Transformation— A Beginning Not an Ending

It has been previously noted that one typical element within the limits-to-growth position consisted of calls by the critics of industrial civilization for an alternate social vision to correct the erroneous and dangerous paradigm and social order. For example, the president of the Club of Rome, Aurelio Peccei, wrote in the early 1980s about the upcoming "decisive decade" and appealed for "the human revolution" to conclude an analysis of the possible catastrophes facing humanity unless the industrial perspective is replaced.[24] This necessary revolution, according to Peccei, would entail:

> *A basically new way of thinking*...it must encourage the rise of new value systems to redress our inner balance, and of new spiritual, ethical, philosophical, social, political, esthetic, and artistic motivations to fill the emptiness of our life; it must be capable of restoring within us—as our most precious possession and need—love, friendship, understanding, solidarity, a spirit of sacrifice, conviviality....[25]

This retrospective volume by one of the Club of Rome's leading thinkers about the work and internationally influential publications of this organization which made the limits-to-growth argument famous, provides an illustration of both the strengths and weaknesses of its limits-to-growth position. Sharp, ecologically based attacks were levelled against industrial civilization and its worldview, with the accompanying projected threats of mankind's self-destruction requiring a transformation in industrial thinking and social structure. However, as I have tried to show, this important literature is itself characterized by deficiencies including the absence-of-means fallacy. One instance of this unfortunate weakness typical of the entire limits-to-growth writings is remarkable only for its explicit formulations: after claiming the need for a "profound change in values," the limits-to-growth advocate writes:

> It is not for this book to advise people, once they have seen the hazard of continuing the course we have been following, how they should reflect their new realization in their personal actions, or how they should go about changing the policies that currently dominate and direct our society.[26]

One major goal of my work is to correct this serious political omission by provoking political theorists who up to now have been largely absent from the limits-to-growth controversy to recognize the profound political questions raised by the limits to economic growth as a critique of industrial society. Now that we are at the end of Peccei's "decisive decade" of the 1980s, have begun the 1990s, and are quickly approaching the end of the millennium, we must, I contend, go beyond the well-intentioned, often admirable, but politically naive pleas for visions of a new, anti-industrial society appearing in the last chapters of limits-to-growth analyses. Political theorists as well as other students of societal change, postindustrial policy makers, and the public must now address the controversial issue of the prescribed transformation of industrial civilization and begin to prove that the entreaties for social revolution by limits-to-growth theorists are not merely pure rhetoric or utopian musings to be confined to the narrow academic realm, devoid of practical significance.

In my discussion, I have examined the limits-to-growth genre: mostly ecological diagnoses, full of threatened disasters followed by vague remedies with little or no discussion at all of how the imperative social changes are to be realized. I recommend extending the breadth of the limits-to-growth position by emphasizing the first importance of the normative political foundations of industrial civilization, what is wrong with its basic values, and what alternative values should be substituted. Errors of omission within the limits-to-growth literature have worked against its effectiveness as a source for transforming industrial society. Its contributors have concentrated too much on environmental criticism of industrialism and have neglected the nature of the next transindustrial civilization and the means to its establishment.

Regarding the shortcomings of the limits-to-growth advocates, a political scientist writing about the apocalyptic visions of nuclear holocaust and ecocatastrophe in contemporary science fiction concludes his discussion with a statement that I think is significant to the assessment of the limits-to-growth position and the challenge it presents to advanced industrial society: "I believe that too often the various contemporary ecological and peace movements have grounded their public appeals on platforms of hopelessness."[27] He goes on to describe his own involvement in the peace movement and to characterize its visions of disaster which, I suggest, can be compared to the limits-to-growth doom and gloom analyses:

These megadeath scenarios may have brought some concrete understanding to the experience of nuclear war in the late twentieth century. But, in and of themselves, they have also tended to produce a psychologically numbing and politically immobilizing effect upon many in the audience...negative critique is not enough.

The first step beyond this sense of despair and hopelessness is to carry the critique [of] the harm and threat of nuclear war to its political foundations and encourage people to "reflect on how that danger is inseparable from the deep structure of politics in American society."[28]

In an essential sense, these remarks also illustrate one of the main themes of this book when applied to the current postindustrial crisis and the limits-to-growth analysis of it. In my presentation of the "death of industrial civilization" I have attempted to understand the nature of the threats produced by the industrial social value of unlimited economic growth. I am aware, as this author observed about the peace movement, of the "psychologically numbing and politically immobilizing effect" of much of the limits-to-growth "doomsday" critique of industrial society. Therefore, it must be accompanied by some positive and realizable recommendations of what to do to avoid the impending disaster. This is why the profoundest importance ought to be accorded the political foundations of these threats and the political nature of their dissolution. I have attempted to demonstrate this point by showing that the threats to industrial civilization have connections with the "deep political structure," not in American capitalist politics or growth-based, socialist societies alone, but within broader—and deeper—industrial politics itself.

The question of how the transindustrial social order is to be created is inherent in this carrying the limits-to-growth critique of industrialism to its political foundations and deep structure. In this part, I began a sketch of the kind of normative bases an alternative, sublimated industrial or transindustrial society should possess. Before I conclude this discussion, the possibilities of this transindustrial society becoming a reality must be considered. In short, can advanced industrial society really be transformed?

I have dutifully enumerated the many powerful sources of pessimism for such an imposing political project. Nonetheless, I wish to avoid giving an excessively negative impression that will engender only total political despair and fatalistic escapism, prolonging the deadly industrial social values, institutions, and mode of thinking. Let us ask at this point: What transformational forces exist *currently* to counteract the powerful conservative ones?

The recognition of the death of our industrial fantasies including unlimited economic growth is, first of all, enlightening. Second, no matter how painful such recognition might be, it is only at times of crisis that transformation, both personal and social, is possible. With recognition comes opportunity, albeit dangerous—as the Chinese and Slater realize.

I have emphasized the role of the worldwide social movements in transforming advanced industrial society.[29] Their creation and expansion, and the goals of those founding and joining them, provide substantial grounds for optimism, I believe, regarding the effort to transform industrial civilization to a desirable social order which is sustainable and recognizes limits. I have made reference to such varied sources of encouragement for industrial transformation as: the increased vote for the German Greens in the 1987 elections and for Green parties throughout Europe in the 1989 European parliamentary election; Inglehart's empirical research showing that a postmaterialist "silent [value] revolution"—not surprisingly "silent" given the little prominence accorded it by the growth-based industrial media of communication—has occurred and, perhaps more importantly, continues to increase in supporters despite inhospitable economic and electoral developments; Milbrath's latest data showing membership in environmental groups of between fifteen and thirty million Americans with between 400,000 and 500,000 people active as environmentalists plus worldwide support for environmentalism;[30] further survey data supporting the adoption of transindustrial values by a significant portion of the advanced industrial population, as represented by America;[31] and the high public visibility of serious environmental threats during the extraordinary summer of 1988 in the United States.

A staunch progrowth defender of industrial values would probably object here that such indications of the beginnings of a possible transformation of industrial society are, even if observable in the late 1980s, outdated in light of events following the apparent peak of public interest in the limits to growth in the 1970s. This objector might continue by indicating a rejection of the limits-to-growth literature's central thrust and implied call for revolutionary change by posing the following challenge: "Look at the stunning election victories of Reagan (and in 1988 of his vice-president, George Bush), and Thatcher (including her unprecedented third straight victory in 1987); the obvious materialism and self-preoccupation symbolized by Yuppies; and the "greed is in" era. Do not these all indicate the defeat of any transformational movement by the massive return of industrial citizens to the industrial, competitive, materialist, progrowth worldview?" This hypothetical critic might add: "Is not Jimmy Carter's 1979 'malaise' speech now viewed as part of the mistaken negativism of an administration that was fundamentally inadequate—as indicated by the successful attack by its progrowth opponent in the electoral debacle of 1980—and whose deficiencies were corrected by the extreme growth-dominated policies of the Reagan administration? Furthermore, does not the sharp decline in the price of petroleum, plus the apparent loss of power and disunity of OPEC, in addition to the oil glut of the 1980s, all demonstrate that the limits-to-growth critique was a faulty analysis just like its doomsday predecessors?" I could invent more progrowth challenges but will stop here because I think that the nature of the challenges would not differ in their essence: the illustrations would change but not the basic support for the industrial value of limitless economic growth.

In reply to the charge of obsoletism, I refer to the annual reports published by the Worldwatch Institute on *The State of the World*. Begun in 1984, they show that the threats of ecological catastrophe first projected by the Club of Rome reports are still valid in all too many areas of population, resources, and the environment. Clearly, ecological dangers are increasing, and new ones such as the depletion of the stratospheric ozone are being discovered. The strong interest shown in these annual reports—as reflected in sales and excerpts in the scholarly literature and popular press—do show the *increasing* public and scholarly concern about biophysical limits to growth denied by progrowth critics. Consider also the spate of articles and television broadcasts on ocean pollution, global warming, the garbage removal crisis and antigrowth movements in California (now spread to other Western cities), all in 1988.[32]

Reinforcing the political impact of these developments, President Bush has emphasized environmental problems, proposing policy correctives and declaring himself "an environmentalist" during the presidential campaign of 1988. He has even gone beyond mere rhetoric with his Clean Air Act reform proposed in the spring of 1989.

Everyday we approach and begin to transgress environmental and human limits in "noise, air pollution, water pollution, over population, solid waste disposal, toxic wastes, nuclear waste, destruction of land and townscapes, depletion of natural resources [and] energy."[33] As these negative consequences become inescapable, spreading Wildean tragedy, Hirschean frustration, and Hirschmanean disappointment, citizens in advanced industrial societies will increasingly sense the need for social transformation. We will seek organizational expressions of our concern and discontent as well as ways of social remediation through revolutionary change. If anyone doubts the possibility of basic change occurring within advanced industrial nations or the relative speed of the social reaction caused by a serious threat to their social order's quality of life, consider the AIDS crisis and the breadth, speed, and depth of both public and elite responses. Basic value, behavioral, and public policy changes have already occurred and are projected to occur within a few short years!

Miles ends his book on the social and political limits to growth (essentially administrative issues of managing a complex advanced industrial society) with the following assertion: "What Americans need is not a blueprint for survival, but a profound change in values and a compass that will take them in a new direction."[34] Mishan echoes these transformational sentiments when he says that

some readers may complain of a lack of detailed proposals, or, worse, a lack of politically practicable proposals. But, at a time when the decencies of civilized living are daily beset by the exigencies of rapid material development, detailed proposals are secondary to what I deem to be the main task: that of convincing people of the need of radical changes in our habitual ways of looking at economic events.[35]

While I would expand Miles's statement to include all advanced industrial citizens, and broaden Mishan's to include radical change in more than just economic events, I agree with the basic point of both passages: at the heart of the industrial crisis lie the basic values of industrial civilization; we cannot save ourselves or our planet unless we transform these industrial values. Like Miles and Mishan, I have not produced a "blueprint" or specific political program of institutional or policy change. To do so would be premature since these questions, as important as they are, are derived from value judgments; the values that our institutions are intended to advance must be decided first. Each transindustrial community must form and decide such issues democratically for itself, hopefully following the transindustrial values presented here.

We must go beyond the recognition of the limits to growth and the concomitant need for a global steady-state with regard to economic growth and material wealth, and begin to emphasize growth in noneconomic, nonmaterial realms. We need a transindustrial society where the quest for material things and materially-indicative, competitive status is replaced by an environmentally sound, cooperative, self-fulfilling, self-developing democratic values for all.

In this book I have tried to suggest some answers to two crucial questions: What values should replace industrial civilization's primary goal of unlimited economic growth? How do we implement our ideas about what transindustrial humanity should value to achieve the transformation of postindustrial society?

First, I have intended to provoke political philosophers to take up these questions aided with greater appreciation of the political significance of the limits-to-growth controversy so that the assertion that we are "working a revolution with little guidance from political philosophers"[36] will no longer be true. Milbrath takes up this challenge in his 1989 publication and I, too, have tried to make some contribution to this effort. Second, I have sought to awaken the public and policy makers to the need for a radical change in our industrial worldview involving the way we define our life goals, social life, relationships to others, and the roles of competition and cooperation. Third, I have attempted to demonstrate the nature and importance of politics to human satisfaction and development in an effort to overcome the reductionism and attempted suppression of politics in our society.

I cannot resolve completely the complex and wide-ranging life-and-death issues raised by the limits-to-growth critique of industrial civilization. Even if this book were successful in achieving its goal of inspiring fellow political philosophers to apply their analytical skills and tradition of thought to these questions, we are not likely to complete such a large task alone. The nature of such questions is vast; it pertains to the character of humanity and the fabric of social life. The questions have existed since Western civilization began. They require the best minds of our entire culture to address them.

The fundamental issues raised by the limits-to-growth controversy, the ensuing critique of industrialism, and prescriptions for its transindustrial replacement, and, indeed, the entire history of political philosophy with its "perennial questions,"[37] remind me of the words of a sage. In reference to studying the sacred Jewish text, the Torah, Rabbi Tarfon is reported to have said:

"it is not your part to finish the task;
yet neither are you free to desist from it."[38]

Preceding this quoted remark is another, with which I conclude:

"Rabbi Tarfon said: The day [life] is short; the task is great; the workmen [human beings] are lazy; the reward is great, and the Master is insistent."[39]

Life is, indeed, short, and the task facing postindustrial citizens is, in fact, great. Human beings are, indeed, lazy: we succumb easily to inertia, we fear change, and the pain and insecurity it brings. Furthermore, we are reluctant to challenge the dominant worldview and social structure of our existing social order. Our goals are difficult to formulate and intimidating to achieve. However, if enlightened postindustrial citizens can overcome these obstacles and meet these demanding tasks, the reward of a sustainable, just and humane world is also great. For Rabbi Tarfon, the Master was insistent. For us, the urgent, limits-to-growth issues confronting contemporary humanity are no less compelling.

Notes

Chapter 1

1. *Earthwalk* (Garden City, N.Y.: Anchor Books, 1974), p. 44.

2. *The Economic Growth Debate: An Assessment* (London: George Allen and Unwin, 1977), pp. 266–267.

3. Quoted in: Robert Byrne, *The 637 Best Things Anybody Ever Said* (New York: Atheneum, 1982), p. 79, #386.

4. "The Limits to Economic Growth: Politicizing Advanced Industrialized Society." *Philosophy and Social Criticism* 8 (Spring 1981), p. 89.

5. The following is a mere sample list of such works beginning with the famous, first Club of Rome report: Donella H. Meadows, Dennis L. Meadows, Jorgen Randers, and William W. Behrens III, *The Limits to Growth: A Report to the Club of Rome's Project on the Predicament of Mankind*, 2nd ed. (New York: New American Library, 1975), from which this literature takes its name. This volume was followed by subsequent reports including: Mihajlo Mesarovic and Eduard Pestel, *Mankind at the Turning Point: The Second Report to the Club of Rome* (New York: E. P. Dutton, 1974); Jan Tinbergen, coord., *Rio: Reshaping the International Order: A Report to the Club of Rome* (New York: New American Library, 1976).

These three reports to the international group of academic and business people known as the Club of Rome, and the great popular and scholarly reaction to the first report, may be considered the catalysts to the limits-to-growth and industrial-crisis literature.

Other notable contributors to this voluminous literature are: Robert L. Heilbroner, *An Inquiry into the Human Prospect* (New York: W. W. Norton, 1975); Robert L. Heilbroner, *Business Civilization in Decline* (New York: W. W. Norton, 1976); E. F. Schumacher, *Small is Beautiful: Economics as if People Mattered* (New York: Harper and Row, 1975); Edward Goldsmith, Robert Allen, Michael Allaby, John Davoll, and Sam Lawrence, *Blueprint for Survival* (New York: New American Library, 1972); Paul R. Ehrlich and Anne H. Ehrlich, *The End of Affluence: A Blueprint for Your Future* (New York: Ballantine Books, 1974); Alvin Toffler, *The Eco-Spasm Report* (New York: Bantam Books, 1975); Lewis Mumford, *The Myth of the Machine*, 2 vols. (New York: Harcourt, Brace Jovanovich, 1967, 1970); Rufus E. Miles, Jr., *Awakening from the American Dream: The Social and Political Limits to Growth* (New York: Universe Books, 1976); William Ophuls, *Ecology and the Politics of Scarcity: A Prologue to a Political Theory of the Steady State* (San Francisco: W. H. Freeman, 1977); Fred Hirsch, *Social Limits to Growth* (Cambridge:

Harvard University Press, 1976); Murray Bookchin, *Toward an Ecological Society* (Montreal: Black Rose Books, 1980); Murray Bookchin, *The Modern Crisis* (Philadelphia: New Society Publishers, 1986); Dennis C. Pirages and Paul R. Ehrlich, *Ark II: Social Response to Environmental Imperatives* (San Francisco: W. H. Freeman, 1974); Lester R. Brown, *The Twenty-Ninth Day: Accommodating Human Needs and Numbers to the Earth's Resources* (New York: W. W. Norton, 1978); W. Jackson Davis, *The Seventh Year: Industrial Civilization in Transition* (New York: W. W. Norton, 1979); Joseph A. Camilleri, *Civilization in Crisis: Human Prospects in a Changing World* (Cambridge: Cambridge University Press, 1976); William R. Catton, Jr., *Overshoot: The Ecological Basis of Revolutionary Change* (Urbana: University of Illinois Press, 1982); Herman E. Daly, *Steady-State Economics: The Economics of Biophysical Equilibrium and Moral Growth* (San Francisco: W. H. Freeman, 1977); Herman E. Daly, ed., *Toward a Steady-State Economy* (San Francisco: W. H. Freeman, 1973); Gerald O. Barney, study director, *The Global 2000* Report to the President: Entering the Twenty-First Century (Charlottesville: Blue Angel, 1981); and, finally, for the best and most comprehensive presentation of the ecological issues, see Paul R. Ehrlich, Anne H. Ehrlich, and John P. Holdren, *Ecoscience: Population, Resources, Environment* (San Francisco: W. H. Freeman, 1977).

To update the Ehrlich, Ehrlich, and Holdren volume with current ecological developments and data, I recommend: Charles H. Southwick, ed., *Global Ecology* (Sunderland, Mass.: Sinauer Associates, 1985); Jessica Tuchman Mathews, Project Director, *World Resources 1986*, A Report by The World Resources Institute and The International Institute for Environment and Development (New York: Basic Books, 1986), as well as its *World Resources 1988–1989* edition, directed by J. Alan Brewster (New York: Basic Books, 1988); *Our Common Future* by The United Nations' Appointed World Commission on Environment and Development (Oxford: Oxford University Press, 1987); and, finally, the continuing series of annual reports begun in 1984 by the Worldwatch Institute, written by Lester R. Brown and his colleagues at The Worldwatch Institute, published by W. W. Norton, entitled: *State of the World*, with changing topics each year. For the latest report see, Lester R. Brown et al., *State of the World 1989: A Worldwatch Institute Report on Progress Toward a Sustainable Society* (New York: W. W. Norton, 1989).

Mention should also be made of a companion volume in this State University of New York Press Series in Environmental Public Policy: Lester W. Milbrath, *Envisioning a Sustainable Society: Learning Our Way Out* (Albany: State University of New York Press, 1989). Unfortunately, this volume became available after my own discussion was completed; hence, I was able only to refer to it briefly.

To appreciate the profound effect the recent ecological awareness—since the 1970s—has had upon the industrial-crisis literature, contrast the foregoing volumes with, Norman Birnbaum, *The Crisis of Industrial Society* (New York: Oxford University Press, 1969), where ecological concerns are totally absent.

    6. Some leading critics of the limits-to-growth, industrial-crisis position are: B. Bruce-Biggs, "Against the Neo-Malthusians," *Commentary* (July 1974), pp. 25–29; Rudolph Klein, "Growth and Its Enemies," *Commentary* (June 1972), pp. 37–44; H. S. D. Cole, Christopher Freeman, Marie Jahoda and K. L. R. Pavitt, *Models*

of Doom: A Critique of the Limits of Growth (New York: Universe Books, 1975); John Maddox, The Doomsday Syndrome (London: Macmillan, 1972); Peter Passell and Leonard Ross, The Retreat from Riches: Affluence and its Enemies (New York: Viking Press, 1974); Herman Kahn, William Brown, and Leon Martel, The Next 200 Years: A Scenario for America and the World (New York: William Morrow, 1976); Herman Kahn, World Economic Development: 1979 and Beyond (New York: William Morrow, 1979); Wilfred Beckerman, Two Cheers for the Affluent Society: A Spirited Defense of Economic Growth (New York: Saint Martin's Press, 1975); Julian L. Simon, The Ultimate Resource (Princeton: Princeton University Press, 1981); Edward Walter, The Immorality of Limiting Growth (Albany: State University of New York Press, 1981); Charles Maurice and Charles W. Smithson, The Doomsday Myth: 10,000 Years of Economic Crises (Stanford, Cal.: Hoover Institution Press, 1984); and Julian L. Simon and Herman Kahn, eds., The Resourceful Earth: A Response to Global 2000 (New York: Basil Blackwell, 1984), pp. 1–49 for a specific attack upon the Global 2000 Report.

For progrowth and much more optimistic ecological perspectives contesting the ecological-crisis literature cited in the previous footnote, see the remainder of the Simon and Kahn volume, The Resourceful Earth as well as: Robert Repetto, ed., The Global Possible: Resources, Development and the New Century (New Haven: Yale University Press, 1985); and, Robert Repetto, World Enough and Time: Successful Strategies for Resources Management (New Haven: Yale University Press, 1986).

A detailed examination and critique of what are termed "postindustrial utopians" is provided in: Boris Frankel, The Postindustrial Utopians (Madison: The University of Wisconsin Press, 1987). And, finally, for a nonpolemical, clearheaded assessment of the limits-to-growth controversy, see John S. Dryzek, Rational Ecology: Environmenta and Political Economy (New York: Basil Blackwell, 1987), especially chapter 2, "Is There an Ecological Crisis?" pp. 14–24.

7. Kirkpatrick Sale, Human Scale (New York: G. P. Putnam's Sons, 1982), pp. 21–22.

8. See Kahn, op. cit., p. 70. The Harris data were taken from The Harris Survey, December 25, 1975.

9. For an example of such a criticism see Johan Galtung, "'The Limits to Growth' and Class Politics," Journal of Peace Research, nos. 1–2 (1973), pp. 112–113, fn. 3.

10. President Jimmy Carter's Address to the Nation, July 15, 1979; transcript, New York Times, July 16, 1979, p. A10.

11. Data cited in Sale, op. cit., p. 420.

12. Frank Levy, Washington Post National Weekly Edition, December 29, 1986, p. 19.

13. Felix Rohatyn, "On the Brink," New York Review of Books, June 11, 1987, p. 3.

14. Levy, *op. cit.*, p. 18.

15. Kurt Vonnegut, Jr., "Only Kidding Folks?" *Nation*, May 13, 1978, p. 575.

16. *Ibid.*

17. Christopher Flavin, "Reassessing Nuclear Power," in Lester R. Brown *et al.*, *State of the World 1987* (New York: W. W. Norton, 1987), p. 67.

18. Arpad von Lazar, Foreward, in Dennis Pirages, *The New Context for International Relations: Global Ecopolitics* (North Scituate, Mass.: Duxbury Press, 1978), p. vii.

19. Thomas R. Pickering and Gus Speth, "Letter of Transmittal," in *The Global 2000 Report to the President*, *op. cit.*, p. iii.

20. See Simon and Kahn, *op. cit.*, p. 45.

21. Heilbroner, *An Inquiry into the Human Prospect*, *op. cit.*, p. 22.

22. Kahn, *op. cit.*, p. 185, table 4.1 and pp. 260–294.

23. See volumes by Maddox, *op. cit.*, and, Maurice and Smithson, *op. cit.*

24. An example of such a position, in addition to the Simon and Kahn volume, is: Mancur Olson, Hans H. Lansberg, and Joseph L. Fisher, Epilogue, in Mancur Olson and Hans H. Landsberg, eds., *The No-Growth Society* (New York: W. W. Norton, 1973), pp. 229–241.

25. Beckerman, *op. cit.*, p. 23.

26. *Ibid.*, see the entire chapter 2, pp. 24–48. The specific quotes are from pp. 27–28, 30, 35, and 37.

27. Kahn, *op. cit.*, p. 54.

28. *Ibid.*, p. 141, table 3.2, for a listing of these antigrowth values and pp. 153–177 for Kahn's elaboration upon this list.

29. *Ibid.*

30. Immanuel Wallerstein, "Crisis as Transition," in Samir Amin, Giovanni Arrighi, Andre Gunder Frank, and Immanuel Wallerstein, *Dynamics of Global Crisis* (New York: Monthly Review Press, 1982)., p. 11.

31. Charles Krauthammer, "On Nuclear Morality," in James E. White, ed., *Contemporary Moral Problems*, 2nd ed. (St. Paul: West, 1988), pp. 403–404.

32. Richard Falk, Foreward, in David W. Orr and Marvin S. Soroos, eds., *The Global Predicament: Ecological Perspectives on World Order* (Chapel Hill: The University of North Carolina Press, 1979), p. xii.

33. The source for this story and the quote is Sale, *op. cit.*, p. 20.

34. See K. L. R. Pavitt, "Malthus and Other Economists: Some Doomsdays Revisited," in Cole *et al.*, pp. 137–143.
For the "moral problem of commercial society, and to argue that it was clearly recognized and understood at the birth of commercial [industrial] society in the 18th century," see Thomas A. Horne, "Envy and Commercial Society: Mandeville and Smith on 'Private Vices, Public Benefits,'" *Political Theory* 9 (November 1981), pp. 551–569. Also, Horne's *The Social Theory of Bernard Mandeville: Virtue and Commerce in Early Eighteenth Century England* (New York: Columbia University Press, 1978). For insightful historical studies, full of details on the "birth of a consumer society," see Neil McKendrick, John Brewer and J. H. Plumb, *The Birth of a Consumer Society: The Commercialization of Eighteenth-Century England* (Bloomington, Ind.: Indiana University Press, 1985).

35. See Gerald Alonzo Smith, "The Teleological View of Wealth: A Historical Perspective," in Herman E. Daly, ed., *Economics, Ecology, Ethics: Essays Toward a Steady-State Economy* (San Francisco: W. H. Freeman, 1980), pp. 215–237; and the references to all four thinkers' works provided by Smith. Also, see Gerald Alonzo Smith, "Epilogue: Malthusian Concern from 1800 to 1962," in William M. Finnin, Jr. and Gerald Alonzo Smith, eds., *The Morality of Scarcity: Limited Resources and Social Policy* (Baton Rouge: Louisiana State University Press, 1979), pp. 107–128.

36. See Martin J. Wiener, *English Culture and the Decline of the Industrial State: 1850–1980* (Cambridge: Cambridge University Press, 1981), chapter 3, "A Counterrevolution of Values," pp. 27–40.
For other cultural critics of industrialism see, Arthur O. Lewis, Jr., *Of Men and Machines* (New York: E. P. Dutton, 1963), part 4, "The Machines as Enemy," pp. 183–291.

37. Galtung, *op. cit.*, p. 112, fn. 2.

38. William Watts, Foreward, 2d ed. of *The Limits to Growth*, Meadows *et al.*, *op. cit.*, pp. x–xi.

39. *Ibid.*, p. 26, footnote.

40. See, for example, Mesarovic and Pestel, *op. cit.*, Tinbergen, *op. cit.*, Ervin Laszlo, *et al.*, *Goals for Mankind: A Report to the Club of Rome on the New Horizons of Global Community* (New York: New American Library, 1978); and, James W. Botkin, Mahdi Elmandjra, and Mircea Malitza, *No Limits to Learning: Bridging the Human Gap: A Report to the Club of Rome* (Oxford: Pergamon Press, 1981).

41. Beckerman, *op. cit.*, p. viii.

42. Kahn, *op. cit.*, pp. 59–60.

43. Henry C. Wallich, "More on Growth," *Newsweek*, March 13, 1972, p. 86.

44. Jay Forrester, "New Perspectives on Economic Growth," in Dennis L. Meadows, ed., *Alternatives to Growth—I: A Search for Sustainable Futures* (Cambridge, Mass.: Ballinger Publishing, 1977), p. 121.

45. Mesarovic and Pestel, *op. cit.*, p. 11 (emphasis on original).

46. Joan Davis and Samuel Mauch, "Strategies for Societal Development," in Meadows, ed., *op. cit.*, p. 225.

47. Joseph A. Schumpeter, *Capitalism, Socialism and Democracy*, 3rd ed. (New York: Harper and Row, 1962), p. 61.

48. Albert O. Hirshman, "Rival Interpretations of Market Society: Civilizing, Destructive or Feeble?" *Journal of Economic Literature* XX, (December 1982), p. 1469.

49. Quoted in Michael Harrington, *The Twilight of Capitalism* (New York: Simon and Shuster, 1976), pp. 321–322.

50. Quoted in David S. Landes, *The Unbound Prometheus: Technological Change and Industrial Development in Western Europe from 1750 to the Present* (Cambridge: Cambridge University Press, 1977), pp. 536–537 (emphasis in original).

51. Hirschman, "Rival Interpretations of Market Society," *op. cit.*, p. 1469.

52. See Schumpeter, *op. cit.*, chapter 13, especially p. 143. For some other thinkers who take this view see, R. H. Tawney, *The Acquisitive Society* (New York: Harcourt, Brace and World, 1948), chapter 4; Mumford, *op. cit.*, volume 1, Technics and Human Development, *op. cit.*, p. 277; and Hirsch, *op. cit.*, part 3, "The Depleting Moral Legacy," pp. 115–158.

53. Pirages and Ehrlich, *op. cit.*, p. 47.

54. See my, "Limits to Economic Growth," *op. cit.*, p. 90.

55. Henry David Thoreau, *Walden* in *Walden and Civil Disobedience*, ed. Owen Thomas (New York: W. W. Norton, 1966), p. 51.

56. See Dickinson McGraw and George Watson, *Political and Social Inquiry* (New York: John Wiley, 1976), chapter 4, pp. 84–107.

57. See among Popper's many works: "The Nature of Philosophical Problems and Their Roots in Science," and "Truth, Rationality and the Growth of Scientific Knowledge," both in: Karl R. Popper, *Conjectures and Refutations: The Growth of Scientific Knowledge* (New York: Harper and Row, 1968), pp. 66–96 and 215–250, respectively.

58. For a chronicle of the increasing awareness of the American public and political leaders to ecological concerns, and the resistance that such awareness and proposed remedial action encountered during the 1970s, consult a volume written by an original member of the President's Council on Environmental Quality: Robert Cahn, *Footprints on the Planet: A Search for an Environmental Ethic* (New York: Universe Books, 1978), *Passim*.

For a brief history of the industrial policy of continuous economic growth see, H. W. Arndt, *The Rise and Fall of Economic Growth: A Study in Contemporary Thought* (Chicago: University of Chicago Press, 1978).

59. For a succinct description of these and other events of this era engendering "the dark moon of our time," (p. 20), see Heilbroner, *An Inquiry into the Human Prospect*, *op. cit.*, chapter 1, 2; pp. 13–58.

On the important year of 1973, see, Catton, *op. cit.*, chapter 4, "Watershed Year [1973]: Modes of Adaptation," pp. 58–74.

60. The original citation for this article by Hardin is: *Science* 162 (13 December 1968), pp. 1243–1248. One source for its many reprintings is: Daly, *Economics, Ecology, Ethics*, *op. cit.*, pp. 100–114. Subsequent references to this article will be to this reprint.

61. *Ibid.*, p. 100.

62. *Ibid.*, pp. 100–101.

63. Regarding the important problem of population growth see, Lester R. Brown, "Stopping Population Growth," in Lester R. Brown *et al.*, *State of the World 1985* (New York: W. W. Norton, 1985), pp. 200–221. In this discussion Brown addresses the social influences upon fertility wherein he states: "It [World Fertility Survey] looked at the many economic and social influences on fertility, considered the role of social gains in reducing family size, and concluded that improved education and employment opportunities for women were correlated more closely with fertility decline than any other social indicator," p. 202.

64. Quoted in Wiener, *op. cit.*, p. ix.

65. Perhaps the most prominent, conscious bracketing out of political factors within a scientific ecological analysis of the industrial crisis occurs in *The Limits to Growth* volume where the authors omit what they term "social" necessities for economic growth, such as: "peace, social stability, education and employment, and steady technological progress," because "these factors are much more difficult to assess or to predict. Neither this book nor our world model at this stage in its development can deal explicitly with these social factors...." Meadows *et al.*, *op. cit.*, p. 55.

It should be pointed out that at other places within their work these authors do recognize the importance of social values (e.g., p. 186), but this omission of political factors because they cannot be "dealt with explicitly" within their models is typical of this error of omission within the biophysically based, limits-to-growth literature.

66. See Daniel Bell, *The Coming of the Post-Industrial Society* (New York: Basic Books, 1976).

67. (San Francisco: W. H. Freeman, 1976).

68. *Ibid.*, p. vii.

69. Ehrlich and Ehrlich, *op. cit.*, p. 1. How particularly apt this Chinese concept is to contemporary events; China has experienced great calamities yet retains the hope of these calamities constituting great opportunities to transform the society for the better. The latest in this unfortunate sequence is the brutal suppression of the student democratic movement in June 1989.

70. Andre Gunder Frank, "Crisis of Ideology and Ideology of Crisis," in Amin, Arrighi, Frank, and Wallerstein, *op. cit.*, p. 109.

71. See Tawney's statement: "Societies, like individuals, have their moral crises and their spiritual revolutions," in his *Religion and the Rise of Capitalism* (New York: New American Library, 1961), p. 227.

72. Herbert Marcuse, *One-Dimensional Man: Studies in the Ideology of Advanced Industrial Society* (Boston: Beacon Press, 1970), p. 7.

73. Slater, *op. cit.*, p. 2.

74. See Mustafa Tolba's Foreward to: John McHale and Magda Cordell McHale, *Basic Human Needs: A Framework for Action* (New Brunswick, N.J.: Transaction Books, 1978), p. 21.

75. Slater, *op. cit.*, pp. 1–2.

76. See *Los Angeles Times*, four-part, front-page series entitled: "A Slow Growth Revolt," July 31, 1988–August 3, 1988; as well as, Timothy Egan, "Like the West Coast City It is, Seattle is Tired of Developing," *New York Times*, May 7, 1989; Week in Review section.

77. Slater, *op. cit.*, p. 3.

78. Ophuls, *op. cit.*, p. 243.

79. Toffler, *op. cit.*, pp. 104–105.

Chapter 2

1. Erich Fromm, *To Have or to Be?* (New York: Harper and Row, 1976), p. 40.

2. *Ibid.*, pp. 39–40.

3. See among Popper's many works on epistemology: "On the Sources of Knowledge and of Ignorance," and "Science: Conjectures and Refutations," in

Popper, *op. cit.*, pp. 3–30 and 33–65, respectively.

4. Popper, "On the Sources of Knowledge and of Ignorance," *ibid.*

5. For additional sources on Popper's epistemology see his *Objective Knowledge: An Evolutionary Approach* (Oxford: Oxford University Press, 1972), and Paul Arthur Schilpp, ed., *The Philosophy of Karl Popper*, 2 vols. (La Salle, Ill.: Open Court, 1974), *Passim.*, for the large secondary literature Popper's works have inspired.

6. For one discussion among the many that could be cited here on Western philosophy's quest for absolutely certain knowledge, see Richard J. Bernstein's account of what he calls "The Cartesian Anxiety" and the contemporary postempiricist challenges to this highly influential but misguided view in his *Beyond Objectivism and Relativism: Science, Hermeneutics, and Praxis* (Phila.: University of Pennsylvania Press, 1985), pp. 16–34.

7. Davis and Mauch, *op. cit.*, pp. 221–222.

8. See Albert O. Hirschman, *Shifting Involvements: Private Interest and Public Policy* (Princeton: Princeton University Press, 1982), *passim.*

9. *Ibid.*, p. 16.

10. *Ibid.* (emphasis in original). The phrase "driving force in human affairs" used to characterize disappointment is taken from p. 15.

11. *Ibid.*, pp. 16–17.

12. For vivid illustrations of the popular recognition of the environmental crises at hand see: Robert H. Boyle, "Forecast for Disaster," *Sports Illustrated*, November 16, 1987, pp. 78–92; and, during one week in January 1988 The Public Broadcasting System television network showed three different programs on the "garbage crisis" (viewed on its New York station). Also in the broadcast media, The American Broadcasting Company's nightly news devoted an entire week during the first week of September 1988 to reports on various environmental crises capped by a one-hour special on the environment, and in 1989 devotes at least one segment per week to its "American Agenda" series to the environment.

Many media accounts describing the drought, heat, and ocean pollution of the summer of 1988 in the United States could be cited here. A sample restricted to the print medium includes newsmagazine cover stories on: the greenhouse effect and global warming in *Newsweek*, July 11, 1988, pp. 16–24; and *New Republic*, September 12–19, 1988, pp. 5–8; on ocean pollution in *Time*, August 1, 1988, pp. 44–50; and *Newsweek*, August 1, 1988, pp. 42–48. The powerful effects of the summer of 1988's various visible environmental crises and the mobilizing of American public opinion to both support the environmental groups and consider changes in public policies because of environmental threats are reported in: Clifford D. May, "Pollution Ills Stir Support for Environment Groups," *New York Times*, August 21, 1988, p. 30. And, finally, the *Los Angeles Times* series of four articles on the slow-growth political movement within California wherein: "Both friends and enemies call it [slow-growth movement] the most important political and socio-economic phenomenon to sweep the state since Proposition 13, the property tax-cutting initiative, a decade ago." See, William Trombley, "Slow-Growth Sentiment Builds Fast," *Los Angeles Times*, July 31, 1988, p. 1.

It may not be an exaggeration to say that the summer of 1988's environmental disasters may constitute the catalyst to achieve a change in the American public's views toward the problems created by the postindustrial status quo. Environmentalist Lester R. Brown and his colleagues at the Worldwatch Institute, publishers of the best-selling, annual series, *The State of the World*, agree on the profound, public significance of the environmental threats of 1988. In their 1989 volume they write: "Historians looking back on 1988 may well mark it as a watershed year both for the environment and the public's concern about it. The earth's deteriorating condition moved into the limelight. . . . " See Lester R. Brown, Christopher Flavin, and Sandra Postel, "A World at Risk," in Lester R. Brown *et al.*, *State of the World: 1989* (New York: W. W. Norton, 1989), p. 3.

For the continuation of this dramatic increase in public awareness of environmental crises and support for environmental groups continuing throughout 1989 see Howard Youth, "Boom Time for Environmental Groups," *World Watch*, 2 (Nov.-Dec. 1989), p. 33.

13. Jeremy Rifkin (with Ted Howard), *Entropy: A New World View* (New York: Bantam Books, 1980), pp. 63–64.

14. Fromm, *op. cit.*, p. 6.

For a succinct presentation of recent data on the contemporary problems of increasing debt among poor countries and rapidly increasing population and declining grain production per capita, see the tables and figures provided by Lester R. Brown in his: "Analyzing the Demographic Trap," in Brown *et al.* *State of the World 1987*, *op. cit.*, pp. 28–29. Also, see McHale and McHale, *op. cit.*, p. 33, figure 3, for a brief table summarizing the plight of the world's poor according to 1976 data, including such shocking figures as: 1,300 million of the world's people earn less than $90 per year or 1,030 million need adequate housing.

For a more recent, detailed description of the impoverished quality of life of the world's poor without counseling despair, see the following two contributions to Repetto, ed., *op. cit.*, Robert Repetto, "Population, Resource Pressures, and Poverty," and Jorge E. Hardoy and David E. Satterthwaite, "Third World Cities and the Environment of Poverty," pp. 131–169 and 171–210, respectively.

15. Albert Camus, *The Rebel: An Essay on Man in Revolt*, trans. Anthony Bower (New York: Alfred A. Knopf, 1956), p. 11.

16. See Camus's discussion of "absurd reasoning" in his *The Myth of Sisyphus and Other Essays*, trans. Justin O'Brien (New York: Alfred A. Knopf, 1955), pp. 3–8, especially p. 7.

17. *Ibid.*, p. 36.

18. *Ibid.*, p. 37.

19. *Ibid.*, p. 2.

20. *Ibid.*

21. See Camus, *The Rebel*, *op. cit.*, *passim.*, but especially pp. 24–25 and 100–111.

22. See Camus's characterization of the first half of the twentieth century as a "period which, in a space of fifty years, uproots, enslaves, or kills seventy million human beings. . . ." *Ibid.*, p. 3.

23. Camus, *The Myth of Sisyphus*, *op. cit.*, pp. 89–91.

24. Daniel Bell, *The Cultural Contradictions of Capitalism* (New York: Basic Books, 1976), pp. 49–50.

25. Mumford, *op. cit.*, vol. 1, p. 203.

26. See Mumford, *op. cit.*, vol. 2, *The Pentagon of Power*, *passim.*

27. Jean Jacques Rousseau, *The Social Contract*, trans. G. D. H. Cole, in *The Social Contract and Discourses* (New York: E. P. Dutton, 1950), chapter 3, pp. 6–7.

28. Fromm, *op. cit.*, pp. 1–2.

29. Richard E. Edwards, "The Logic of Capital Accumulation," in Richard C. Edwards, Michael Reich, Thomas E. Weisskopf, eds., *The Capitalist System: A Radical Analysis of American Society*, 2d ed. (Englewood Cliffs, N.J.: Prentice-Hall, 1978), p. 100.

30. William Leiss, *The Limits to Satisfaction: An Essay on the Problem of Needs and Commodities* (Toronto: University of Toronto Press, 1976), p. 4 (my emphasis). And we can now add post-Maoist China to Leiss's list of nation's resting their legitimacy upon a "permanently rising level of consumption," at least as an aspiring "industrialized socialist nation." Also, this point is reinforced by the Soviet Union under Gorbachev.

31. See John Kenneth Galbraith, *The New Industrial State*, 2d ed. rev. (New York: New American Library, 1972), pp. 374–376.

32. Bell, *The Cultural Contradictions of Capitalism*, *op. cit.*, p. 238.

33. Ophuls, *op. cit.*, p. 203. On this point of environmental limits and threats in socialist societies as well as capitalist ones, see Sabine Rosenbladt, "Is Poland Lost? Pollution and Politics in Eastern Europe," *Greenpeace* 13, no. 6 (November/December 1988), pp. 14–19.

34. Herman Arthur, "The Japan Gap: A Country Moves Ahead—But At What Price?" *American Educator* (Summer 1983), p. 44 (emphasis in original).

35. Camilleri, *op. cit.*, p. 137.

36. Herman E. Daly, "The Steady-State Economy: Toward a Political Economy of Biophysical Equilibrium and Moral Growth," in Daly, *Toward a Steady-State Economy, op. cit.,* pp. 149–151.

37. See Patricia Springborg, *The Problem of Human Needs and the Critique of Civilization* (London: George Allen and Unwin, 1981), *Passim.*, and the literature cited therein. For a detailed report on the nature of basic human needs, see McHale and McHale, *op. cit., passim.*

38. Daly, *Steady-State Economics, op. cit.,* p. 99 (emphasis in original).

39. Jess Stein, ed., *The Random House Dictionary of the English Language* unabr. ed. (New York: Random House, 1969), p. 626.

40. Mesarovic and Pestel, *op. cit.,* p. 8. "Brief on Growth," figure D, "Growth of Human."

41. *Ibid.* Note that even in the plant world where growth occurs throughout the entire lives of plants: "towards the end of their lives their growth rate decreases. An oak tree, even after a lifetime of 150 years, grows about three inches per year. In the beginning, as with a human embryo, plant growth appears to be exponential. But after having achieved a certain critical living mass, this phase is over, and organic—tapered—growth sets in;" p. 8, figure B, "Growth of an Oak Tree."

42. Quoted in: Richard Neuhaus, *In Defense of People: Ecology and the Seduction of Radicalism* (New York: Macmillan, 1971), p. 18.

43. Mesarovic and Pestel, *op. cit.,* chapter 1, pp. 1–9.

44. *Ibid.,* pp. 3–4.

45. *Ibid.,* pp. 7–9.

46. For just a sample list of the authors who make this elitist charge, see Neuhaus, *op. cit.,* Beckerman, *op. cit.,* Kahn, *op. cit.,* Olson, Landsberg and Fisher, *op. cit.,* and Passell and Ross, *op. cit.*

47. See "Commentary," by the Executive Committee of the Club of Rome, in Meadows *et al., op. cit.,* pp. 197–198.

48. On the *prima facie*, overriding obligation to save people from preventable death, see William Aiken, "World Hunger and Foreign Aid: The Morality of Mass Starvation," in Burton M. Leiser, ed., *Values in Conflict: Life, Liberty and the Role of Law* (New York: Macmillan, 1981), pp. 189–201.

Chapter 3

1. "Economic Possibilities for Our Grandchildren," in John Maynard Keynes, *Essays in Persuasion* (New York: W. W. Norton, 1963), p. 273.

2. *The Politics of the Solar Age: Alternatives to Economics* (Garden City, N.Y.: Anchor Press/Doubleday, 1981), p. 124, fn. 11; and p. 181.

3. The notable exceptions to this statement are the works of William Ophuls and Lester Milbrath. For the former, see his "Leviathan or Oblivion?" in Daly, *Toward a Steady-State Economy, op. cit.*, pp. 215-230; "The Politics of the Sustainable Society," in Dennis Clark Pirages, ed., *The Sustainable Society: Implications for Limited Growth* (New York: Praeger, 1977), pp. 157-172; in addition to, *Ecology and the Politics of Scarcity, op. cit.*

Milbrath's works include: *Environmentalists: Vanguard for a New Society* (Albany: State University of New York Press, 1984), and *Envisioning a Sustainable Society, op. cit.*

Furthermore, the names of Lynton K. Caldwell, Harold and Margaret Sprout, and Dennis C. Pirages, should be mentioned. These political scientists have written extensively on the environment. See Lynton K. Caldwell, *Man and His Environment: Policy and Administration* (New York: Harper and Row, 1975); Harold and Margaret Sprout, *The Ecological Perspective in Human Affairs with Special Reference to International Politics* (Princeton: Princeton University Press, 1965), and, *The Context of Environmental Politics: Unfinished Business for America's Third Century, op. cit.*; and, Pirages and Ehrlich, *Ark II, op. cit.*; Pirages, *The New Context for International Relations, op. cit.*, and, "Introduction: A Social Design for Sustainable Growth," in Pirages, *The Sustainable Society, op. cit.*, pp. 1-13.

What should be noted here for the purposes of this point about the absence of political analyses of economic growth is that these political scientists emphasize environmental concerns *exclusively*. To the extent that political scientists may be said to have contributed to the limits-to-growth literature at all it has been with respect to an ecologically informed view of politics with little or no discussion of economic growth *per se*, much less its desirability. For example, in none of the cited works above by Caldwell, the Sprouts, and Pirages, was the subject of economic growth listed in the index for more than twelve pages! This is where Milbrath's latest volume is distinctive.

To further support this lack of political scientists' involvement in research on the limits-to-growth issue, I refer the reader to the fact that of the more than one hundred advisers to the Federal Government's massive two-volume work, *The Global 2000 Report to the President, op. cit.*, the only political scientists that I can identify from the institutional affiliations given is Dennis Pirages. See, list of "Informal Advisers to the Study," volume II, The Technical Report, pp. xiii–xviii.

4. On the intentionally misleading implications of establishing "the Nobel Prize for Economics" for the purpose of enhancing the scientific image of this discipline, see Henderson, *op. cit.*, p. 175, where she writes that the Nobel Prize for Economics "is, in fact, not a Nobel Prize at all. In reality, this prize was set up in 1968 by the Central Bank of Sweden in the amount of $145,000, in the memory of Alfred Nobel, and is the only one of the prizes that was not set up by Nobel himself."

5. "Reductionist" is used here to mean "the criticism that a claimed reduc-

tion of one subject matter (or explanation) to another is false," as in the title of the following volume: *Beyond Reductionism: New Perspectives in the Life Sciences*, edited by Arthur Koestler and J. R. Smythies (New York: Macmillan, 1969).

Although the nature of scientific reduction in general, and related to some subject matter (like biology), is quite controversial (although uniformly valued by scientists when genuine) within the philosophy of science, I offer the following natural scientific definition as a point of reference: "a reduction is effected when the experimental laws of the secondary science [reduced science] (and if it has an adequate theory, its theory as well) are shown to be the logical consequences of the theoretical assumptions (inclusive of the coordinating definitions) of the primary science [reducing science]...[In addition] it does seem reasonable to impose as a nonformal requirement that the theoretical assumptions of the primary science be supported by empirical evidence possessing some degree of probative force." See Ernest Nagel, *The Structure of Science: Problems in the Logic of Scientific Explanation* (New York: Harcourt, Brace and World, 1961), pp. 352, 358.

6. Hannah Arendt, *The Human Condition: A Study of the Central Dilemmas Facing Modern Man* (Garden City, N.Y.: Doubleday/Anchor Books, 1959), p. 29.

7. *Ibid.*, pp. 31, 34.

8. Ernest Barker, Introduction to *The Politics of Aristotle* (New York: Oxford University Press, 1965), p. lvi (my emphasis).

9. Arendt, *op. cit.*, p. 35. Henderson (*op. cit.*, p. 162) informs her readers that the word "private" originates from the Latin word "*privare*," "which means to *deprive* others, showing the widespread ancient view that property was first and foremost *communal*" (Henderson's emphasis).

10. For a volume-length discussion of this modern demise of politics, see Richard Sennett, *The Fall of Public Man: On the Social Psychology of Capitalism* (New York: Random House, 1978). See, also, any standard text on American public opinion and behavior for the very low political participation by Americans, which just briefly surpassed fifty percent of those eligible to vote in the most recent presidential election in 1988.

11. See, for example, Ludwig von Mises, "Introduction: Why Read Adam Smith Today?" in Adam Smith, *The Wealth of Nations* (Chicago: Henry Regnery, 1953), p. v; and, Louis Dumont, *From Mandeville to Marx: The Genesis and Triumph of Economic Ideology* (Chicago: The University of Chicago Press, 1977), p. 38.

12. Dumont, *ibid.*, pp. 34, 38 (emphasis in original).

13. See William J. Barber, *A History of Economic Thought* (New York: Penguin Books, 1977), p. 25.

14. See Daniel Bell's comment that for Smith, "economics...is inextricably normative and moral," in Daniel Bell, "Models and Reality in Economic Dis-

course," in Daniel Bell and Irving Kristol, eds., *The Crisis in Economic Theory* (New York: Basic Books, 1981), p. 56.

15. Quoted by Albert O. Hirschman in his *The Passions and the Interests: Political Arguments for Capitalism Before its Triumph* (Princeton: Princeton University Press, 1978), p. 103.

16. *Ibid.*, pp. 103–104.

17. On these other classical economists, see Barber, *op. cit.*, chapters 2–4; and, Maurice Dobb, *Theories of Value and Distribution Since Adam Smith: Ideology and Economic Theory* (Cambridge: Cambridge University Press, 1973), Chapters 3–5.

18. Arendt, *op. cit.*, p. 39.

19. For an excellent study of the differences between the medieval and modern worldviews, see Tawney, *Religion and the Rise of Capitalism, op. cit.*

20. For this point on the dependence of modern economics upon the existence of a society founded on the market and the latter's late development, see Adolphe Lowe, *On Economic Knowledge: Toward a Science of Political Economy*, Enlarged Edition (Armonk, N.Y.: M. E. Sharpe, 1983), pp. 31–32. Also, on modern society's dependence upon the market, see Karl Polanyi, *The Great Transformation: The Political and Economic Origins of Our Time* (Boston: Beacon Press, 1957).

21. Dumont, *op. cit.*, p. 33 (emphasis in original).

22. Barber, *op. cit.*, p. 17.

23. Tawney, *Religion and the Rise of Capitalism, op. cit.*, p. 34.

24. Polanyi, *op. cit.*, p. 71.

25. This expression is taken from Dumont, *op. cit.*, p. 7, where it was italicized.

26. These expressions are taken from Tawney, *Religion and the Rise of Capitalism, op. cit.*, p. 227. Although the literature on the industrial revolution is immense, I would recommend starting with Polanyi, *op. cit.*, and Tawney's *Religion and the Rise of Capitalism*.

27. Mumford, *op. cit.*, volume 1, p. 277.

28. See Daly, *Steady-State Economics, op. cit.*, p. 3, fn., from which this quote of Malthus was borrowed.

29. See Bell, "Models and Reality in Economic Discourse," *op. cit.*, p. 47.

30. Dumont, *op. cit.*, pp. 26, 36.

31. For this discussion of neoclassical economics I rely upon Dobb, *op. cit.*,

chapter 7, pp. 166–210; wherein the author attributes credit to the neoclassical revolution from classical economics to W. S. Jevons; Barber, *op. cit.*, part 3, pp. 163–221; where the author emphasizes the contributions of Alfred Marshall as a "giant without equal . . . among the Anglo-Saxon neoclassical pioneers," p. 168; and, finally, Lowe, *op. cit.*, chapter 8, pp. 194–216.

32. Paul R. and Anne H. Ehrlich, "Humanity at the Crossroads," in Daly, *Economics, Ecology, Ethics, op. cit.*, p. 43.

33. Dobb, *op. cit.*, p. 15 (emphasis in original).

34. Warren J. Samuels, "Ideology in Economics," in Sidney Weintraub, ed., *Modern Economic Thought* (Phila.: University of Pennsylvania Press, 1980), p. 469. See this entire article for a review of how economists have attempted to deal with the issue of ideology (or value judgments) in their supposedly scientific discipline. We shall discuss this subject below in connection with value noncognitivism.

35. The quoted phrase in Piero Straffa's, the editor of the writings of Ricardo, and is cited by Dobb, *op. cit.*, p. 84.

36. Barber, *op. cit.*, p. 165. The commentator quoted here by Barber is the noted economic theorist, Joan Robinson.

37. Sidney Weintraub, "Introduction," to Distribution Theory section, in, Weintraub, *op. cit.*, p. 392.

38. On this important shift that occurred within neoclassical economics, see Dobb, *op. cit.*, pp. 34–35, 168.

39. James A. Caporaso, "Pathways Between Economics and Politics: Possible Foundations for the Study of Global Political Economy," paper delivered at the Annual Meeting of the American Political Science Association, 1983, Chicago, p. 7.

40. See, *ibid.*, pp. 27–28. Also, see Creel Froman, *The Two American Political Systems: Society, Economics, and Politics* (Englewood Cliffs, N.J.: Prentice-Hall, 1984), *passim*, but especially chapters three, five and seven.

41. Thomas S. Kuhn, *The Structure of Scientific Revolutions*, 2d ed., Enlarged (Chicago: The University of Chicago Press, 1970). A large literature commenting upon and utilizing Kuhn's discussion has developed particularly on the importance of disciplinary frameworks, or, "paradigms" as Kuhn called them, upon the products of knowledge, and the mostly sociological and political process of paradigm crisis and transformation. For just one example of such an application of Kuhn's work, see Gary Gutting, ed., *Paradigms and Revolutions: Applications and Appraisals of Thomas Kuhn's Philosophy of Science* (Notre Dame, Ind.: University of Notre Dame Press, 1980); especially the chapter pertaining to economics: Mark Blaug, "Kuhn versus Lakatos, or Paradigms versus Research Programmes in the History of Economics," pp. 137–159.

42. For this information and further discussion of the conservative aspects of economists' training and unusual professional rewards, when compared to the other

social sciences, see Gunnar Myrdal, *Against the Stream: Cultural Essays in Economics* (New York: Random House, 1975), pp. 59–64.

43. *Ibid.*, p. 62.

44. Henderson, *op. cit.*, p. 79 for both quotes here.

45. Caporaso, *op. cit.*, p. 6.

46. Neuhaus, *op. cit.*, p. 150.

47. See Tawney, *Religion and the Rise of Capitalism, op. cit.*, pp. 227–228, and Henderson, *op. cit.*, p. 187.

48. Henderson, *op. cit.*, p. 187.

49. Polanyi, *op. cit.*, p. 30.

50. See Tawney, *Religion and the Rise of Capitalism, op. cit.*, pp. 227–228, and Henderson, *op. cit.*, p. 228.

51. The separation of politics and political science from their moral submersion is usually credited to Machiavelli and, in this regard, he should be considered the founder of modern autonomous political science. For a presentation of this interpretation of Machiavelli, see, Claude Lefort, "On the Concept of Politics and Economics in Machiavelli," in C. B. Macpherson, comp., *Political Theory and Political Economy*, papers from the Annual Meeting of the Conference for the Study of Political Thought, April 1974, p. 1; and, Sheldon S. Wolin, *Politics and Vision: Continuity and Innovation in Western Political Thought* (Boston: Little, Brown, 1960), chapter 7, pp. 195–238.

52. Bookchin, *Toward an Ecological Society, op. cit.*, p. 31.

53. Hans Peter Dreitzel, "On the Political Meaning of Culture," in Norman Birnbaum, ed., *Beyond the Crisis* (New York: Oxford University Press, 1977), p. 90, (emphasis in original).

54. C. B. Macpherson, *Democratic Theory: Essays in Retrieval* (Oxford: Oxford University Press, 1973), p. 29.

55. For an historically rich account of the origin of the industrial, consumption-based society, see McKendrick, Brewer and Plumb, *op. cit.*, *passim*.

Chapter 4

1. Henry C. Wallich, "Zero Growth," *Newsweek*, January 24, 1972, p. 62.

2. Herman E. Daly, "The Steady-State Economy," in Daly, *Toward a Steady-State, op. cit.*, p. 167.

3. Albert O. Hirschman, *Essays in Trespassing: Economics of Politics and*

Beyond (Cambridge: Cambridge University Press, 1981), p. 23.

4. Lee Rainwater, "Equity, Income, Inequality, and the Steady State," in Pirages, *The Sustainable Society*, *op. cit.*, pp. 263–264.

5. Bruce M. Shefrin, *The Future of U.S. Politics in an Age of Economic Limits* (Boulder, Colo.: Westview Press, 1980), p. 4 and abstract page.

6. This label is a paraphrase from: Charles S. Maier, "The Politics of Inflation in the Twentieth Century," in Fred Hirsch and John H. Goldthorpe, eds., *The Political Economy of Inflation* (Cambridge: Harvard University Press, 1979), p. 70, where he writes: "The concept of growth as a surrogate for redistribution appears, in retrospect, as the great conservative idea of the last generation." I would merely add that I think that the conservative aspects of the idea of economic growth as a surrogate for redistribution go back further than the last generation, as I shall attempt to show in my subsequent discussion of liberalism.

7. Herman E. Daly, "The Steady-State Economy," in Daly, *Toward a Steady-State Economy*, *op. cit.*, p. 171 (emphasis in original).

8. See title of a volume by Lester C. Thurow, *The Zero-Sum Society: Distribution and the Possibilities for Economic Change* (New York: Basic Books, 1980), wherein the author discusses a society deprived of the "miracle"—I would say "illusion"—of economic growth fraught with political conflict as a result of a winner-take-all-loser-give-up-everything economic system.

I shall subsequently argue that this undesirable set of zero-sum traits only characterize a no-growth society if our current progrowth values remain in place. Such a negative result need not occur if our current values change in the direction I suggest in part 4.

9. Walter W. Heller, "Coming to Terms with Growth and the Environment," in Sam H. Schurr, ed., *Energy, Economic Growth, and the Environment* (Baltimore: Johns Hopkins University Press, 1973), p. 11 (emphasis in original).

10. Lowe, *op. cit.*, p. 340.

11. Neuhaus, *op. cit.*, p. 151.

12. Bell, *The Cultural Contradictions of Capitalism op. cit.*, p. 80, fn. 31.

13. For such an analysis see Peter S. Albin, *Progress Without Poverty: Socially Responsible Growth* (New York: Basic Books, 1978).

14. For the dramatic data supporting this conclusion see Froman, *op. cit.*, chapter 4, pp. 51–66.

15. Hirsch, *op. cit.*, p. 174. For a collection of critical essays upon this work by Hirsch, see Adrian Ellis and Krishan Kumar, eds., *Dilemmas of Liberal Democracies: Studies in Fred Hirsch's Social Limits to Growth* (London: Tavistock Publications, 1983).

16. For examples see Beckerman, *op. cit.*; Kahn, *op. cit.*; and, Passell and Ross, *op. cit.*

17. See Albin, *op. cit.*, Hirsch, *op. cit.*, Froman, *op. cit.*, and Thomas R. Dye and Harmon Zeigler, "Socialism and Equality in Cross-National Perspective," *PS: Political Science and Politics* XXI (Winter 1988), pp. 45–56 and the sources of such data cited therein. These authors' cross-national data lead them to make the following important conclusion for our discussion: "After a certain threshold level of economic development is achieved, further increases in development do not necessarily produce additional increases in equality. The recent experience in the United States provides an illustration of the threshold notion; continued economic growth over the past few decades has not significantly reduced the remaining inequality," p. 51.

18. See Herman E. Daly, "Electric Power, Employment, and Economic Growth: A Case Study in Growthmania," in Daly, *Toward a Steady-State Economy, op. cit.*, p. 275; and, also, Dobb, *op. cit.*, p. 242.

19. Amartya K. Sen, *Collective Choice and Social Welfare*, cited in: Gary Gappert, *Post-Affluent America: The Social Economy of the Future* (New York: Franklin Watts, 1979), p. 99. Also, see the critique of Pareto optimality contained in: Mark A. Lutz and Kenneth Lux, *The Challenge of Humanistic Economics* (Menlo Park, Cal.: Benjamin/Cummings, 1979), pp. 92–101.

20. Bell, in Bell and Kristol, *op. cit.*, p. 50 (emphasis in original).

21. See Barber, *op. cit.*, p. 171.

22. See Walter W. Weisskopf, "Economic Growth versus Existential Balance," in Daly, *Toward a Steady-State Economy, op. cit.*, p. 243.

23. Kassiola, *op. cit.*, p. 94 where this statement was italicized.

24. Adam Smith, *An Inquiry into the Nature and Causes of the Wealth of Nations, op. cit.*, Book 1, chapter 8; p. 145 of this edition.

25. See Olson and Landsberg, *op. cit.*, *passim.*, but especially Olson's "Introduction," pp. 1–13 and the "Epilogue," by Olson, Landsberg, and Fisher, *op. cit.*, p. 229–241.
Even those economists who accept the limits-to-growth general position fall prey to this point of the alleged undesirable political traits of a no-growth society; see Kenneth E. Boulding, "New Goals for Society?" in Schurr, *op. cit.*, pp. 149–150. The Meadows team itself appears to associate the no-growth or negative growth of central cities' populations and their poor quality of life; see, Meadows *et al.*, *op. cit.*, p. 156.

26. Robert L. Heilbroner, *The Limits of American Capitalism* (New York: Harper and Row, 1967), p. 72.

27. Jürgen Habermas, *Legitimation Crisis*, trans. Thomas McCarthy (Boston: Beacon Press, 1973), p. 21.

28. Alan Wolfe, *America's Impasse: The Rise and Fall of the Politics of Growth* (New York: Pantheon, 1981). See also, Arndt, *op. cit.*

29. Wolfe, *ibid.*, p. 10.

Chapter 5

1. Wolin, *op. cit.*, p. 290.

2. *Ibid.*, p. 291. Dumont (*op. cit.*) makes the same point about Locke in a chapter entitled: "Locke's *Two Treatises*: Emancipation from Politics," where he writes: "perhaps the most revealing aspect in this configuration [of Locke's ideas] is that economics is not simply juxtaposed to politics but is hierarchically superior to it...." (pp. 59–60).

3. For another discussion of liberalism that is compatible with Wolin's and my presentation here, see the work of Macpherson, especially: *Democratic Theory*, *op. cit.*, and, *The Political Theory of Possessive Individualism: Hobbes to Locke* (Oxford: Oxford University Press, 1965).

4. Wolin, *op. cit.*, p. 291.

5. *Ibid.*, pp. 293–294.

6. Smith, *The Theory of Moral Sentiments*, cited in Wolin, *op. cit.*, p. 330. The opening phrase is Wolin's.
For a detailed account of the various forms of pain and despair suffered by contemporary Americans who experience downward mobility, see Katherine S. Newman, *Falling From Grace: The Experience of Downward Mobility in the American Middle Class* (New York: Free Press, 1988).

7. Wolin, *ibid.*, pp. 329, 331. The quote by Smith is from *The Wealth of Nations*, Book 5, chapter 2.

8. Wolin, *ibid.*, pp. 294–297.

9. Quoted in *ibid.*, p. 297.

10. *Ibid.*, pp. 297, 299. Here the devastating effect of value noncognitivism upon modern and contemporary political thought should be mentioned. This important point will be discussed shortly.

11. *Ibid.*, p. 300.

12. *Ibid.*

13. Robert A. Isaak and Ralph P. Hummel, *Politics for Human Beings* (North Scituate, Mass.: Duxbury Press, 1975), pp. 299, 14.

14. Brown, *The Twenty-Ninth Day, op. cit.*, p. 323.

15. This is a major theme of Polanyi's work (*op. cit.*) which stresses the fact that: "A self-regulating market demands nothing less than the institutional separation of society into an economic and political sphere" (p. 71).

16. Wolin, *op. cit.*, p. 347. See also, Lowe, *op. cit.*, pp. 30–31.

17. Wolin, *ibid.*, p. 301.

18. *Ibid.* Here Wolin cites Smith's *Wealth of Nations*, Book 1, chapters 7–8 and Book IV, chapter 2.

19. Wolin, *op. cit.*, p. 302.

20. C. B. Macpherson, "The Economic Penetration of Political Theory," in Macpherson, *Political Theory and Political Economy, op. cit., passim.*

21. The terms in quotes were borrowed from progrowth literature wherein the same metaphors appear frequently.

22. Wolin, *op. cit.*, p. 312.

23. G. A. Cohen, "The Structure of Proletarian Unfreedom," *Philosophy and Public Affairs* 12, No. 1 (Winter 1983), pp. 12–13 (emphasis in original). The phrase "extra-economic coercion" is from Marx's *Capital.*

24. John Firor, "Interconnections and the 'Endangered Species' of the Atmosphere," World Resources Institute, *Journal '84*, p. 20.

25. Wolin, *op. cit.*, p. 312.

26. Bell, *Cultural Contradictions of Capitalism, op. cit.*, p. 28 (emphasis in original).

27. *Ibid.*, p. 25. Bell here refers to "Western society," however, I think he means: "modern industrial and postindustrial society."

28. See Walter A. Weisskopf, *Alienation and Economics* (New York: Dell, 1971), chapter 2, especially p. 36.

29. Daly, in Smith, *op. cit.*, p. 67.

30. David Mermelstein, Introduction to part 3; in David Mermelstein, ed., *Economics: Mainstream Readings and Radical Critiques*, 2d ed. (New York: Random House, 1973), p. 230.

31. Value noncognitivism also reveals the shift by economists from objec-

tively defined, value-based, human needs to subjectively defined, analyst-neutral *wants*. For the important role of wants in economic thought see Tibor Scitovsky, *The Joyless Economy: An Inquiry into Human Satisfaction and Consumer Dissatisfaction* (Oxford: Oxford University Press, 1976).

32. Sidney S. Alexander, "Human Values and Economists' Values," in Hook, *op. cit.*, p. 107.

33. Keynes, *op. cit.*, p. 365.

Chapter 6

1. Jean Jacques Rousseau, "A Discourse on the Origin of Inequality," in Jean Jacques Rousseau, *The Social Contract and Discourses*, trans. G. D. H. Cole (New York: E. P. Dutton, 1950), p. 270.

2. Hirsch, *op. cit.*, p. 2–3.

3. On the crucial role of the insatiability of relative goods in advanced industrial societies, see Scitovsky, *op. cit.*, Leiss, *The Limits to Satisfaction, op. cit.*, and Kimon Valaskakis *et al.*, *The Conserver Society: A Workable Alternative for the Future* (New York: Harper and Row, 1979), especially part 1.

For the first contemporary economist who emphasized this relativity of modern goods termed "relative income hypothesis," see James S. Duesenberry, *Income, Saving and the Theory of Consumer Behavior* (Cambridge: Harvard University Press, 1949).

4. For this distinction between absolute "destitution" and relative "poverty," see Andre Gorz, *Ecology as Politics*, trans. by Patsy Vigderman and Jonathan Cloud (Boston: South End Press, 1980), p. 29.

5. Galbraith, *The New Industrial State, op. cit.*, p. 24.

On the great social significance of advertising and its relation to material consumption see Stuart Ewen, *Captains of Consciousness: Advertising and the Social Roots of the Consumer Culture* (New York: McGraw-Hill, 1977). For one deceptive way—through subliminal messages—that modern advertising achieves this large influence within advanced industrial society see Wilson Bryan Key, *Subliminal Seduction: Ad Media's Manipulation of a Not so Innocent America* (New York: New American Library, 1974).

6. Rousseau, *op. cit.*, pp. 241–242.

7. For illustrative examples see Beckerman, *op. cit.*; Kahn, *op. cit.*; Passell and Ross, *op. cit.*; and, perhaps the most extreme progrowth position, Simon, *op. cit.*

8. Marion J. Levy, Jr., *Modernization and the Structure of Societies: A Setting for International Affairs*, 2 vols. (Princeton: Princeton University Press,

1966), vol. 2, pp. 784–785 (my emphasis). Levy cites as the originator of the "trickle effect," L. A. Fallers, "A Note on the Trickle Effect," *Public Opinion Quarterly* 18, no. 3 (Fall 1954), pp. 314–321. He also notes that this work and its conception of the "trickle effect" is seldom used by other students of society, p. 784, fn. 18.

I agree with Levy's remark here about the lack of analysis of this often-referred-to phenomenon despite the popular use of the term "trickle down" by members of the political elite. A thorough analysis of the nature and implications of this important "trickle down" assumption of contemporary political economic thinking and policy is rare. In fact, Levy's discussion is the only one I have encountered!

   9. Tawney, *The Acquisitive Society, op. cit.*, p. 40.

   10. See Macpherson, *Possessive Individualism op. cit.*, *passim.*

   11. Mishan, *Economic Growth Debate, op. cit.*, pp. 119–120.

   12. Mishan, *Technology and Growth, op. cit.*, pp. 83–84.

   13. Passell and Ross, *op. cit.*, p. 14.

   14. See Ted Robert Gurr, *Why Men Rebel* (Princeton: Princeton University Press, 1972), especially pp. 24–30 and the literature cited therein. For a more recent discussion and application of this theory, see Abraham H. Miller, Louis H. Bolce, and Mark Halligan, "The J-Curve Theory and the Black Urban Riots: An Empirical Test of Progressive Relative Deprivation Theory," *American Political Science Review* 71, no. 3 (September 1977), pp. 964–982.

   15. Thomas Hobbes, *Leviathan*, chapter 8; cited in Macpherson, *Possessive Individualism, op. cit.*, p. 34.

   16. Thorstein Veblen, *The Theory of the Leisure Class: An Economic Study of Institutions* (New York: New American Library, 1963), pp. 39–40. The term "pecuniary emulation" appears on p. 40.

   17. See, Hirsch, *op. cit.*, p. 7.

   18. Hirsch, *ibid.*, p. 5.

   19. *Ibid.* The first term is introduced on p. 4 and the second on p. 35.

   20. *Ibid.*, p. 2.

   21. *Ibid.*, p. 4.

   22. For a discussion of the importance of community in nineteenth and twentieth century political thought see, Wolin, *op. cit.*, chapter 10. For this value in Western political thought in general see, Glenn Tinder, *Community: Reflections on a Tragic Ideal* (Baton Rouge: Louisiana State University Press, 1980) and the literature cited therein.

Chapter 7

1. Polanyi, *op. cit.*, p. 40.

2. Marcuse, *op. cit.*, p. 9.

3. Quoted in: Wolin, *op. cit.*, p. 286.

4. Lutz and Lux, *op. cit.*, p. 301, fn. (emphasis in original).

5. See Arendt, *op. cit.*, section 61, "The Rise of the Social," pp. 35–45. See p. 15 for the first quoted phrase.

6. *Ibid.*, pp. 34–35. For Arendt's perhaps too weak formulation of the mere "coincidence" between the rise of modern society and economics, see p. 39. Based upon our discussion above, the relation between modern, reductionist, depoliticizing economics and modern, reductionist, depoliticizing, materialist society is probably stronger than mere coincidence as this part will attempt to delineate.

7. E. K. Hunt, "The Transition from Feudalism to Capitalism," in Edwards, Reich and Weisskopf, *op. cit.*, p. 57.

8. Social anthropologist Louis Dumont expresses the normative revolutionary character of industrialism as follows: "In most societies, and in the first place in the higher civilizations, which I shall designate henceforth as the 'traditional societies,' the relations between men are more important, more highly valued, than the relations between and things. This primacy is reversed in the modern type of society, in which relations between men are subordinated to relations between men and things... This is the decisive shift that distinguishes the modern civilization from all others and that corresponds to the primacy of the economic view in our ideological universe...." See Dumont, *op. cit.*, pp. 5, 81. This work by Dumont is an intellectual historical tracing of this materialist reversal of industrial society within the political and economic thought of Locke, Mandeville, Hume, Smith, and Marx.

For another intellectual history of what the author terms "political hedonism" (what I call "industrial materialism"), begun in the sixteenth and seventeenth centuries with modernity and industrialization, and its revolutionary stance against the values of the long-dominant, ancient-Scholastic, moral-political tradition, see Frederick Vaughan, *The Tradition of Political Hedonism: From Hobbes to J. S. Mill* (New York: Fordham University Press, 1984).

9. Macpherson, *Democratic Theory, op. cit.*, pp. 17–18.

10. For a history of the opposition to Western thought to what the author calls "luxury" from the ancient Hebrews until 1700, see, John Sekora, *Luxury: The Concept in Western Thought, Eden to Smollet* (Baltimore: Johns Hopkins University Press, 1977), chapter 1. Sekora asserts that "the concept of luxury is one of the oldest, most important, and most pervasive negative principles for organizing society Western history has known," pp. 1–2.

The modern denial of limits violates the two millennia of Western thought opposed to luxury or, in other words, recognizing our limits. That the industrial value of unlimited growth and its materialism are characterized both by "luxury" in Sekora's sense and "hedonism" in Vaughan's should be clear.

11. Bruce-Biggs, *op. cit.*, p. 29.

12. See Fromm, *op. cit.*, p. 77. In this volume Fromm attacks this "having mode," or materialism, of modern industrial society. He captures the insecurity that such materialism engenders when he pointedly poses the question: "If I am what I have and if what I have is lost who then am I?" p. 109.

13. On the concept of "dominant social paradigm" as "the prominent worldview, model, or frame of reference, through which individuals, or, collectively, a society, interpret the meaning of the external world;" wherein this worldview consists of "norms, beliefs, values, habits and so on...." see Pirages and Ehrlich, *op. cit.*, p. 43.

14. Although brief in length, the following list of normative limits-to-growth works is broadly defined indicating the paucity of this approach within the overall limits-to-growth position: Heilbroner, *An Inquiry into the Human Prospect*, *op. cit.*, Schumacher, *op. cit.*, Hirsch, *op. cit.*, Camilleri, *op. cit.*, Miles, *op. cit.*, Ophuls, *op. cit.*, Milbrath, *Envisioning*, *op. cit.*, and, Robert L. Stivers, *The Sustainable Society: Ethics and Economic Growth* (Philadelphia: Westminster Press, 1976).

15. Beckerman, *op. cit.*, pp. 79, 81.

16. Thurow, *op. cit.*, p. 120 (the emphasis is mine).

17. See Richard A. Easterlin, "Does Economic Growth Improve the Human Lot? Some Empirical Evidence," in Paul A. David and Melvin W. Reder, eds., *Nations and Households in Economic Growth: Essays in Honor of Moses Abramovitz* (New York: Academic Press, 1974), p. 119.

18. Ronald Inglehart, *The Silent Revolution: Changing Values and Political Styles Among Western Publics* (Princeton: Princeton University Press, 1977), p. 176.

19. Morgan Reynolds and Eugene Smolensky, "Welfare Economics: Or, When is a Change an Improvement?" in Weintraub, *op. cit.*, pp. 447–448.

20. See Daly, "The Steady-State Economy: Toward a Political Economy of Biophysical Equilibrium and Moral Growth," *op. cit.*

21. John Stuart Mill, *Principles of Political Economy with some of Their Applications to Social Philosophy*, 2 vols., volume 2, Book 4, chapter 6 (New York: D. Appleton, 1872), p. 336.

22. *Ibid.*, p. 337. Today with the sexual revolution and feminist movement, we might revise Mill's statement about America to read: "the lives of *both* sexes are devoted to dollar-hunting!"

23. *Ibid.*

24. This list of the "things[?] that make people happy" is taken from Robert E. Lane, "Markets and the Satisfaction of Human Wants," *Journal of Economic Issues* 12 (December 1978), p. 815.

For a creative and influential discussion of how the materialist postindustrial society, because of its preoccupation with material acquisition, puts time pressure on such crucial but nonmaterial aspects of human experience as Lane's list or child-care or care of the elderly, all made to suffer because of their time-intensiveness, see Staffan Burenstam Linder, *The Harried Leisure Class* (New York: Columbia University Press, 1970), especially Chapters 4 and 5.

25. Schumacher, *op. cit.*

26. On the concept of "voluntary simplicity," see Duane Elgin, *Voluntary Simplicity: Toward a Way of Life That is Outwardly Simple, Inwardly Rich* (New York: William Morrow, 1981) and the references contained therein.

On the concept of the "simple life" in American thought, see David E. Shi, *The Simple Life: Plain Living and High Thinking in American Culture* (New York: Oxford University Press, 1986).

27. Slater, *op. cit.*, pp. 62–63 (emphasis in original).

28. Fromm, *op. cit.*, p. 149.

29. A discussion of the primary representative of this philosophical tradition, from the pre-Socratics until the twentieth century is provided by, Wilhem Windelband, *A History of Philosophy*, 2 vols. (New York: Harper and Row, 1958).

30. See, C. H. Whitely, *An Introduction to Metaphysics* (London: Methuen, 1966), p. 12.

31. Hereafter when the terms "material commodities" or "material goods" are used, I shall include within this category the provision of services in exchange for monetary payment. To further support this treatment of services-for-a-fee as falling within the materialist component of industrial society, I cite William Leiss's discussion of all human needs having a materialist element within them "in the sense that the life-requirements of individuals and societies necessarily entail a constant 'material exchange' of organic and inorganic substances governed by the structure of nature;" see Leiss, *op. cit.*, p. 64. This important point about the (material) nature of social goods, including goods within postindustrial society, shall be addressed and expanded upon shortly.

32. This point is often overlooked especially by economists who we saw in the previous part were mostly characterized by value noncognitivism as well as assuming the "bedrock truth of [modern] economics" which, according to Irving Kristol, consists of materialism or the belief that "the overwhelming majority of men and women are naturally and incorrigibly [ever-increasingly? unlimitedly?] interested in improving their material conditions. . . . " see Kristol, in Bell and Kristol, *op. cit.*, p. 218.

33. See Valaskakis *et al.*, *op. cit.*, p. 15. The first sentence quoted from this source regarding "the first belief of mass-consumption society" is taken from the section title on this page and is capitalized in the original text.

Chapter 8

1. *Leviathan*, part 1, chapter 11. See Herbert W. Schneider, ed., The Library of Liberal Arts Edition, Parts 1 and 2 (Indianapolis: Bobbs-Merrill, 1958), p. 85.

2. See *Emile*, Book 4, trans. Barbara Foxley, Everyman's Library Edition (London: J. M. Dent, 1963), pp. 174–175.

3. Fromm, *op. cit.*, p. 27.

4. For an influential presentation of this interpretation of Hobbes's political philosophy and its modern significance, see Leo Strauss, *The Political Philosophy of Hobbes: Its Basis and its Genesis*, trans. Elsa M. Sinclair (Chicago: University of Chicago Press, 1966), especially the Introduction, pp. 1–5.

5. Cited in Vaughan, *op. cit.*, p. 107. The quotation from Hobbes in single quotes is from *De Cive* and cited in Vaughan as: I, 2, 5, 7; 13, 4–6 (see, p. 112, fn. 136). In my edition of *De Cive* (*The Citizen*) the pertinent passage reads: the Sovereign's duty is "to furnish their subjects abundantly, not only with the good things belonging to life, but also with those which advance to delectation." See Thomas Hobbes, *Man and Citizen*, ed. Bernard Gert (Garden City: Anchor Books, 1972), *The Citizen*, 13, 4; p. 259.

6. Hobbes, *Leviathan*, *op. cit.*, Introduction, p. 23 of Library of Liberal Arts edition.

7. George H. Sabine, *A History of Political Theory*, 4th ed., rev. by Thomas Landon Thorson (Hinsdale, Ill.: Dryden Press, 1973), p. 424.

8. A brief list of such intellectual historical analyses which would make, along with the references contained in them, a good starting point for such an inquiry is: Hirschman, *Passions and Interests*, *op. cit.*, Hirschman, "Rival Interpretations of Market Society," *op. cit.*, Horne, "Envy and Commercial Society," *op. cit.*; in addition to the previously cited historical studies of modern thought and society: Dumont, *op. cit.*, Macpherson, *Possessive Individualism*, *op. cit.*, and Vaughan, *op. cit.*

9. For our earlier discussion of this competitive or relative nature of goods in advanced industrial society necessitating dissatisfaction for most of its members see part 2 above.

10. Jean Jacques Rousseau, *A Discourse on the Origin of Inequality* in *The Social Contract and Discourses*, *op. cit.*, p. 223, fn. 2.

11. See *ibid.*, especially pp. 241–242 where this account of Rousseau's was quoted earlier.

12. *Ibid.*, p. 197.

13. Albert Camus, *The Myth of Sisyphus and Other Essays, op. cit.*, p. 4.

14. Isaak and Hummel, *op. cit.*, p. 42.

14. Rousseau, *Second Discourse on Inequality, op. cit.*, p. 270 (my emphasis).

15. *Ibid.*, p. 271.

17. It is, I think, instructive to recall that Rousseau's examples of the origin of inequality or social esteem concern excellence at skillful activities like singing, dancing, speaking or physical traits such as, beauty, strength or dexterity—and not material possessions yet! See the previously quoted passage from his *Second Discourse on Inequality.* It was left to Smith to make this essential materialist connection.

18. Adam Smith, *The Theory of Moral Sentiments*, vol. 1, quoted in Hirschman, *The Passions and the Interests, op. cit.*, p. 108 (emphasis in original).

19. Adam Smith, *An Inquiry into the Nature and Cause of the Wealth of Nations*, Book 1, chapter 12, Modern Library College Editions (New York: Random House, 1985), p. 15.

20. *Ibid.*, Book 2, chapter 3, p. 147.

21. Weisskopf, "Economic Growth versus Existential Balance," in Daly, ed., *Toward a Steady-State Economy, op. cit.*, p. 242.

22. Hirschman, *The Passions and the Interests, op. cit.*, p. 109.

23. Horne, *op. cit.*, p. 553.

24. *Ibid.*, See also his volume, *The Social Theory of Bernard Mandeville, op. cit.*

25. Horne, "Envy and Public Benefits," *ibid.*

26. E. J. Mishan, *Technology and Growth*, quoted in Goldian VandenBroeck, ed., *Less is More: The Art of Voluntary Poverty* (New York: Harper & Row, 1978), p. 289.

27. Both quotes may be found in Springborg, *op. cit.*, p. 29.

28. Abram N. Shulsky, "Economic Doctrine in Aristotle's *Politics*," in Macpherson, *Political Economy and Political Theory, op. cit.*, pp. 20–24 for Shulsky's entire discussion; the quoted phrases at the beginning of this paragraph were taken from pp. 20 and 23–24 respectively, and the lengthier statement from p. 20 of this work.

29. *Ibid.*, pp. 22–23.

30. *Ibid.*, p. 24.

31. See, Dusan Pokorny, "Professor Shulsky on Aristotle's Economic Doctrine," in Macpherson, *ibid.*, pp. 6–9.

32. Hobbes, *Leviathan*, part 1, chapter 13, *op. cit.*, p. 107.

33. Mumford, vol. 1, *op. cit.*, p. 203. See also, Mumford's discussion of industrialization as the "removal of limits" in a section with that name in vol. 2, pp. 172–175.

34. Macpherson, *Democratic Theory, op. cit.*, p. 31.

35. Smith, "The Teleological View of Wealth: A Historical Perspective," in Daly, ed., *Economics, Ecology, Ethics, op. cit.*, p. 215. The mention of narcissism in the previous paragraph is taken from: Christopher Lasch, *The Culture of Narcissism: American Life in an Age of Diminishing Expectations* (New York: Warner Books, 1979).

36. Philip Slater, *Wealth Addiction* (New York: E. P. Dutton, 1980), pp. 18, 23, and 144 (emphasis in original).

37. Scitovsky, *op. cit.*, p. 125.

38. *Ibid.*, pp. 128–129.

39. *Ibid.*, p. 128.

40. *Ibid.*, pp. 130–131.

41. Cited in Keith Thomas, "The Social Origins of Hobbes's Political Thought," in K. C. Brown, ed., *Hobbes Studies* (Cambridge: Harvard University Press, 1965), p. 191.

42. *Ibid.*

43. Veblen, *op. cit.*, p. 39. It should be noted that Veblen, like Hirsch, fails to cite any of the (mostly political) previous thinkers who recognized this competitive emulation or *amour propre* quality of industrial life. Are these omissions by economists Veblen and Hirsch the result of the lack of appreciating political philosophy by economists, along with its key emphasis upon social values?

44. Springborg, *op. cit.*, p. 45.

45. See Karl Marx, *Capital*, vol. 1, part 1, chapter 1, section 4 entitled: "The Fetishism of Commodities and The Secret Thereof." I have used the selections from this work by Marx contained in: Robert C. Tucker, ed., *The Marx-Engels Reader* (New York: W. W. Norton, 1972). In this edition this section is found on pp. 215–225.

46. Marx, *Capital, ibid.*, p. 215.

47. See *ibid.*, part 1, chapter 1, "Commodities," pp. 198–225.

48. See John G. Gurley, "The Theory of Surplus Value," in Edwards, Reich, and Weisskopf, *op. cit.*, pp. 88–90.

49. Cited in *ibid.*, p. 89; no source is given here for this quote of Marx.

50. Marx, *op. cit.*, p. 217.

51. Gurley, *op. cit.*, p. 89.

52. Thomas E. Weisskopf, "The Irrationality of Capitalist Economic Growth," in Edwards, Reich and Weisskopf, *op. cit.*, p. 401.

53. Marx, *op. cit.*, p. 217.

54. See Engels's attempt at clarifying what he and Marx thought on this issue, in his letters during the last years of his life, contained in Lewis S. Feuer, ed., *Marx & Engels: Basic Writings on Politics & Philosophy* (Garden City: Doubleday, 1959), pp. 395–412. Essentially, these notes by Engels claim a *qualified* materialist view. Some of the same letters are provided by Tucker in his volume, *op. cit.*, pp. 640–650.

55. Cited in Lutz and Lux, *op. cit.*, p. 10 with no citation given (emphasis in original).

56. Linder, *op. cit.*, p. 124.

57. *Ibid.*

58. Easterlin, *op. cit.*, pp. 90, 121.

59. See Mary Douglas and Baron Isherwood, *The World of Goods: Towards an Anthropology of Consumption* (New York: W. W. Norton, 1979). The phrase "materialist approach to consumption" and its rejection are taken from p. 202; the phrase "communication approach to consumption" is borrowed from p. 10; and, see part 1 of this volume wherein the authors analyze industrial "Goods as an Information System."

60. *Ibid.*, p. 5.

61. Leiss, *op. cit.*, p. 64 (emphasis is mine).

62. *Ibid.*, p. 80. Leiss discusses Lancaster's theory of consumption involving commodities as "collections of characteristics" on pp. 79–82. Lancaster's main work is: *Consumer Demand: A New Approach* (New York: Columbia University Press, 1971).

63. Quoted in Leiss, *ibid.*, p. 80.

64. *Ibid.*

65. *Ibid.*, p. 82.

66. See *ibid.*, p. 80.

67. *Ibid.*, p. 81.

68. Thomas Hobbes, *De Cive, The English Version*, edited by Howard Warrender (Oxford: Oxford University Press, 1983), pp. 43–44. The translation in brackets was supplied by the editor in footnote a, p. 44.

69. Hobbes, *Leviathan, op. cit.*, part 1, chapter 6, p. 57.

70. Marcuse, *op. cit.*, p. 58.

Chapter 9

1. Daniel Bell, "The Return of the Sacred: The Argument about the Future of Religion," in Gabriel A. Almond, Marvin Chodorow, and Roy Harvey Pearce, eds., *Progress and its Discontents* (Berkeley: University of California Press, 1982), pp. 522–523.

2. Willis W. Harman, *An Incomplete Guide to the Future* (New York: W. W. Norton, 1979), pp. 144–145.

3. See Bell, *The Cultural Contradictions of Capitalism, op. cit.*, p. 49.

4. Dennis Clark Pirages, "Introductions: A Social Design for Sustainable Growth," in Dennis Clark Pirages, ed., *The Sustainable Society: Implications for Limited Growth, op. cit.*, p. 5.

5. See *ibid.*, pp. 5–10, but especially p. 8 for this list.

6. *Ibid.*, p. 8.

7. Victor Ferkiss, "Nature, Technology and Political Society," paper delivered at the 1982 Annual Meeting of the American Political Science Association, Denver, pp. 12, 15.

8. The phrase "politics as a way of living," has been borrowed from the subtitle of chapter 6 of: Benjamin Barber, *Strong Democracy: Participatory Politics for a New Age* (Berkeley: University of California Press, 1984), p. 117. On this title page Barber provides the following quotation from Aristotle (no other information is given regarding its source) which serves as part of the chapter's epigraph: "We have in mind men whose state of virtue does not rise above that of ordinary people . . . who seek not an ideally perfect constitution, but first a way of living."

I have added here the term "human development" to Barber's (and Aristotle's) "way of living" as a characterization of the highest form of politics within a desirable society following Marx and Engels's envisioned superior replacement for the capitalist social order. They wrote: "In place of the old bourgeois society, with its classes and class antagonisms, we shall have an association, in which the free development of each is the condition of the free development of all." See Karl Marx and Friedrich Engels, "Manifesto of the Communist Party," in Tucker, *op. cit.*, p. 353.

For a discussion of the crucial causal relation between political activity and human development, see the wide-ranging literature on participatory democracy whose advocates usually emphasize the educative function of political participation on the part of all citizens. See, for example, in addition to Barber's volume above, Carole Pateman, *Participation and Democractic Theory* (London: Cambridge University Press, 1972), especially chapter 2; and, Ronald Mason, *Participatory and Workplace Democracy: A Theoretical Development in Critique of Liberalism* (Carbondale: Southern Illinois University Press, 1982), especially chapter 1; as well as the participationist theorists cited or discussed in these three works.

9. See Sam Dolgoff, ed., *Bakunin on Anarchy: Selected Works by the Anarchist-Founder of World Anarchism* (New York: Vintage Books/Random House, 1972).

10. *The Republic of Plato*, trans. Allan Bloom (New York: Basic Books, 1968), 369a; p. 45 of this edition. See also, 369c, p. 46, where the text refers to a "city in speech."

11. One example of such a work is Ehrlich and Ehrlich, *op. cit.* The final chapter of this work is entitled: "A Brighter Future: It's Up to You," pp. 217–257.

12. See 471c, p. 151 of the Bloom translation of *The Republic*, *op. cit.*, and for Socrates' reply: 472a, p. 152. Bloom provides the information regarding the Greek view of the third wave in note 35, p. 460.

13. Alvin W. Gouldner, *Enter Plato: Classical Greece and the Origins of Social Theory*, part 2 (New York: Harper and Row, 1971), p. 125.

14. See Milbrath, *Envisioning*, *op. cit.*, pp. xii, 59, 71 and 87.

15. *Ibid.*, pp. 35, 71.

16. For an example, see his discussion on p. 353, *ibid.*

17. See *ibid.*, pp. 367–368.

18. Neuhaus, *op. cit.*, pp. 15–16 and 117.

19. See Milbrath, *Envisioning*, figure 4.1, p. 72.

20. On the dangers of a monistic value structure and the need for a pluralist one, see Isaiah Berlin, *Four Essays on Liberty* (London: Oxford University Press, 1969), *passim.*, but especially pp. xlix–li and the essay, "John Stuart Mill and the Ends of Life," pp. 173–206. On the naturalistic fallacy, see any introductory text in

moral philosophy. For one of the most thorough discussions see, John Hospers, *Human Conduct: An Introduction to the Problems of Ethics* (New York: Harcourt, Brace and World, 1961), pp. 532–538.

21. See Milbrath's typology of social change approaches on pp. 354–356 of *Envisioning, op. cit.*

22. See *ibid.*, pp. 366–380.

23. Niccolo Machiavelli, *The Prince*, trans. Luigi Ricci (New York: New American Library, 1962), Chapter 6, pp. 49–50.

24. See quote by Henry C. Wallich cited earlier. See, also the large body of data showing the greater conservatism of the lower calss as compared to the younger members of the middle class in Inglehart's research; for example, his: *The Silent Revolution: Changing Values and Political Styles Among Western Publics, op. cit.* For two contemporary Marxists' recognition of this important development for Marxist theory see Gorz, *op. cit.*, and Habermas, *Legitimation Crisis, op. cit.* Again, this development supports Machiavelli's point about the incredulity of humanity toward anything (socially) new.

25. On the Greens, their political philosophy, and social action to realize it, see Werner Hulsberg, *The German Greens: A Social and Political Profile*, trans. Gus Fagan (London: Verso, 1988); Charlene Spretnak and Fritjof Capra, *Green Politics* (Santa Fe, N.M.: Bear and Co., 1986); Rudolf Bahro, *Building the Green Movement*, trans. Mary Tyler (Philadelphia: New Society Publishers, 1986); Jonathon Porritt, *Seeing Green: The Politics of Ecology Explained* (New York: Basil Blackwell, 1985); and, the speeches and writings of the German Greens' leader, Petra Kelly, contained in: Petra Kelly, *Fighting for Hope*, trans. Marianne Howarth (Boston: South End Press, 1984).

Spretnak and Capra provide a list of Green parties and their addresses around the world which include: Austria, Belgium, Canada, France, Ireland, Luxembourg, Sweden, the United Kingdom, and the United States, in addition to West Germany; see pp. 251–252 of their volume.

For an example of the increasing academic and public interest in the Greens, see the 1986 Annual Meeting of the American Political Science Association in Washington, D.C. where three papers on the Greens were delivered: Mary M. McKenzie, "Toward a New Political Consciousness: A Preliminary Report on New Social Movements in the Federal Republic of Germany;" John Ely, "The Greens of West Germany: An Alternative Modernity (or: How German is It?)"; and, Herbert Kitschelt, "The West German Green Party in Comparative Perspective: Explaining Innovation in Competitive Party Systems." This continued through the 1989 Annual Meeting where there were no less than five papers on the Greens. Also, see special issue of *Social Research* 52 (Winter 1985) devoted to "Social Movements." Guest edited by Jean L. Cohen, which contains six articles on the new social movements, including the Greens, by contemporary social theorists.

This academic flurry of interest in the Greens and the other new anti-industrial social movements (of which more discussion shall be provided later) should increase even further given the Green party's electoral improvement in the 1987 West German parliamentary elections, gaining 8.3 percent of the vote—up from 5.6 in 1983 (see James M. Markham, "West German Vote: Kohl Wins 4 Years as Umpire," *New York Times*, January 27, 1987, p. a3, for the election results); and a significant increase in the 1989 European Parliament elections held in June 1989 (see Serge Schmemann, "Environmentalists and Socialists Gain in European Vote," *New York Times*, June 19, 1989, p. a1). For an analysis of the European elections and the Green parties' performance, see E. Gene Frankland, "Does Green Politics Have a Future in Britain?" Paper delivered at the 1989 Annual Meeting of the American Political Science Association, Atlanta, pp. 13–23, especially Table 3.

26. Other examples of biophysical limits-to-growth works that do not consider industrial values are: Mesarovic and Pestel, *op. cit.*, Davis, *op. cit.*, Goldsmith *et al.*, *op. cit.*, Catton, *op. cit.*, and finally, Barney, *op. cit.*

27. See Daly, *Steady-State Economics, op. cit.*, pp. 53–56.

28. *Ibid.*, pp. 56–61. This idea was first proposed by Kenneth Boulding in his, *The Meaning of the 20th Century: The Great Transition* (New York: Harper and Row, 1964), pp. 135–136; whom Daly cites.

29. Botkin, Elmandjra, and Malitza, *op. cit.*, pp. 93–94.

30. Mishan, *The Economic Growth Debate, op. cit.*, p. 122 for the quoted phrase and pp. 122–125 for the author's entire attack upon modern transportation.

31. Pirages and Ehrlich, *op. cit.*, p. 280. This proposal is part of the final section of this volume entitled, "A New Society" and consisting of three pages! (pp. 279–282)

32. Hirsch, *op. cit.*, p. 183.

33. Joshua Cohen and Joel Rogers, *On Democracy: Toward a Transformation of American Society* (New York: Penguin Books, 1983), p. 179.

34. Michael E. Kraft, "Political Change and the Sustainable Society," in Dennis Clark Pirages, ed., *The Sustainable Society: Implications for Limited Growth* (New York: Praeger, 1977), pp. 173–196.

35. *Ibid.*, p. 177.

36. *Ibid.*, pp. 186–187.

37. Lane Davis, "The Cost of Realism: Contemporary Restatement of Democracy," *Western Political Quarterly* 17 (1964), pp. 40–41.

38. See Introduction by Lionel Trilling to works by Arnold in: *Major British Writers*, Enlarged Edition, G. B. Harrison *et al.*, eds. (New York: Harcourt, Brace, 1959), vol. 2, pp. 579–592.

39. John Stuart Mill, "The Spirit of the Age," in J. B. Schneewind, ed., *Mill's Essays on Literature and Society* (New York: Collier Books, 1965), p. 30. See the editor's discussion of Mill's two stage view of history: either a "natural" stage which is stable and where social consensus exists, or a "transitional" era where social agreement breaks down; see, pp. 14–15; also Mill's "Spirit of the Age" essay, pp. 36, 46.

40. John Stuart Mill, *On Liberty*, ed. Currin V. Shields (Indianapolis: Bobbs-Merrill, 1956), Ch. II, p. 27.

41. See Peter L. Berger and Thomas Luckman, *The Social Construction of Reality: A Treatise in the Sociology of Knowledge* (Garden City, N.Y.: Doubleday, 1966) for the central role of social factors in defining our experienced reality.

42. See for just one illustration of this very large literature, Roger Trigg, *Reality at Risk: A Defence of Realism in Philosophy and the Sciences* (Sussex, Great Britain: The Harvester Press, 1980) and the references cited therein. For a political perspective on this debate see Bernstein, *op. cit.*

43. Trilling, *op. cit.*, pp. 585–586.

44. Matthew Arnold, *Stanzas from the Grande Chartreuse*, in Harrison *et al.*, *op. cit.*, vol. 2, p. 613. In the passage quoted in the text, "these" refers to the monks of the French town of Chartreuse. See Trilling's note on p. 612.

45. Philip Green, *Retrieving Democracy: In Search of Civic Equality* (Totawa, N.J.: Rowman and Allanheld, 1985), p. viii (emphasis in original).

46. *Ibid.*, p. 266.

47. Camilleri, *op. cit.*, p. 250.

48. George Orwell, *1984* (New York: New American Library, 1961), p. 61 where it is italicized.

49. For the quoted passage see, Camilleri, *op. cit.*, p. 250. For the references to Freire see footnote 8 on p. 292 of this work by Camilleri.

50. On the Greek view where it is asserted that "the Hellenic impulse always emphasized limit, and the *polis* was always limited by what the Greek could take in 'at a single view,' " see Murray Bookchin, *Toward an Ecological Society, op. cit.*, p. 143. On the Hebrew view, see Sekora, *op. cit.*, pp. 23–24.

For the first Greek political philosophical attack upon the "unlimited acquisition of money" as "overstepping the boundary of the necessary;" see Plato's *Republic*, 372d–373d, pp. 49–50 of the Bloom edition; the quoted phrases are from 373d, p. 50.

51. Herman E. Daly, "Introduction," in Daly, *Toward a Steady-State Economy, op. cit.*, p. 281.

52. Peter L. Berger, Brigitte Berger, and Hansfried Kellner, *The Homeless Mind: Modernization and Consciousness* (New York: Random House, 1973), p. 185.

53. William H. Chafe, *Women and Equality: Changing Patterns in American Culture* (New York: Oxford University Press, 1978), p. 101. See Chafe's citation to Smelzer's influential, *Theory of Collective Behavior*, in a note on p. 99.

54. Mark N. Hagopian, *The Phenomenon of Revolution* (New York: Mead, 1974), p. 166.

55. Cohen and Rogers, *op. cit.*, p. 183.

56. This is the theme of Inglehart's work; see references to his work provided earlier. Also, see various crises in the environment during the summer of 1988 and the public's possible change of values and increased support for environmental groups and antigrowth policies. For one such report, see May, *op. cit.*, p. 30.

57. See Introduction to Wilde's play, *Lady Windermere's Fan*, from which the epigraph is taken, by the editors to the volume: J. S. P. Tatlock and R. G. Martin, *Representative English Plays: From the Miracle Plays to Pinero*, 2d ed., revised and enlarged (New York: Appleton-Century-Crofts, 1938), p. 843. The text of Wilde's play may be found on pp. 844–871, with the remarks used for the epigraph for this volume on p. 863.

58. Given Wilde's predilection to comment upon human nature in general in this play (according to the editors, Tatlock and Martin, see *ibid.*), it probably is the former; however I do not believe that either interpretation will jeopardize the analysis which is to follow for reasons that I hope will be evident.

59. The quoted passage from Tocqueville is cited in: Robert N. Bellah, Richard Madsen, William M. Sullivan, Ann Swidler, and Steven M. Tipton, *Habits of the Heart: Individualism and Commitment in American Life* (Berkeley: University of California Press, 1985), p. 117. The original source is Tocqueville's *Democracy in America*. For full citation, see p. 318, note 5 of this work.

60. CBS Television Network, October 13, 1970; quoted in Stavrianos, *op. cit.*, p. 165.

61. Nicholas Rescher, "What is Value Change?" A Framework for Research," in Kurt Baier and Nicholas Rescher, eds., *Values and the Future: The Impact of Technological Change on American Values* (New York: Free Press, 1971), p. 74 (emphasis in original). See p. 82 for Rescher's term "realization erosion".

62. Alfie Kohn, *No Contest: The Case Against Competition* (Boston: Houghton Mifflin, 1986), p. 111 (my emphasis for the first emphasis of the commentator, the second emphasis is in the original). The original source is: George Leonard, "Winning Isn't Everything, It's Nothing," *Intellectual Digest* (October 1973), p. 46.

63. See Lutz and Lux, *op. cit.*, p. 11, figure 1-1.

64. David Vogel, "Business and the Politics of Slowed Growth," in Pirages, ed., *op. cit.*, p. 249.

65. For this latter point of the relation between the existence of discrepancies between our values and reality, and social transformation see Wilbert E. Moore's analysis of social change whose "universal source" is said by Moore to be, "in its most general form . . . the *lack of close correspondence between the 'ideal' and the 'actual'* in many and pervasive contexts of social behavior." See Wilbert E. Moore, *Social Change* (Englewood Cliffs, N.J.: Prentice-Hall, 1965), p. 18 (emphasis in original).

66. On the logical or conceptual impossibilities of everyone succeeding competitively see Hirsch, *op. cit.*, and Kohn, *op. cit.* In addition, for an empirical indication of the necessary futility of materially poor nations catching up with the materially affluent nations I cite the data provided by Jerome Segal in his "Income and Development," *QQ—Report from the Center for Philosophy and Public Policy*, University of Maryland, vol. 5, no. 4 (Fall 1985), pp. 9–12, in a table entitled: "The GNP Race," p. 11. In this table comparing the GNP (in dollars) per capita in 1983, the annual growth rate of GNP per capita 1965–1983, and the number of years until the gap closes between the rich and poor nations if the 1965–1983 rates continue, the reader is startled to learn the following: that such newly industrialized countries as the Republic of Korea and Brazil will take 42 and 73 years respectively to catch up to the materially affluent countries (called by Segal: "industrial market economies"); poor Third World countries such as Sri Lanka and Cameroon, 902 and 1334.7 years respectively; and, most stunning of all, the extremely poor, "Fourth World" countries (to indicate their even worse poverty than Third World countries) enumerated by Segal as: Costa Rica, Kenya, India, Bangladesh, Zaire, Burma, Tanzania, Haiti, Pakistan, Bolivia, Peru, and 38 nonspecified really poor nations, have no chance of catching up with the rich nations; Segal writes "never" next to each country in the table under the column "number of years until the gap closes if 1965–1983 rates continue"!

Segal considers his data "horrifying" (p. 11) in their implications because: "the world is being enmeshed in our [United States'] consumption styles. There is no Third World country today in which the lifestyle of the rich countries is not known and in which the tastes of the poor are not shifting toward appetites for what they do not have and will *never* attain," p. 11 (my emphasis).

67. Milbrath, *Envisioning, op. cit.*, p. 312.

68. Oleg Zinam, "The Myth of Absolute Abundance: Economic Development as a Shift in Relative Scarcities," *American Journal of Economics and Sociology* 41, no. 1 (January 1982), p. 73.

69. Horne, "Envy and Commercial Society," *op. cit.*, pp. 553–554.

70. Kohn, *op. cit.*, pp. 74–75 (emphasis in original).

71. *Ibid.*, p. 142 (my emphasis).

72. For a favorable discussion of the nature and value of community, see John Friedmann, *The Good Society: A Personal Account of its Struggle With the World of Social Planning and a Dialectical Inquiry into the Roots of Radical Practice* (Cambridge: The MIT Press, 1982), especially chapters 4–5, and, Michael J. Sandel, *Liberalism and the Limits of Justice* (New York: Cambridge University Press, 1983), especially chapter 4; also, see, Barber, *op. cit.*, chapter 9. For an analysis that claims that community is an unattainable and therefore a "tragic ideal" see Tinder, *op. cit.* For further reading on this important political value, consult the works referred to in these four discussions.

73. The works cited in *ibid.*, with the exception of Tinder, discuss these values at greater length.

74. Gurr, *op. cit.*, p. 24.

75. See James C. Davies, "Toward a Theory of Revolution," *American Sociological Review* 27 (Feb. 1962), pp. 5–19; cited in Gurr, *ibid.*, p. 39, note 49.

For a discussion of the J-curve hypothesis applied to America, see Miller, Bolce, and Halligan, *op. cit.* For a critique of this article by Miller, Bolce, and Halligan, see Faye Crosby, "Relative Deprivation Revisited: A Response to Miller, Bolce and Halligan," *American Political Science Review* 73, no. 1 (March 1979), pp. 103–112. For Miller and Bolce's reply, Crosby's rejoinder, and a comment upon the debate by James Davies, see "Communications," *American Political Science Review*, vol. 73, no. 3 (Sept. 1979), pp. 818–830.

76. See Book 5 of *The Politics* devoted to the "Causes of Revolution and Constitutional Change," where Aristotle writes: "There are some who stir up sedition because their minds are filled by a passion for equality, which arises from their thinking that they have the worst of the bargain in spite of being the equals of those who have got the advantage. There are others who do it because their minds are filled with a passion for inequality (i.e., superiority), which arises from their conceiving that they get no advantage over others (but only an equal amount, or even a smaller amount) although they are really more than equal to others...Thus inferiors become revolutionaries in order to be equals, and equals in order to be superiors." Book 5, chapter 2, p. 207 of, *The Politics of Aristotle*, Barker edition. *op. cit.* This reference to Aristotle's relative deprivation theory of revolution is also made by Gurr, *ibid.*, p. 37.

77. Cited as the epigraph to chapter 2 of: Gurr, *ibid.*, p. 22. The original source is, Marx and Engels's *Wage Labor and Capital*.

78. Cited in Springborg, *op. cit.*, p. 109.

79. This latter point about the dread of failure and the fear of losing in competitive America was vividly brought home to me one day when I approached a crying, three year-old, nursery school classmate of my daughter's. When I inquired as to what the problem was, she pointed to another three year-old and sobbed: "He called me a loser!"

80. Bell, *The Cultural Contradictions of Capitalism*, *op. cit.*, p. 22.

81. On the J-curve hypothesis, see Gurr, *op. cit.*, pp. 46–58; Miller, Bolce, and Halligan, *op. cit.*, and Crosby, *op. cit.*, and their respective replies to each other cited earlier.

82. Quoted in: Charles Tilly, *Big Structures, Large Processes, Huge Comparisons* (New York: Russell Sage Foundation, 1984), p. 103. The original citation is: James C. Davies, *When Men Revolt and Why* (New York: Free Press, 1971), p. 133.

83. See Cohan, *op. cit.*, p. 205.

84. Tilly, *op. cit.*, p. 104.

85. *Ibid.*, pp. 104–105.

86. See Inglehart's research; recent election data on support for West German Greens; Elgin's research; and, data on who supports environmental organizations cited earlier, especially Milbrath's two volumes, *Environmentalists*, *op. cit.*, and *Envisioning*, *op. cit.*

87. Hirsch, *op. cit.*, p. 9.

88. Quoted in Wolin, *op. cit.*, p. 330. The first part of the quotation is Wolin's interpretation.

Chapter 10

1. George Lakey, *Strategy for a Living Revolution* (San Francisco: W. H. Freeman, 1973), p. 28.

2. Walter Kaufmann, *Hegel: A Reinterpretation* (Garden City, N.Y.: Anchor Books/Doubleday, 1966), p. 144 (emphasis in original).

3. Georg Wilhelm Friedrich Hegel, *The Science of Logic*, chapter 1, note. The passage quoted is taken from *ibid.*, pp. 180–181 (emphasis in original).

4. Klaus Eder, "The 'New Social Movements': Moral Crusades, Political Pressure Groups, or Social Movements?" *Social Research* 52, no. 4 (Winter 1985), p. 890.

5. Peter Laslett, *The World We Have Lost: England Before the Industrial Age*, 2d ed. (New York: Charles Scribner's Sons, 1973), p. 3.

6. *Ibid.*, p. 96, and the supporting data presented on p. 97.

7. Inglehart, "Post-Materialism in an Environment of Insecurity," *op. cit.*, p. 890.

8. *Ibid.*, p. 894, table 7 and *passim*.

9. *Ibid.*, p. 895.

10. Porritt, *op. cit.*, pp. 216–217. This is only a partial list of Porritt's contrasts between these two worldviews.

11. See Spretnak and Capra, *op. cit.*, pp. 229–233. Also these "Ten Key Values" are available from the American Greens' headquarters: Committees of Correspondence, P.O. Box 30208, Kansas City, Missouri, 64112.

12. Quoted in Spretnak and Capra, *ibid.*, p. xxvi.

13. *Ibid.*, pp. 229–230. For a detailed presentation and elaboration of the American Greens' values, see their Strategy and Policy Approaches in Key Areas, Constituting "Green Program USA," Special Edition, *Green Letter* and *Greener Times*, Autumn 1989.

14. *Ibid.*, p. 230.

15. See *ibid.*, chapter 2 on: "Principles of a New Politics," where the Greens' four basic values or "pillars" are discussed.

16. Porritt, *op. cit.*, p. 223.

17. *Ibid.*, p. 219.

18. See Ted Becker and Richard Scarce, "Teledemocracy Emergent: State of the Art and Science." Paper delivered at the 1984 Annual Meeting of The American Political Science Association, Washington, D.C.; and Barber, *op. cit.*, pp. 273–279; and the literature cited in each of these works.

19. See Barber, *op. cit.*, pp. 276–279.

20. Porritt, *op. cit.*, p. xvi.

21. Claus Offe, "New Social Movements: Challenging the Boundaries of Institutional Politics," *Social Research* 52, no. 4 (Winter 1985), p. 849 (the first emphasis is mine).

22. *Ibid.*, p. 848.

23. Ely, *op. cit.*, p. 46.

24. See Aurelio Peccei, *One Hundred Pages for the Future: Reflections of the President of the Club of Rome* (New York: New American Library, 1982). The phrase "decisive decade" is taken from the title of the first chapter in part 2, p. 125.

25. *Ibid.*, p. 180 (emphasis in original).

26. Miles, *op. cit.*, p. 236.

27. Ernest J. Yanarella, "Slouching Toward the Apocalypse: Visions of

Nuclear Holocaust and Eco-Catastrophe in Contemporary Science Fiction," paper delivered at the 1984 Annual Meeting of The American Political Science Association, Washington, D.C., p. 34.

28. *Ibid.*, the last quoted phrase is from an article by Sheldon Wolin; see Yanarella's full citation on p. 43, note 113.

29. For an interesting analysis of the revolutionary political nature of the new social groups, see Timothy W. Luke, "The New Social Movements: An Analysis of Conflict, Social Cleavages and Class in the Emergent Informational Society." Paper delivered at the 1984 Annual Meeting of The American Political Science Association, Washington, D.C. He describes seven traits of these groups (see pp. 10–11 for summary), such as: "post-Marxism," "postproletariat," and "postindustrial" (p. 10). Luke's conclusion is most pertinent to the view presented here: "their [the new social movements] joint program largely is one of politicization" and "these new mobilizations of popular protest are much more than merely neoromantic/neopopulist reactions to secular social changes;" see pp. 39, 52.

30. See Milbrath, *Envisioning, op. cit.*, p. 361.

31. Consult as sources for this empirical claim: Spretnak and Capra, *op. cit.*, p. 195; Daniel Yankelovich, *New Rules: Searching for Self-Fulfillment in a World Turned Upside Down* (New York: Bantam Books, 1982), *passim.*, and, Elgin, *op. cit.*, p. 132, in addition to Inglehart's and Milbrath's data along these lines.

32. See Lester R. Brown et al., *State of the World:* 1985, A Worldwatch Institute Report on Progress Toward a Sustainable Society, *op. cit.*, and the subsequent annual reports.

33. Milbrath, *Environmentalists, op. cit.*, p. 83.

34. Miles, *op. cit.*, p. 236.

35. Mishan, *op. cit.*, p. x.

36. Milbrath, *Environmentalists, op. cit.*, p. 64.

37. See Glenn Tinder, *Political Thinking: The Perennial Questions*, 4th ed. (Boston: Little, Brown, 1986).

38. Bell, "The Return of the Sacred: The Argument About the Future of Religion," *op. cit.*, p. 523 (no citation is given by Bell). The exact quote, according to my edition of the *Ethics of the Fathers* is as follows: "He [Rabbi Tarfon] used to say: You are not called upon to complete the work [of Torah study], yet you are not free to evade it...." See Philip Birnbaum, translator and annotator, *Ethics of the Fathers* (New York: Hebrew Publishing, 1949), chapter two, verse 21, p. 16. (The words in the second brackets were provided in the text of this edition.)

39. *Ethics of the Fathers, ibid.*, chapter two, verse 20, p. 16. (The words in the brackets were provided in the text of this edition.)

Bibliography

Abramson, Paul R. and Ronald Ingelhart. "Generational Replacement and Value Change in Six West European Societies." Paper delivered at the Annual Meeting of the American Political Science Association, 1984, Washington, D.C.

Aiken, William. "World Hunger and Foreign Aid: The Morality of Mass Starvation," in Burton M. Leiser, ed., *Values in Conflict: Life, Liberty and the Rule of Law*. New York: Macmillan, 1981, pp. 189-201.

Albin, Peter S. *Progress without Poverty: Socially Responsible Growth*. New York: Basic Books, 1978.

Alexander, Sidney S. "Human Values and Economists' Values," in Sidney Hook, *Human Values and Economic Policy: A Symposium*. New York: New York University Press, 1967, pp. 101-116.

Allen, Woody. Quotation in: Robert Byrne, *The 637 Best Things Anybody Ever Said*. New York: Atheneum, 1982, p. 79, #386.

Almond, Gabriel A., Marvin Chodorow, and Roy Harvey Pearce, eds. *Progress and Its Discontents*. Berkeley: University of California Press, 1982.

Amin, Samir, Giovanni Arrighi, Andre Gunder Frank, and Immanuel Wallerstein. *Dynamics of Global Crisis*. New York: Monthly Review Press, 1982.

Applebaum, Eileen. "Radical Economics," in Sidney Weintraub, ed., *Modern Economic Thought*. Phila.: University of Pennsylvania Press, 1977, pp. 559-574.

Arendt, Hannah. *The Human Condition: A Study of the Central Dilemmas Facing Modern Man*. Garden City: Doubleday/Anchor Books, 1959.

Aristotle. *The Politics of Aristotle*. Ernest Barker, ed. and trans. New York: Oxford University Press, 1962.

Arndt, H. W. *The Rise and Fall of Economic Growth: A Study of Contemporary Thought*. Chicago: University of Chicago Press, 1978.

Arnold, Matthew. *Stanzas from the Grande Chartreuse*, in G. B. Harrison *et al.* eds. *Major British Writers*. Enlarged Edition, Two Volumes. New York: Harcourt, Brace, 1959, Vol. 2, pp. 612-615.

Arthur, Herman. "The Japan Gap: A Country Moves Ahead—But At What Price?" *American Educator*. Summer 1983, pp. 38-44.

Bahro, Rudolf. *Building the Green Movement*. Mary Tyler, trans. Phila.: New Society Publishers, 1986.

Baier, Kurt and Nicholas Rescher, eds. *Values and the Future: The Impact of Technological Change on American Values*. New York: Free Press, 1971.

Bakunin, Mikhail. *Bakunin on Anarchy: Selected Works by the Anarchist-Founder of World Anarchism*. Sam Dolgoff, ed. New York: Vintage Books/Random House, 1972.

Barber, Benjamin. *Strong Democracy: Participatory Politics for a New Age*. Berkelely: University of California Press, 1984.

Barber, William J. *A History of Economic Thought*. New York: Penguin Books, 1977.

Barker, Ernest. Introduction to *The Politics of Aristotle*. Ernest Barker, ed. and trans. New York: Oxford University Press, 1962, pp. xi–lxxvi.

Barney, Gerald O., Study director. *The Global 2000 Report to the President: Entering the Twenty-first Century*. Charlottesville: Blue Angel, 1981.

Becker, Ted and Richard Scarce. "Teledemocracy Emergent: State of the Art and Science." Paper delivered at the Annual Meeting of the American Political Science Association, 1984, Washington, D.C.

Beckerman, Wilfred. *Two Cheers for the Affluent Society: A Spirited Defense of Economic Growth*. New York: Saint Martin's Press, 1975.

Bell, Daniel. *The Coming of the Post-Industrial Society: A Venture in Social Forecasting*. New York: Basic Books, 1976.

———. *The Cultural Contradictions of Capitalism*. New York: Basic Books, 1976.

———. "Models and Reality in Economic Discourse," in Daniel Bell and Irving Kristol, eds. *The Crisis in Economic Theory*. New York: Basic Books, 1981, pp. 46–80.

———. "The Return of the Sacred: The Argument about the Future of Religion," in Gabriel A. Almond, Marvin Chodorow, and Roy Harvey Pearce, eds. *Progress and Its Discontents*. Berkeley: University of California Press, 1982, pp. 501–523.

——— and Irving Kristol, eds. *The Crisis in Economic Theory*. New York: Basic Books, 1981.

Bellah, Robert N., Richard Madsen, William M. Sullivan, Ann Swidler, and Steven M. Tipton. *Habits of the Heart: Individualism and Commitment in American Life*. Berkeley: University of California Press, 1985.

Berger, Peter L. and Thomas Luckmann. *The Social Construction of Reality: A Treatise in the Sociology of Knowledge*. Garden City: Doubleday, 1966.

_____ and Brigitte Berger, and Hansfried Kellner. *The Homeless Mind: Moderni- zation and Consciousness*. New York: Random House, 1973.

Berlin, Isaiah. *Four Essays on Liberty*. London: Oxford University Press, 1969.

Bernstein, Richard J. *Beyond Objectivism and Relativism: Science, Hermeneutics, and Praxis*. Phila.: University of Pennsylvania Press, 1985.

Birnbaum, Norman. *The Crisis of Industrial Society*. New York: Oxford University Press, 1969.

_____, ed. *Beyond the Crisis*. New York: Oxford University Press, 1977.

Birnbaum, Philip, trans. and annotator. *Ethics of the Fathers*. New York: Hebrew Publishing, 1949.

Blaug, Mark. "Kuhn versus Lakatos, or Paradigms versus Research Programmes in the History of Economics," in Gary Gutting, ed. *Paradigms and Revolutions: Applications and Appraisals of Thomas Kuhn's Philosophy of Science*. Notre Dame: University of Notre Dame Press, 1980, pp. 137–159.

Bookchin, Murray. *Toward an Ecological Society*. Montreal: Black Rose Books, 1980.

_____. *The Modern Crisis*. Phila.: New Society Publishers, 1986.

Botkin, James W., Mahdi Elmandjra, and Mircea Malitza. *No Limits to Learning: Bridging the Human Gap: A Report to the Club of Rome*. Oxford: Pergamon Press, 1981.

Boulding, Kenneth E. *The Meaning of the Twentieth Century: The Great Transition*. New York: Harper and Row, 1964.

_____. "New Goals for Society?" in Sam H. Schurr, ed. *Energy, Economic Growth, and the Environment*. Baltimore: Johns Hopkins University Press, 1973, pp. 139–151.

Boyle, Robert H. "Forecast for Disaster." *Sports Illustrated*. November 16, 1987, pp. 78–92.

Brewster, J. Alan, director. *World Resources 1988–1989*. A Report by The World Resources Institute and The International Institute for Environment and Development. New York: Basic Books, 1988.

Brown, K. C., ed. *Hobbes Studies*. Cambridge: Harvard University Press, 1965.

Brown, Lester R. *The Twenty-ninth Day: Accommodating Human Needs and Numbers to the Earth's Resources*. New York: W. W. Norton, 1978.

_____. "Stopping Population Growth," in Lester R. Brown *et al. State of the World 1985*. New York: W. W. Norton, 1985, pp. 200–221.

———. "Analyzing the Demographic Trap," in Lester R. Brown *et al. State of the World 1987*. New York: W. W. Norton, 1987, pp. 20–37.

——— and Christopher Flavin, and Sandra Postel. "A World at Risk," in Lester R. Brown *et al. State of the World 1989*. New York: W. W. Norton, 1989, pp. 3–20.

——— *et al. State of the World Annuals*. New York: W. W. Norton, 1985, 1987, and 1989.

Bruce-Biggs, B. "Against the Neo-Malthusians," *Commentary*, July 1974, pp. 25–29.

Byrne, Robert, ed. *The 637 Best Things Anybody Ever Said*. New York: Atheneum, 1982.

Cahn, Robert. *Footprints on the Planet: A Search for an Environmental Ethic*. New York: Universe Books, 1978.

Caldwell, Lynton K. *Man and His Environment: Policy and Administration*. New York: Harper and Row, 1975.

Camilleri, Joseph A. *Civilization in Crisis: Human Prospects in a Changing World*. Cambridge: Cambridge University Press, 1976.

Camus, Albert. *The Myth of Sisyphus and Other Essays*. Justin O'Brien, trans. New York: Alfred A. Knopf, 1955.

———. *The Rebel: An Essay on Man in Revolt*. Anthony Bower, trans. New York: Alfred A. Knopf, 1956.

Caporaso, James A. "Pathways Between Economics and Politics: Possible Foundations for the Study of Global Political Economy." Paper delivered at the Annual Meeting of the Amercian Political Science Association, 1983, Chicago.

Carter, Jimmy. "Address to the Nation," July 15, 1979. Transcript, *New York Times*, July 16, 1979, p. A10.

Catton, William R. Jr. *Overshoot: The Ecological Basis of Revolutionary Change*. Urbana: University of Illinois Press, 1982.

Chafe, William H. *Women and Equality: Changing Patterns in American Culture*. New York: Oxford University Press, 1978.

Cohan, A. S. *Theories of Revolution: An Introduction*. New York: John Wiley, 1975.

Cohen, G. A. "The Structure of Proletarian Unfreedom." *Philosophy and Public Affairs*, 12, Winter 1983, pp. 3–33.

Cohen, Jean L., ed. "Social Movements." *Social Research*, Special Issue, Vol. 52, Winter 1985.

Cohen, Joshua and Joel Rogers. *On Democracy: Toward a Transformation of American Society.* New York: Penguin Books, 1983.

Cole, H. S. D., Christopher Freeman, Marie Jahoda, and K. L. R. Pavitt. *Models of Doom: A Critique of the Limits to Growth.* New York: Universe Books, 1975.

Crosby, Faye. "Relative Deprivation Revisited: A Response to Miller, Bolce and Halligan," *American Political Science Review,* 73, March 1979, pp. 103–112.

_____. "Rejoinder," in "Communications." *American Political Science Review,* 73, September 1979, pp. 822–825.

Daly, Herman E. "The Steady-State Economy: Toward a Political Economy of Biophysical Equilibrium and Moral Growth," in Herman E. Daly, ed. *Toward a Steady-State Economy.* San Francisco: W. H. 1973, pp. 149–174.

_____. "Electric Power, Employment, and Economic Growth: A Case Study in Growthmania," in Herman E. Daly, ed. *Toward a Steady-State Economy.* San Francisco: W. H. Freeman, 1973, pp. 252–277.

_____. *Steady-State Economics: The Economics of Biophysical Equilibrium and Moral Growth.* San Francisco: W. H. Freeman, 1977.

_____. "Entropy, Growth, and the Political Economy of Scarcity," in V. Kerry Smith, ed. *Scarcity and Growth Reconsidered.* Baltimore: Johns Hopkins University Press, 1979, pp. 67–94.

_____, ed. *Toward a Steady-State Economy.* San Francisco: W. H. Freeman, 1973.

_____, ed. *Economics, Ecology, Ethics: Essays Toward a Steady-State Economy.* San Francisco: W. H. Freeman, 1980.

David, Paul A. and Melvin W. Reder, eds. *Nations and Households in Economic Growth: Essays in Honor of Moses Abramovitz.* New York: Academic Press, 1974.

Davies, James C. "Toward a Theory of Revolution," *American Sociological Review,* 27 Feb. 1962, pp. 5–19.

_____. *When Men Revolt and Why.* New York: Free Press, 1971.

_____. "Comment," in "Communications." *American Political Science Review,* 73, September 1979, pp. 825–830.

Davis, Joan and Samuel Mauch. "Strategies for Societal Development," in Dennis L. Meadows, ed. *Alternatives to Growth-I: A Search for Sustainable Futures.* Cambridge, Mass.: Ballinger, 1977, pp. 217–242.

Davis, Lane. "The Cost of Realism: Contemporary Restatement of Democracy." *Western Political Quarterly,* 17, March 1964, pp. 37–46.

Davis, W. Jackson. *The Seventh Year: Industrial Civilization in Transition*. New York: W. W. Norton, 1979.

Dobb, Maurice. *Theories of Value and Distribution since Adam Smith: Ideology and Economic Theory*. Cambridge: Cambridge University Press, 1973.

Douglas, Mary and Baron Isherwood. *The World of Goods: Towards an Anthropology of Consumption*. New York: W. W. Norton, 1979.

Dreitzel, Hans Peter. "On the Political Meaning of Culture," in Norman Birnbaum, ed. *Beyond the Crisis*. New York: Oxford University Press, 1977, pp. 83–129.

Dryzek, John S. *Rational Ecology: Environment and Political Economy*. New York: Basil Blackwell, 1987.

Duesenberry, James S. *Income, Saving and the Theory of Consume Behavior*. Cambridge: Harvard University Press, 1949.

Dumont, Louis. *From Mandeville to Marx: The Genesis and Triumph of Economic Ideology*. Chicago: University of Chicago Press, 1977.

Dye, Thomas R. and Harmon Zeigler. "Socialism and Equality in Cross-National Perspective." *PS: Political Science and Politics*. XXI, Winter 1988, pp. 45–56.

Easterlin, Richard A. "Does Economic Growth Improve the Human Lot? Some Empirical Evidence," in Paul A. David and Melvin W. Reder, eds. *Nations and Households in Economic Growth: Essays in Honor of Moses Abramovitz*. New York: Academic Press, 1974, pp. 89–125.

Eder, Klaus. "The 'New Social Movements': Moral Crusades, Political Pressure Groups, or Social Movements?" *Social Research*. 52, Winter 1985, pp. 869–890.

Edwards, Richard C. "The Logic of Capital Accumulation," in Richard C. Edwards, Michael Reich, and Thomas E. Weisskopf, eds. *The Capitalist System: A Radical Analysis of American Society*. Second Edition, Englewood Cliffs, N.J.: Prentice-Hall, 1978, pp. 99–105.

_____, Michael Reich, and Thomas E. Weisskopf, eds. *The Capitalist System: A Radical Analysis of American Society*. Second Edition, Englewood Cliffs, N.J.: Prentice-Hall, 1978.

Egan, Timothy. "Like the West Coast City It is, Seattle is Tired of Developing." *New York Times*, May 7, 1989, Week in Review section.

Ehrlich, Paul R. and Anne H. Ehrlich. *The End of Affluence: A Blueprint for Your Future*. New York: Ballantine Books, 1974.

_____. "Humanity at the Crossroads," in Herman E. Daly, ed. *Economics, Ecology, Ethics*. San Francisco: W. H. Freeman, 1980, pp. 38–43.

_____, and John P. Holdren. *Ecoscience: Population, Resources, Environment.* San Francisco: W. H. Freeman, 1977.

Elgin, Duane. *Voluntary Simplicity: Toward a Way of Life that is Outwardly Simple, Inwardly Rich.* New York: William Morrow, 1981.

Ellis, Adrian and Krishan Kumar, eds. *Dilemmas of Liberal Democracies: Studies in Fred Hirsch's SOCIAL LIMITS TO GROWTH.* London: Tavistock Publications, 1983.

Ely, John. "The Greens of West Germany: An Alternative Modernity (or, How German is It?)." A Paper delivered at the Annual Meeting of the American Political Science Association, 1986, Washington, D.C.

Ewen, Stuart. *Captains of Consciousness: Advertising and the Social Roots of the Consumer Culture.* New York: McGraw-Hill, 1977.

Executive Committee of the Club of Rome. "Commentary," in Donella H. Meadows, Dennis L. Meadows, Jorgen Randers, and William W. Behrens, III.*The Limits to Growth: A Report for the Club of Rome's Project on the Predicament of Mankind.* Second Edition, Revised. New York: New American Library, 1975, pp. 189–200.

Falk, Richard A. Foreward to: David W. Orr and Marvin S. Soroos, eds. *The Global Predicament: Ecological Perspectives on World Order.* Chapel Hill: University of North Carolina Press, 1979, pp. ix–xvi.

Fallers, L. A. "A Note on the Trickle Effect." *Public Opinion Quarterly,* 18, Fall 1954, pp. 314–321.

Ferkiss, Victor. "Nature, Technology and Political Society." A Paper delivered at the Annual Meeting of the American Political Science Association, 1982, Denver.

Feuer, Lewis S., ed. *Marx and Engels: Basic Writings on Politics and Philosophy.* Garden City: Doubleday, 1959.

Finnin, William M. Jr. and Gerald Alonzo Smith, eds. *The Morality of Scarcity: Limited Resources and Social Policy.* Baton Rouge: Louisiana State University Press, 1979.

Firor, John. "Interconnections and the 'Endangered Species' of the Atmosphere." World Resources Institute, *Journal '84,* pp. 16–26.

Flavin, Christopher. "Reassessing Nuclear Power," in Lester R. Brown *et al. State of the World 1987.* New York: W. W. Norton, 1987, pp. 57–80.

Forrester, Jay. "New Perspectives on Economic Growth," in Dennis L. Meadows, ed. *Alternatives to Growth-I.* Cambridge, Mass.: Ballinger, 1977, pp. 107–121.

Frank, Andre Gunder. "Crisis of Ideology and Ideology of Crisis," in Samir Amin,

Giovanni Arrighi, Andre Gunder Frank, and Immanuel Wallerstein. *Dynamics of Global Crisis*. New York: Monthly Review Press, pp. 109–165.

Frankel, Boris. *The Post-Industrial Utopias*. Madison: University of Wisconsin Press, 1987.

Frankland, E. Gene. "Does Green Politics Have a Future in Britain?" A Paper delivered at the Annual Meeting of the American Political Science Association, 1989, Atlanta.

Friedmann, John. *The Good Society: A Personal Account of Its Struggle with the World of Social Planning and a Dialectical Inquiry into the Roots of Radical Practice*. Cambridge: MIT Press, 1982.

Froman, Creel. *The Two American Political Systems: Society, Economics, and Politics*. Englewood Cliffs, N.J.: Prentice-Hall, 1984.

Fromm, Erich. *To Have or to Be?* New York: Harper and Row, 1976.

Galbraith, John Kenneth. *The New Industrial State*. Second Edition, Revised. New York: New American Library, 1972.

Galtung, Johan. "'The Limits to Growth' and Class Politics," *Journal of Peace Research*, 1–2, 1973, pp. 101–114.

Gappert, Gary. *Post-Affluent America: The Social Economy of the Future*. New York: Franklin Watts, 1979.

Goldsmith, Edward, Robert Allen, Michael Allaby, John Davoll, and Sam Lawrence. *Blueprint for Survival*. New York: New American Library, 1972.

Gorz, Andre. *Ecology as Politics*. Patsy Vigderman and Jonathan Cloud, trans. Boston: South End Press, 1980.

Gouldner, Alvin W. *Enter Plato: Classical Greece and the Origins of Social Theory, Part II*. New York: Harper and Row, 1971.

Green, Philip. *Retrieving Democracy: In Search of Civic Equality*. Totowa, N.J.: Rowman and Allanheld, 1985.

Gurley, John G. "The Theory of Surplus Value," in Richard C. Edwards, Michael Reich, and Thomas E. Weisskopf, eds. *The Capitalist System*. Englewood Cliffs, N.J.: Prentice-Hall, 1978, pp. 80–92.

Gurr, Ted Robert. *Why Men Rebel*. Princeton: Princeton University Press, 1972.

Gutting, Gary, ed. *Paradigms and Revolutions: Applications and Appraisals of Thomas Kuhn's Philosophy of Science*. Notre Dame: University of Notre Dame Press, 1980.

Habermas, Jürgen. *Legitimation Crisis*. Thomas McCarthy, trans. Boston: Beacon Press, 1973.

Hagopian, Mark N. *The Phenomenon of Revolution*. New York: Dodd, Mead, 1974.

Hardin, Garrett. "The Tragedy of the Commons," in Herman E. Daly, ed. *Economics, Ecology, Ethics*. San Francisco: W. H. Freeman, 1980, pp. 100–114.

Hardoy, Jorge E. and David E. Satterthwaite. "Third World Cities and the Environment of Poverty," in Robert Repetto, ed. *The Global Possible: Resources, Development and the New Century*. New Haven: Yale University Press, 1985, pp. 171–210.

Harman, Willis W. *An Incomplete Guide to the Future*. New York: W. W. Norton, 1979.

Harrington, Michael. *The Twilight of Capitalism*. New York: Simon and Shuster, 1976.

Harrison, G. B. *et al.*, eds. *Major British Writers*. Enlarged Edition, Two Volumes. New York: Harcourt, Brace, 1959.

Heilbroner, Robert L. *The Limits of American Capitalism*. New York: Harper and Row, 1967.

_____. *An Inquiry into the Human Prospect*. New York: W. W. Norton, 1975.

_____. *Business Civilization in Decline*. New York: W. W. Norton, 1976.

Heller, Walter W. "Coming to Terms with Growth and the Environment," in Sam H. Schurr, ed. *Energy, Economic Growth, and the Environment*. Baltimore: Johns Hopkins University Press, 1973, pp. 3–29.

Henderson, Hazel. *The Politics of the Solar Age: Alternatives to Economics*. Garden City: Anchor Press/Doubleday, 1981.

Hirsch, Fred. *Social Limits to Growth*. Cambridge: Harvard University Press, 1976.

_____ and John H. Goldthorpe, eds. *The Political Economy of Inflation*. Cambridge: Harvard University Press, 1979.

Hirschman, Albert O. *The Passions and the Interests: Political Arguments for Capitalism Before Its Triumph*. Princeton: Princeton University Press, 1978.

_____. *Essays in Trespassing: Economics to Politics and Beyond*. Cambridge: Cambridge University Press, 1981.

_____. *Shifting Involvements: Private Interest and Public Policy*. Princeton: Princeton University Press, 1982.

_____. "Rival Interpretations of Market Society: Civilizing, Destructive or Feeble?" *Journal of Economic Literature*, XX, Dec. 1982, pp. 1463–1484.

Hobbes, Thomas. *Man and Citizen*. Bernard Gert, ed. Garden City: Anchor Books, 1972.

_____. *DE CIVE, The English Version.* Howard Warrender, ed. Oxford: Oxford University Press, 1983.

_____. *Leviathan.* Herbert W. Schneider, ed. The Library of Liberal Arts Edition. Indianapolis: Bobbs-Merrill, 1958.

Hook, Sidney, ed. *Human Values and Economic Policy: A Symposium.* New York: New York University Press, 1967.

Horne, Thomas A. *The Social Theory of Bernard Mandeville: Virtue and Commerce in Early Eighteenth Century England.* New York: Columbia University Press, 1978.

_____. "Envy and Commercial Society: Mandeville and Smith on 'Private Vices, Public Benefits.'" *Political Theory.* 9, November 1981, pp. 551–569.

Hospers, John. *Human Conduct: An Introduction to the Problems of Ethics.* New York: Harcourt, Brace and World, 1961.

Hulsberg, Werner. *The German Greens: A Social and Political Profile.* Gus Fagan, trans. London: Verso, 1988.

Hunt, E. K. "The Transition from Feudalism to Capitalism," in Richard C. Edwards, Michael Reich, and Thomas E. Weisskopf, eds. *The Capitalist System.* Englewood Cliffs, N.J.: Prentice-Hall, 1978, pp. 55–64.

Inglehart, Ronald. *The Silent Revolution: Changing Values and Political Styles among Western Publics.* Princeton: Princeton University Press, 1977.

Isaak, Robert A. and Ralph P. Hummel. *Politics for Human Beings.* North Scituate, Mass.: Duxbury Press, 1975.

Kahn, Herman. *World Economy Development: 1979 and Beyond.* New York: William Morrow, 1979.

_____, William Brown, and Leon Martel. *The Next 200 Years: A Scenario for America and the World.* New York: William Morrow, 1976.

Kaplan, Abraham. *The Conduct of Inquiry: Methodology for Behavioral Science.* San Francisco: Chandler, 1964.

Kassiola, Joel. "The Limits to Economic Growth: Politicizing Advanced Industrialized Society." *Philosophy and Social Criticism.* 8, Spring 1981, pp. 87–113.

Kaufmann, Walter. *Hegel: A Reinterpretation.* Garden City: Anchor Books/Doubleday, 1966.

Kelly, Petra. *Fighting for Hope.* Marianne Howarth, trans. Boston: South End Press, 1984.

Key, Wilson Bryan. *Subliminal Seduction: Ad Media's Manipulation of a Not so Innocent America.* New York: New American Library, 1974.

Keynes, John Maynard. "Economic Possibilities for Our Grandchildren," in John Maynard Keynes, *Essays in Persuasion*. New York: W. W. Norton, 1963, pp. 358–373.

_____. *Essays in Persuasion*. New York: W. W. Norton, 1963.

Kitschelt, Herbert. "The West German Green Party in Comparative Perspective: Explaining Innovation in Competitive Party Systems." A Paper delivered at the Annual Meeting of the American Political Science Association, 1986, Washington, D.C.

Klein, Rudolph. "Growth and Its Enemies." *Commentary*. June 1972, pp. 37–44.

Koestler, Arthur and J. R. Smythies, eds. *Beyond Reductionism: New Perspectives in the Life Sciences*. New York: Macmillan, 1969.

Kohn, Alfie. *No Contest: The Case Against Competition*. Boston: Houghton Mifflin, 1986.

Kraft, Michael E. "Political Change and the Sustainable Society," in Dennis Clark Pirages, ed. *The Sustainable Society: Implications for Limited Growth*. New York: Praeger, 1977, pp. 173–196.

Krauthammer, Charles. "On Nuclear Morality," in James E. White, ed. *Contemporary Moral Problems*. Second Edition. St. Paul: West, 1988, pp. 403–409.

Irving Kristol. "Rationalism in Economics," in Daniel Bell and Irving Kristol, eds. *The Crisis in Economic Theory*. New York: Basic Books, 1981, pp. 201–218.

Kuhn, Thomas S. *The Structure of Scientific Revolutions*. Second Edition, Enlarged. Chicago: University of Chicago Press, 1970.

Lakey, George. *Strategy for a Living Revolution*. San Francisco: W. H. Freeman, 1973.

Lancaster, Kelvin. *Consumer Demand: A New Approach*. New York: Columbia University Press, 1971.

Landes, David S. *The Unbound Prometheus: Technological Change and Industrial Development in Western Europe from 1750 to the Present*. Cambridge: Cambridge University Press, 1977.

Lane, Robert E. "Markets and the Satisfaction of Human Wants," *Journal of Economic Issues*. 12, December 1978, pp. 799–827.

Lasch, Christopher. *The Culture of Narcissism: American Life in an Age of Diminishing Expectations*. New York: Warner Books, 1979.

Laslett, Peter. *The World We Have Lost: England Before the Industrial Age*. Second Edition. New York: Charles Scribner's Sons, 1973.

Laszlo, Ervin *et al*. *Goals for Mankind: A Report to the Club of Rome on the New Horizons of Global Community*. New York: New American Library, 1978.

Lefort, Claude. "On the Concept of Politics and Economics in Machiavelli," in C. B. Macpherson, comp. *Political Theory and Political Economy.* Papers from the Annual Meeting of the Conference for the Study of Political Thought, April 1974.

Leiser, Burton M., ed. *Values in Conflict: Life, Liberty and the Rule of Law.* New York: Macmillan, 1981.

Leiss, William. *The Limits to Satisfaction: An Essay on the Problem of Needs and Commodities.* Toronto: University of Toronto Press, 1976.

Leonard, George. "Winning Isn't Everything, It's Nothing." *Intellectual Digest.* October 1973, pp. 45–47.

Letter, Green/Greener Times. Newsletter of the U.S. Greens Committees of Correspondence. Autumn 1989.

Levy, Frank. "We're Running Out of Gimmicks to Sustain Our Prosperity: Decline Began in 1973, But We Have Concealed It." *Washington Post National Weekly Edition*, December 26, 1986, pp. 18–19.

Levy, Marion J. Jr. *Modernization and the Structure of Societies: A Setting for International Affairs.* Two Volumes. Princeton: Princeton University Press, 1966.

Lewis, Arthur O. Jr., ed. *Of Men and Machines.* New York: E. P. Dutton, 1963.

Linder, Staffan Burenstam. *The Harried Leisure Class.* New York: Columbia University Press, 1970.

Lowe, Adolphe. *On Economic Knowledge: Toward a Science of Political Economy.* Enlarged Edition. Armonk, N.Y.: M. E. Sharpe, 1983.

Luke, Timothy W. "The New Social Movements: An Analysis of Conflict, Social Cleavages and Class in the Emergent Informational Society," A Paper delivered at the Annual Meeting of the American Political Science Association, 1984, Washington, D.C.

————. "The Political Economy of Social Ecology and Voluntary Simplicity," A Paper delivered at the Annual Meeting of the American Political Science Association, 1984, Washington, D.C.

Lutz, Mark A. and Kenneth Lux. *The Challenge of Humanistic Economics.* Melo Park, Cal.: Benjamin/Cummings, 1979.

Machiavelli, Niccolo. *The Prince.* Luigi Ricci, trans. New York: New American Library, 1962.

Macpherson, C. B. *The Political Theory of Possessive Individualism: Hobbes to Locke.* Oxford: Oxford University Press, 1965.

_____. *Democratic Theory: Essays in Retrieval*. Oxford: Oxford University Press, 1973.

_____. "The Economic Penetration of Political Theory," in C. B. Macpherson, comp. *Political Theory and Political Economy*. Papers from the Annual Meeting of the Conference for the Study of Political Thought, April 1974.

_____, comp. *Political Theory and Political Economy*. Papers from the Annual Meeting of the Conference for the Study of Political Thought, April 1974.

Maddox, John. *The Doomsday Syndrome*. London: Macmillan, 1972.

Maier, Charles S. "The Politics of Inflation in the Twentieth Century," in Fred Hirsch and John H. Goldthorpe, eds. *The Political Economy of Inflation*. Cambridge: Harvard University Press, 1979, pp. 37–72.

Marcuse, Herbert. *One-Dimensional Man: Studies in the Ideology of Advanced Industrial Society*. Boston: Beacon Press, 1970.

Markham, James M. "West German Vote: Kohl Wins 4 Years as Umpire." *New York Times*. January 27, 1987, p. a3.

Marx, Karl and Friedrich Engels. "Manifesto of the Communist Party," in Robert C. Tucker, ed. *The Marx-Engels Reader*. New York: W. W. Norton, 1979, pp. 335–362.

Mason, Ronald. *Participatory and Workplace Democracy: A Theoretical Development in Critique of Liberalism*. Carbondale: Southern Illinois University Press, 1982.

Mathews, Jessica Tuchman, Project Director. *World Resources 1986*. A Report by the World Resources Institute and the International Institute for Environment and Development. New York: Basic Books, 1986.

Maurice, Charles and Charles W. Smithson. *The Doomsday Myth: 10,000 Years of Economic Crises*. Stanford: Hoover Institution Press, 1984.

May, Clifford D. "Pollution Ills Stir Support for Environment Groups," *New York Times*. August 21, 1988, p. 30.

McGraw, Dickinson and George Watson. *Political and Social Inquiry*. New York: John Wiley, 1976.

McHale, John and Magda Cordell McHale. *Basic Human Needs: A Framework for Action*. New Brunswick, N.J.: Transaction Books, 1978.

McKendrick, Neil, John Brewer and J. H. Plumb. *The Birth of a Consumer Society: The Commercialization of Eighteenth-Century England*. Bloomington: Indiana University Press, 1985.

McKenzie, Mary M. "Toward a New Political Consciousness: A Preliminary Report on New Social Movements in the Federal Republic of Germany," A Paper delivered at the Annual Meeting of the American Political Science Association, 1986, Washington, D.C.

Meadows, Dennis, L., ed. *Alternatives to Growth—I: A Search for Sustainable Futures.* Cambridge, Mass.: Ballinger, 1977.

Meadows, Donella H., Dennis L. Meadows, Jorgen Randers, and William W. Behrens III. *The Limits to Growth: A Report to the Club of Rome's Project on the Predicament of Mankind.* Second Edition. New York: New American Library, 1975.

Mermelstein, David. Introduction to part 3, in David Mermelstein, ed. *Economics: Mainstream Readings and Radical Critiques.* Second Edition. New York: Random House, 1973, pp. 29–30.

_____, ed. *Economics: Mainstream Readings and Radical Critiques.* Second Edition. New York: Random House, 1973.

Mesarovic, Mihajlo and Eduard Pestel. *Mankind at the Turning Point: The Second Report to the Club of Rome.* New York: E. P. Dutton, 1974.

Milbrath, Lester W. *Environmentalists: Vanguard for a New Society.* Albany: State University of New York Press, 1984.

_____. *Envisioning a Sustainable Society: Learning Our Way Out.* Albany: State University of New York Press, 1989.

Miles, Rufus E. Jr. *Awakening from the American Dream: The Social and Political Limits to Growth.* New York: Universe Books, 1976.

Mill, John Stuart. *On Liberty.* Currin V. Shields, ed. Indianapolis: Bobbs-Merrill, 1956.

_____. "The Spirit of the Age," in J. B. Schneewind, ed. *Mill's Essays on Literature and Society.* New York: Collier, 1965, pp. 27–78.

_____. *Principles of Political Economy with some of their Applications to Social Philosophy.* Two volumes. New York: D. Appleton, 1872.

Miller, Abraham H., Louis H. Bolce, and Mark Halligan. "The J-Curve Theory and the Black Urban Riots: An Empirical Test of Progressive Relative Deprivation Theory." *American Political Science Review,* 71, September 1977, pp. 964–982.

_____, and _____. "Reply to Crosby," in "Communications." *American Political Science Review,* 73, September 1979, pp. 818–822.

Mishan, E. J. *Technology and Growth: The Price We Pay.* New York: Praeger, 1970.

_____. *The Economic Growth Debate: An Assessment.* London: George Allen and Unwin, 1977.

Moore, Wilbert E. *Social Change*. Englewood Cliffs, N.J.: Prentice-Hall, 1965.

Mumford, Lewis. *The Myth of the Machine*. Two Volumes. New York: Harcourt, Brace Jovanovich, 1967, 1970.

Myrdal, Gunnar. *Against the Stream: Cultural Essays in Economics*. New York: Random House, 1975.

Nagel, Ernest. *The Structure of Science: Problems in the Logic of Scientific Explanation*. New York: Harcourt, Brace and World, 1961.

Neuhaus, Richard. *In Defense of People: Ecology and the Seduction of Radicalism*. New York: Macmillan, 1971.

Newman, Katherine S. *Falling from Grace: The Experience of Downward Mobility in the American Middle Class*. New York: Free Press, 1988.

New Republic. "How to Cool Off the Earth." September 12 and 19, 1988, pp. 5–8.

Newsweek. "The Greenhouse Effect." July 11, 1988, pp. 16–20.

_____. "Don't Go Near the Water." August 1, 1988, pp. 42–48.

Offe, Claus. "New Social Movements: Challenging the Boundaries of Institutional Politics." *Social Research*. 52, Winter 1985, pp. 817–868.

Olson, Mancur. Introduction to: Mancur Olson and Hans H. Landsberg, eds. *The No-Growth Society*. New York: W. W. Norton, 1973, 1–13.

_____, Hans H. Landsberg, and Joseph L. Fisher. Epilogue to: Mancur Olson and Hans H. Landsberg, eds. *The No-Growth Society*. New York: W. W. Norton, 1973, pp. 229–241.

_____ and _____, eds. *The No-Growth Society*. New York: W. W. Norton, 1973.

Ophuls, William. *Ecology and the Politics of Scarcity: A Prologue to a Political Theory of the Steady State*. San Francisco: W. H. Freeman, 1977.

_____. "Leviathan or Oblivion?" in Herman E. Daly, ed. *Toward a Steady-State Economy*. San Francisco: W. H. Freeman, 1973, pp. 215–230.

_____. "The Politics of the Sustainable Society," in Dennis Clark Pirages, ed. *The Sustainable Society: Implications for Limited Growth*. New York: Praeger, 1977, pp. 157–172.

Orr, David W. and Marvin S. Soroos, eds. *The Global Predicament: Ecological Perspectives on World Order*. Chapel Hill: University of North Carolina Press, 1979.

Orwell, George. *1984*. New York: New American Library, 1961.

Our Common Future. Report by the United Nations' Appointed World Commission on Environment and Development. Oxford: Oxford University Press, 1987.

Passell, Peter and Leonard Ross. *The Retreat from Riches: Affluence and Its Enemies*. New York: Viking Press, 1974.

Pateman, Carole. *Participation and Democratic Theory*. London: Cambridge University Press, 1972.

Pavitt, K. L. R. "Malthus and Other Economists: Some Doomsdays Revisited," in H. S. D. Cole *et al*. eds. *Models of Doom*. New York: Universe Books, 1975, pp. 137–158.

Peccei, Aurelio. *One Hundred Pages for the Future: Reflections of the President of the Club of Rome*. New York: New American Library, 1982.

Pickering, Thomas R. and Gus Speth. "Letter of Transmittal," in Gerald O. Barney, Study Director, *The Global 2000 Report to the President: Entering the Twenty-First Century*. Charlottesville: Blue Angel, 1981, pp. iii–v.

Pirages, Dennis. *The New Context for International Relations: Global Ecopolitics*. North Scituate, Mass.: Duxbury Press, 1978.

———. "Introduction: A Social Design for Sustainable Growth," in Dennis Clark Pirages, ed. *The Sustainable Society Implications for Limited Growth*. New York: Praeger, 1977, pp. 1–13.

———, ed. *The Sustainable Society: Implications for Limited Growth*. New York: Praeger, 1977.

——— and Paul R. Ehrlich. *Ark II: Social Response to Environmental Imperatives*. San Francisco: W. H. Freeman, 1974.

Plato. *The Republic of Plato*. Allan Bloom, trans. New York: Basic Books, 1968.

Pokorny, Dusan. "Professor Shulsky on Aristotle's Economic Doctrine," in C. B. Macpherson, comp. *Political Economy and Political Theory*. Papers from the Conference for the Study of Political Thought, April 1974.

Polanyi, Karl. *The Great Transformation: The Political and Economic Origins of Our Time*. Boston: Beacon Press, 1957.

Popper, Karl R. "The Nature of Philosophical Problems and Their Roots in Science," in Karl R. Popper. *Conjectures and Refutations: The Growth of Scientific Knowledge*. New York: Harper and Row, 1968, pp. 66–96.

———. "Truth, Rationality and the Growth of Scientific Knowledge," in Karl R. Popper. *Conjectures and Refutations: The Growth of Scientific Knowledge*. New York: Harper and Row, 1968, pp. 215–250.

———. "On the Sources of Knowledge and of Ignorance," in Karl R. Popper. *Conjectures and Refutations: The Growth of Scientific Knowledge*. New York: Harper and Row, 1968, pp. 3–30.

_____. "Science: Conjectures and Refutations," in Karl R. Popper. *Conjectures and Refutations: The Growth of Scientific Knowledge.* New York: Harper and Row, 1968, pp. 33–65.

_____. *Objective Knowledge: An Evolutionary Approach.* Oxford: Oxford University Press, 1972.

Porritt, Jonathon. *Seeing Green: The Politics of Ecology Explained.* New York: Basil Blackwell, 1985.

Rainwater, Lee. "Equity, Income, Inequality, and the Steady State," in Dennis Clark Pirages, ed. *The Sustainable Society.* New York: Praeger, 1977, pp. 262–273.

Repetto, Robert. *World Enough and Time: Successful Strategies for Resources Management.* New Haven: Yale University Press, 1986.

_____. "Population, Resource Pressures and Poverty," in Robert Repetto, ed. *The Global Possible: Resources, Development, and the New Century.* New Haven: Yale University Press, 1985, pp. 131–169.

_____, ed. *The Global Possible: Resources, Development, and the New Century.* New Haven: Yale University Press, 1985.

Rescher, Nicholas. "What is Value Change? A Framework for Research," in Kurt Baier and Nicholas Rescher, eds. *Values and the Future: The Impact of Technological Change on American Values.* New York: Free Press, 1971, pp. 68–109.

Reynolds, Morgan and Eugene Smolensky. "Welfare Economics: Or, When is a Change an Improvement?" in Sidney Weintraub, ed. *Modern Economic Thought.* Phila.: University of Pennsylvania Press, 1977, pp. 447–466.

Rifkin, Jeremy (with Ted Howard). *Entropy: A New World View.* New York: Bantam Books, 1981.

Rohatyn, Felix. "On the Brink." *New York Review of Books.* June 11, 1987, pp. 3–6.

Rosenbladt, Sabine. "Is Poland Lost? Pollution and Politics in Eastern Europe." *Greenpeace.* 13, November/December 1988, pp. 14–19.

Rousseau, Jean Jacques. "A Discourse on the Origin of Inequality," in Jean Jacques Rousseau, *The Social Contract and Discourses.* G. D. H. Cole, trans. New York: E. P. Dutton, 1950, pp. 175–282.

_____. *The Social Contract and Discourses.* G. D. H. Cole, trans. New York: E. P. Dutton, 1950.

_____. *Emile.* Barbara Foxley, trans. London: J. M. Dent, 1963.

Sabine, George H. *A History of Political Theory.* Fourth Edition, Revised by Thomas

Landon Thorson. Hinsdale, Ill.: Dryden Press, 1973.

Sale, Kirkpatrick. *Human Scale.* New York: G. P. Putnam's Sons, 1982.

Samuels, Warren J. "Ideology in Economics," in Sidney Weintraub, ed. *Modern Economic Thought.* Phila.: University of Pennsylvania Press, 1977, pp. 467–484.

Sandel, Michael J. *Liberalism and the Limits of Justice.* New York: Cambridge University Press, 1983.

Schilpp, Paul Arthur, ed. *The Philosophy of Karl Popper.* Two Volumes. La Salle, Ill.: Open Court, 1974.

Schmemann, Serge. "Environmentalists and Socialists Gain in European Vote." *New York Times.* June 19, 1989, pp. a1, a6.

Schneewind, J. B., ed. *Mill's Essays on Literature and Society.* New York: Collier Books, 1965.

Schultze, Charles L. "Is Economics Obsolete? No, Underemployed," in David Mermelstein, ed. *Economics: Mainstream Readings and Radical Critiques.* New York: Random House, 1973, pp. 16–23.

Schumacher, E. F. *Small is Beautiful: Economics as if People Mattered.* New York: Harper and Row, 1975.

Schumpeter, Joseph A. *Capitalism, Socialism and Democracy.* Third Edition. New York: Harper and Row, 1962.

Schurr, Sam H., ed. *Energy, Economic Growth, and the Environment.* Baltimore: Johns Hopkins University Press, 1973.

Scitovsky, Tibor. *The Joyless Economy: An Inquiry into Human Satisfaction and Consumer Dissatisfaction.* Oxford: Oxford University Press, 1976.

Segal, Jerome. "Income and Development." *QQ—Report from the Center for Philosophy and Public Policy.* University of Maryland, 5, Fall, 1985, pp. 9–12.

Sekora, John. *Luxury: The Concept in Western Thought, Eden to Smollet.* Baltimore: Johns Hopkins University Press, 1977.

Sennett, Richard. *The Fall of Public Man: On the Social Psychology of Capitalism.* New York: Random House, 1978.

Shefrin, Bruce M. *The Future of U.S. Politics in an Age of Economic Limits.* Boulder: Westview Press, 1980.

Shi, David E. *The Simple Life: Plain Living and High Thinking in American Culture.* New York: Oxford University Press, 1986.

Shulsky, Abram N. "Economic Doctrine in Aristotle's *Politics*," in C. B. Macpherson, comp. *Political Economy and Political Theory.* Papers from the Annual Meeting of the Conference for the Study of Political Thought, April 1974.

Simon, Julian L. *The Ultimate Resource.* Princeton: Princeton University Press, 1981.

_____ and Herman Kahn, eds. *The Resourceful Earth: A Response to Global 2000.* New York: Basil Blackwell, 1984.

Slater, Philip. *Earthwalk.* Garden City: Anchor Books, 1974.

_____. *Wealth Addiction.* New York: E. P. Dutton, 1980.

Smith, Adam. *In Inquiry into the Nature and Cause of the Wealth of Nations.* Richard F. Teichgraeber, III, ed. New York: Random House, 1985.

Smith, Gerald Alonzo. "The Teleological View of Wealth: A Historical Perspective," in Herman E. Daly, ed. *Economics, Ecology, Ethics: Essays Toward a Steady-State Economy.* San Francisco: W. H. Freeman, 1980, pp. 215–237.

_____. "Epilogue: Malthusian Concern from 1800 to 1962," in William M. Finnin, Jr. and Gerald Alonzo Smith, eds. *The Morality of Scarcity: Limited Resources and Social Policy.* Baton Rouge: Louisiana State University Press, 1979, pp. 107–128.

Smith, V. Kerry, ed. *Scarcity and Growth Reconsidered.* Baltimore: Johns Hopkins University Press, 1979.

Southwick, Charles H. *Global Ecology.* Sunderland, Mass.: Sinauer Associates, 1985.

Spretnak, Charlene and Fritjof Capra. *Green Politics.* Sante Fe: Bear and Co., 1986.

Springborg, Patricia. *The Problem of Human Needs and the Critique of Civilization.* London: George Allen and Unwin, 1981.

Sprout, Harold and Margaret Sprout. *The Ecological Perspective in Human Affairs with Special Reference to International Politics.* Princeton: Princeton University Press, 1965.

_____ and _____. *The Context of Environmental Politics: Unfinished Business for America's Third Century.* Lexington: The University Press of Kentucky, 1978.

Stavrianos, L. S. *The Promise of the Coming Dark Age.* San Francisco: W. H. Freeman, 1976.

Stivers, Robert L. *The Sustainable Society: Ethics and Economic Growth.* Phila.: Westminster Press, 1976.

Strauss, Leo. *The Political Philosophy of Hobbes: Its Basis and Its Genesis.* Elsa M.

Sinclair, trans. Chicago: University of Chicago Press, 1966.

Tatlock, J. S. P. and R. G. Martin. Introduction to: Oscar Wilde, *Lady Windermere's Fan*, in J. S. P. Tatlock and R. G. Martin, eds. *Representative English Plays: From the Miracle Plays to Pinero*. Second Edition, Revised and Enlarged. New York: Appleton-Century-Crofts, 1938, pp. 843–844.

_____ and _____, eds. *Representative English Plays: From the Miracle Plays to Pinero*. Second Edition, Revised and Enlarged. New York: Appleton-Century-Crofts, 1938.

Tawney, R. H. *The Acquisitive Society*. New York: Harcourt, Brace and World, 1948.

_____. *Religion and the Rise of Capitalism*. New York: New American Library, 1961.

Thomas, Keith. "The Social Origins of Hobbes's Political Thought," in K. C. Brown, ed. *Hobbes Studies*. Cambridge: Harvard University Press, 1965, pp. 185–236.

Thoreau, Henry David. *Walden* in *Walden and Civil Disobedience*. Owen Thomas, ed. New York: W. W. Norton, 1966, pp. 1–221.

Thurow, Lester C. *The Zero-Sum Society: Distribution and the Possibilities for Economic Change*. New York: Basic Books, 1980.

Tilly, Charles. *Big Structures, Large Processes, Huge Comparisons*. New York: Russell Sage Foundation, 1984.

Time. "Our Filthy Seas." August 1, 1988, pp. 44–50.

Times, Los Angeles. "A Slow Growth Revolt." July 31, 1988–August 3, 1988. Four-part, front-page series.

Tinbergen, Jan, coord. *RIO: Reshaping the International Order: A Report to the Club of Rome*. New York: New American Library, 1976.

Tinder, Glenn. *Community: Reflections on a Tragic Ideal*. Baton Rouge: Lousiana State University Press, 1980.

_____. *Political Thinking: The Perennial Questions*. Fourth Edition. Boston: Little, Brown, 1986.

Toffler, Alvin. *The Eco-Spasm Report*. New York: Bantam Books, 1975.

Tolba, Mustafa. Introduction to: John McHale and Magda Cordell McHale. *Basic Human Needs*. New Brunswick, N.J.: Transaction Books, 1978, pp. 1–2.

Trigg, Roger. *Reality at Risk: A Defence of Realism in Philosophy and the Sciences*. Sussex, Great Britain: The Harvester Press, 1980.

Trilling, Lionel. Introduction to works by Matthew Arnold, in: G. B. Harrison *et al.* *Major British Writers.* Two Volumes. Enlarged Edition. New York: Harcourt, Brace, 1959. Volume Two, pp. 579-592.

Trombley, William. "Slow-Growth Sentiment Builds Fast." *Los Angeles Times.* July 31, 1988, p. 1.

Tucker, Robert C., ed. *The Marx-Engels Reader.* New York: W. W. Norton, 1972.

Valaskakis, Kimon *et al.* *The Conserver Society: A Workable Alternative for the Future.* New York: Harper and Row, 1979.

VandenBroeck, Goldian, ed. *Less is More: The Art of Voluntary Poverty.* New York: Harper and Row, 1978.

Vaughan, Frederick. *The Tradition of Political Hedonism: From Hobbes to J. S. Mill.* New York: Fordham University Press, 1984.

Veblen, Thorstein. *The Theory of the Leisure Class: An Economic Study of Institutions.* New York: New American Library, 1963.

Vogel, David. "Business and the Politics of Slowed Growth," in Dennis Clark Pirages, ed. *The Sustainable Society.* New York: Praeger, 1977, pp. 241-256.

von Lazar, Arpad. Foreward to: Dennis Pirages. *The New Context for International Relations.* North Scituate, Mass.: Duxbury Press, 1978, pp. vii-viii.

von Mises, Ludwig. "Introduction: Why Read Adam Smith Today?" in Adam Smith. *An Inquiry into the Nature and Causes of the Wealth of Nations.* Chicago: Henry Regnery, 1953, pp. v-x.

Vonnegut, Kurt, Jr. "Only Kidding Folks?" *Nation.* May 13, 1978, p. 575.

Wallerstein, Immanuel. "Crisis as Transition," in Samir Amin, Giovanni Arrighi, Andre Gunder Frank, and Immanuel Wallerstein, *Dynamics of Global Crisis.* New York: Monthly Review Press, 1982, pp. 11-54.

Wallich, Henry C. "Zero Growth." *Newsweek.* January 24, 1972, p. 62.

_____. "More on Growth." *Newsweek.* March 13, 1972, p. 86.

Walter, Edward. *The Immorality of Limiting Growth.* Albany: State University of New York Press, 1981.

Watts, William. Foreward to: Donella H. Meadows *et al.* *The Limits to Growth.* Second Edition, Revised. New York: New American Library, 1975, pp. ix-xii.

Weintraub, Sidney. Introduction to: Distribution Theory section, in: Sidney Weintraub, ed. *Modern Economic Thought.* Phila.: University of Pennsylvania Press, 1977, pp. 391-393.

————, ed. *Modern Economic Thought*. Phila.: University of Pennsylvania Press, 1977.

Weisskopf, Thomas E. "The Irrationality of Capitalist Economic Growth," in Richard C. Edwards, Michael Reich, and Thomas E. Weisskopf, eds. *The Capitalist System*. Second Edition. Englewood Cliffs, N.J.: Prentice-Hall, 1978, pp. 395–409.

Weisskopf, Walter W. "Economic Growth versus Existential Balance," in Herman E. Daly, ed. *Toward A Steady-State Economy*. San Francisco: W. H. Freeman, 1973, pp. 240–251.

————. *Alienation and Economics*. New York: Dell, 1971.

White, James E., ed. *Contemporary Moral Problems*. Second Edition. St. Paul: West, 1988.

Whitely, C. H. *An Introduction to Metaphysics*. London: Methuen, 1966.

Wiener, Martin J. *English Culture and the Decline of the Industrial State: 1850–1980*. Cambridge: Cambridge University Press, 1981.

Wilde, Oscar. *Lady Windermere's Fan*. in J. S. P. Tatlock and R. G. Martin, eds. *Representative English Plays: From the Miracle Plays to Pinero*. Second Edition, Revised and Enlarged. New York: Appleton-Century-Crofts, 1938, pp. 844–871.

Windelband, Wilhelm. *A History of Philosophy*. Two Volumes. New York: Harper and Row, 1958.

Wolfe, Alan. *America's Impasse: The Rise and Fall of the Politics of Growth*. New York: Pantheon, 1981.

Wolin, Sheldon S. *Politics and Vision: Continuity and Innovation in Western Political Thought*. Boston: Little, Brown, 1960.

Yanarella, Ernest J. "Slouching toward the Apocalypse: Visions of Nuclear Holocaust and Eco-Catastrophe in Contemporary Science Fiction." Paper delivered at the Annual Meeting of the American Political Science Association, 1984, Washington, D.C.

Yankelovich, Daniel. *New Rules: Searching for Self-Fulfillment in a World Turned Upside Down*. New York: Bantam Books, 1982.

Youth, Howard. "Boom Time for Environmental Groups." *World Watch*. 2, November/December 1989, p. 33.

Zinam, Oleg. "The Myth of Absolute Abundance: Economic Development as a Shift in Relative Scarcities." *American Journal of Economics and Sociology*. 41, January 1982, pp. 61–76.

Index

JU